Ney: General of Cavalry
Volume 1
1769-1799

Ney: General of Cavalry
Volume 1
1769-1799
The Early Career of a Marshal
of the First Empire

Antoine Bulos

Ney: General of Cavalry Volume 1 1769-1799:
The Early Career of a Marshal
of the First Empire
by Antoine Bulos

First published under the title
Memoirs of Marshal Ney Volume 1

Leonaur is an imprint
of Oakpast Ltd

Copyright in this form © 2009 Oakpast Ltd

ISBN: 978-1-84677-662-5 (hardcover)
ISBN: 978-1-84677-661-8 (softcover)

http://www.leonaur.com

Publisher's Notes

In the interests of authenticity, the spellings, grammar and place names used have been retained from the original editions.

The opinions of the authors represent a view of events in which he was a participant related from his own perspective, as such the text is relevant as an historical document.

The views expressed in this book are not necessarily those of the publisher.

Contents

Preface	7
First Years of Ney's Life	13
Ney's Character	23
Continuation of the Preceding	31
Ney's First Feat of Arms	39
Battle of the Roer	50
Siege of Maestricht	60
Passage of the Rhine	71
Battle of Altenkirchen	81
Capture of Dierdorf and Montabaur	88
Action at Herborn	96
The Army of the Rhine Begins	100
Operations	100
Feats of Arms by General Ney	111
Continuation of Ney's Feats	119
Occupation of Nuremberg	134
Death of Marceau	146
Distress of the French Troops	157
Hoche Takes Command of the Army of Sambre-et-Meuse	167
Ney is Appointed to the Command of Hussars	179
Ney Taken Prisoner	186
Second Coalition	208
Ney Accepts the Rank of General of Division	218
Action at Winterhur	237
March upon Stuttgard	244
Ney Appointed to the Chief Command of the Army	255
Different Engagements	266
Appendix	282

Marshal Ney

Preface

Marshal Ney was perhaps, next to Napoleon, the greatest of the generals produced by the French Revolution. When the French people, goaded to desperation by the minions of a long line of besotted and voluptuous monarchs, the oppression of an overbearing and privileged aristocracy, and the arrogance of a proud and dissolute hierarchy, at length threw off the yoke under which they had groaned during so many centuries, and proclaimed an equality of political rights, all the other powers of Europe united to put down the principles which had led to this event. The revolutionary spirit, thus pressed upon and hemmed in on all sides, acquired tenfold energy, and burst like a torrent through the barriers opposed to it, overrunning the whole of continental Europe, throwing down the longest established thrones, and sweeping away, in its impetuous course, the very foundations of the most ancient social edifices.

This ill-judged opposition to the rights of between twenty and thirty millions of people, changed the aspect of the whole civilized world, and from it sprang a race of warriors who, seconded by the military spirit inherent in the French nation, subdued every country in Europe, save only Great Britain, protected by her navies and her insular situation. Among the "first and foremost" of these warriors stood Michael Ney, the son of a cooper at Sarrelouis, a small fortified town in the department of Moselle. He was born in 1769, when the debauchery of Louis XV had exhausted the finances of his country—when the mistresses of this monarch appointed his ministers, his ambassadors, and his generals, and made the government of a great and high-minded people pander to their profligacy. Ney became a soldier in 1787, a short time before the meeting of the States-General, and the wonders effected by the eloquence of Mirabeau.

From the moment the privileges of the aristocracy were abolished, and military promotion was opened to all classes of the community, Ney's career was as rapid as it was brilliant. He gave proof of surpassing genius throughout the French campaigns in Germany and in Switzerland; he displayed diplomatic talents of a high order, under the guidance and instructions of the celebrated Charles Maurice Talleyrand, then minister for foreign affairs to the French Republic—and certainly the greatest diplomatist of this or perhaps any former age.

Michael Ney was appointed Marshal of the French Empire, in his thirty-fifth year; and from that period he shared, day by day, in all the glories and perils of Napoleon. As he was no party man, but devoted wholly to his country, whatever its form of government, he lent his sword and talents to the chiefs whom it had chosen. This was his principle through life, and it accounts for his serving Louis XVIII. in 1814, as well as for his joining his former master and friend, when he found his efforts to oppose him unavailing—when the whole of his army had gone over to Napoleon, and the positive will of the nation, afterwards put down by the united armies of Europe, recalled the exile of Elba to the imperial throne.

The talents, the dauntless valour, the high-minded generosity, and the considerate kindness of Ney, are proverbial in the French army; and he dwells in the memory of the veterans who served under him, like one of the heroes or demigods of old.

From Ney's activity and daring spirit, combined with consummate skill and prudence, and from his particular talent in providing for the wants of the troops, without oppressing the inhabitants of the countries overrun by the French armies, he was generally employed in the vanguard—a circumstance which has led to the error, in which even many of his countrymen share, that he was a mere soldier of action, excellent in leading an attack, but devoid of the high acquirements, extensive knowledge, and strategic skill so necessary to wield and manoeuvre large masses of soldiers.

This mistaken notion has been strengthened by some of his old companions in arms, who now attempt to vituperate his memory, because he would not allow them, when under his command, to practise that system of robbery and plunder which disgraced the French armies in the countries through which they passed, whether as friends or foes, and by means of which some of Napoleon's generals acquired immense wealth. These men, since Ney's death, have attempted to undervalue his talents as a commander. Others, with a view of elevating themselves, have sought to found a military reputation at the expense of his; and among the latter, is a certain General Jomini, *aide-de-camp* to the late Emperor Alexander, a Swiss by birth, and a flippant writer about campaigns and battles. Ney, having met with him in Switzerland in an almost destitute condition, made him enter the French service, brought him rapidly forward, and ultimately placed him at the head of his staff.

Jomini now pretends that, while filling this situation, he was Marshal Ney's providence; that he constantly directed all the brilliant achievements of which his general obtained the credit, and got Ney out of the scrapes into which his deficiencies as a commander were continually leading him. Now, supposing this contemptible rodomontade to be true, how happens it that this same General Jomini has never distinguished himself by his military talents since he left Ney to enter the service of Russia? His name is quite unknown, even among the third and fourth-rate generals of the day. Surely he cannot allege the want of opportunity; for in the service of no European state is high military talent made more available than in that of Russia.

The truth is, Ney never asked the advice either of his staff collectively, or of any of its officers in particular, on those grand and extraordinary movements by which he often baffled and defeated an enemy of vastly superior force. They were the rapid inspirations of his own instinctive genius, and to this may perhaps be attributed the almost unvaried success that attended them. With regard to his skill as a theoretical as well as a practical warrior, he was unquestionably superior to every other officer in the French service, even to Masséna, by many considered the best of Napoleon's generals. This may appear to some a very hazardous assertion; it is nevertheless true. Marshal Ney was second only to the Emperor, who, on many important occasions, even yielded to his opinions.

Ney's retreat from Russia, in 1813, was a masterpiece of strategy; it is equal to any thing of the kind ever performed by the greatest generals of ancient or modern times, and will hold a prominent place in the military annals of the nineteenth century. That Ney united profound science to the experience of a life of active warfare, is placed beyond a doubt by the manuscripts left in his own handwriting, containing his observations upon the various campaigns in which he served, and also his military studies for the use of his own officers, when he commanded the camp at Montreuil. To this we may add, that he first improved upon the old system of military tactics, and founded the system now followed by the French armies.

In defiance of a solemn capitulation, Marshal Ney was imprisoned as a traitor, and adjudged to die by the members of a faction who had sold their country. These men had fixed his doom before they came to the judgement-seat; it was sealed by their iniquitous sentence, and "the bravest of the brave" was judicially murdered at the back of the Luxembourg, on the 7th of December 1815. He died as he had lived, a man of heroic courage and unshaken firmness. His death will ever remain a foul blot, not only upon the then government of his country, but upon those foreign governments which might and ought to have interfered to prevent such a catastrophe. This view of the case will doubtless be declared erroneous by men of the present day, imbued with the blind vindictiveness of party-feeling; but it will surely be the one taken in after-ages, when time shall have effaced every vestige of such feeling. Then will the name of Marshal Ney rise pure and imperishable, and justice be done by the whole world to the memory of one who died a felon's death, only because he loved his country too well, and the person of its king less.

The present memoirs are founded upon the papers and documents which he left behind him, consisting of anecdotic and biographical fragments, accounts of his diverse missions and campaigns, and the substance of many extraordinary secrets entrusted to him as a general and a statesman. All these materials throw great light upon the history of the French empire, more especially upon that part of it which relates to the invasion of Spain and the disastrous expedition against Russia.

The work has been put together under the direction and management of the Duke of Elchingen, Marshal Ney's second son, who has affixed his signature to every sheet sent to press.

Chapter 1

First Years of Ney's Life

Michael Ney was born on the 10th of January 1769, at Sarrelouis, a fortified town in the department of Moselle. At an early age he evinced a decided taste for a military life. He was educated at a school kept by the Monks of St. Augustin, where he applied himself sedulously to his studies, but displayed great turbulence of disposition. He constituted himself the avenger of wrongs among his school-fellows, whom he trained and disciplined like soldiers. His father had served during the Seven Years' War, and had afterwards settled in his native town, where he exercised the calling to which he had been bred —that of cooper. He had unintentionally fired the inflammable imagination of his son, by accounts of the battles he had witnessed.

He had distinguished himself by his valour at Rosbach—a circumstance which he always contrived to introduce in his stories of fields lost and won. He used to observe, however, that courage was not alone sufficient to insure the success of a military man: that to obtain command, noble birth was also requisite, and that the son of a poor mechanic had nothing but humiliation to expect in a profession where promotion was granted only to favour and family interest. The recollection, he added, of the perils he had encountered, and the glory of his personal achievements, were the only rewards of men like himself who could not boast of high lineage.

The trade of the elder Ney, though considered respectable on the banks of the Rhine, was not very lucrative, and he was anxious that his son should embrace some profession for which his education qualified him. M. Valette, a notary, much pleased with Michael's capacity and attainments, offered to take him into his office. This appearing eligible, it was determined that the young man should study the law.[1]

Docile to the wishes of his parents, Ney consented without difficulty to this arrangement. Nevertheless, the duties in a notary's office did not exactly harmonize with a mind yearning for the bustle of a military life; and Michael having soon become disgusted with them, obtained an appointment of clerk to the *Procureur de Roi*. But this was still worse; for if he must be pinned to the desk, he by far preferred copying deeds and contracts, to conducting criminal proceedings.

Michael had now completed his fifteenth year; he had a presentiment of his future greatness, and was burning to follow the bent of his inclination. His father, unable to appreciate these workings of a master-spirit, or to share in the hopes which they raised, endeavoured to suppress them. Peter Ney, his eldest son, was already a soldier. Michael's deference to his father's wishes was extreme, and he succeeded for a time, if not in subduing this irresistible propensity, at least in directing his mind to a new pursuit. The mines of Apenwerler were then in full produce; and young Ney was sent thither as an overseer.

The works, and the bustle attendant upon them, at first captivated him; he loved to watch the change in the ore, and to study the different processes it underwent in its transformation. But this knowledge was soon acquired, and his imagination relapsed into its former dreams of campaigns, and battles, and military fame. The entreaties of his father, and the tears of his mother, though they affected him much, could not alter his determination. His vocation was however again checked for a short period. Though young, he was well-informed, punctual, active, and zealous; and an offer was made him to superintend the iron works at Saleck. He accepted this new office, and the novelty of the scenes in which he was now engaged made him, for a while,

---

[1]. Minutes of Ney's handwriting are still preserved in this office as valuable relics.

forget his warlike intentions. He had besides a prospect of future competency, which had never before been held out to him, and he applied himself cheerfully to the fulfilment of the duties he had undertaken.

Two years were spent in this manner; but his military propensities strengthening every day, his office became insupportable to him. The very place in which he lived contributed to develop the passion which raged within him. Almost every town on the Rhine is fortified, and has a garrison. If the superintendent of the Saleck works went to Treves, to Bergheim, or to Deux-Ponts, he was sure to see soldiers performing the platoon exercise, and all those military movements in which he longed to participate as a mere private, though he already felt the instinct of command. His resolution to conform to the wishes of his parents was not powerful enough to overcome the workings of his soul.

He therefore resigned his situation, and set out for Metz, where the regiment of hussars, called the *Régiment de Colonel-Général*, was then quartered. The grief with which this sudden and decided step was likely to afflict his parents, gave him considerable uneasiness, and he long hesitated before he paid them a parting visit; but filial affection triumphed over every other feeling, and quitting the high road, he directed his steps towards Sarrelouis.

The meeting was very painful, and he had to encounter reproaches, tears, entreaties, and even threats. The scene which took place was heart-rending, and he could only put an end to it by abruptly resuming his journey on foot. Though without clothes or money, worn out with fatigue and anxiety, his shoes in holes, his feet lacerated and bleeding—his courage did not forsake him; and by his perseverance at this early stage of his life he already gave proof of that energy of purpose which, in after life, yielded to no obstacle.

Many years elapsed ere he returned to Sarrelouis. Fortune had then rewarded his courage with high rank and honours. When he again visited his birthplace, the cannon roared, and the troops were under arms. The inhabitants of Sarrelouis ran in crowds to behold their illustrious townsman. Marshal Ney, on perceiving the road over which, thirteen years before, he had travelled on foot to become a soldier, related with emotion, to the officers who surrounded him, the history of his first departure from his family.

On his arrival at Metz, on the 1st of February 1787, being then eighteen years of age, he enlisted in the *Régiment de Colonel-Général*, afterwards the 4th Hussars. He entered this regiment under the auspices of one of his countrymen, a lieutenant in the regiment, but who could be of no service to him in the way of promotion. This however was of no consequence at that period. Promotion then belonged only to the aristocracy; interest was therefore of no use, and he must wait until better times should widen the field of glory through which he was destined to run. But he commenced his military career not without certain advantages. He had some knowledge of business, practical natural philosophy, and the resources of industry. His good conduct, his application, and the rapidity with which he made himself master of the duties of a soldier, attracted the attention of his officers; whilst his patient submission to discipline and his orderly conduct elicited their goodwill; and as he wrote a beautiful hand, he was soon employed in the quartermaster's office. This gave him some leisure time, which he devoted to qualifying himself for his new profession.

He distinguished himself among his comrades by his fine, soldier-like appearance, his great dexterity in the use of his weapons, and the ease and boldness with which he rode the most dangerous horses, breaking-in those hitherto considered unmanageable. On account of these qualities, every regimental affair of honour was confided to him. The fencing-master of the *Chasseurs de Vintimille*, a regiment also quartered at Metz, was, like most regimental fencing-masters of those days, a dangerous duellist, and as such dreaded not only by young recruits but by old and experienced soldiers. This man had wounded the fencing-master of *Colonel-Général*, and insulted the whole regiment. The non-commissioned officers having held a meeting to take measures for the punishment of this bully, Ney, just promoted to the rank of brigadier, was selected, as the bravest and cleverest swordsman, to inflict the chastisement deemed necessary. He accepted the mission with joy, but just as the duel was about to commence, he felt some one pull him violently by the tail. On turning his head he perceived the colonel of his regiment, who immediately put him under arrest.

Duelling, at that period, was punishable with death, and Ney was taken in the very act. The matter could not well have been more serious; but the young brigadier was much liked by his officers, and besides, there was no personal quarrel, he having been delegated to fight for the honour of the regiment. The non-commissioned officers waited on the colonel in a body to solicit his pardon, which was soon made an *affaire de corps*. Revolutionary ideas already prevailed in the army to such an extent that a too great severity of discipline was always eluded, lest it should exasperate the men.

A long confinement therefore saved Ney from a court-martial; but he had scarcely obtained his release ere he judged it necessary to satisfy what he deemed a point of honour. The danger he had incurred could not turn him from his purpose; for he scorned to be protected from the peril of a meeting with so formidable an antagonist, by any other means than his own skill and courage. The interrupted duel took place, proper precautions having been taken to keep it secret. Ney was the conqueror; he disabled his adversary by a wound on the wrist, which subsequently led to the discharge of the bully fencing-master from the service. This man was afterwards reduced to great poverty; and Ney, who had become rich, sought him out and settled a pension upon him.

Marshal Ney never forgot his origin. When at the very climax of his fortune, he loved to call to mind the point whence he had started. It grieved him, during his military career, to see old errors revived, the principles of equality lost sight of, and the bearers of ancient names and titles loaded with favours, without any personal merit to justify such partiality. He was much displeased at the eagerness shown to court such individuals; and he required numerous proofs of courage and talent, before he could overcome the unfavourable impression produced by officers who were forced upon him from policy, and in opposition to his own wishes. When in their presence, he always made a point of speaking of his early life. If any officers talked before him of their noble birth, of the pecuniary allowances they received from their families, or of their expectations of hereditary wealth, he would say, "I was less fortunate than you, gentlemen; I received nothing from my family, and I thought myself rich at Metz when I had two loaves of bread upon my shelf."

Soon after he was raised to the rank of Marshal of the empire, being at a large party, every one crowded round him to offer their congratulations on the event. Interrupting the flattering speeches of the company, he addressed an old officer who kept himself at some distance from the rest of the party. "Do you remember, captain," he said, "the time when you used to say to me, as I made my report to you, 'Very well, Ney; continue as you are now going on, and you will make your way, my lad?'"—

"Perfectly well, *Monsieur le Maréchal*," his old captain replied; "I then had the honour to command one better than myself. Such things are not to be forgotten."

The satisfaction which Ney derived from recalling the events of his youth arose as well from the noble pride of having owed his rise solely to his own exertions, as from the recollection of family attachments. He loved to talk about the tender affection of his mother and the paternal advice of his father [2] and whenever he yielded to the impetuosity of his courage, he carefully concealed from his parents the dangers to which he exposed

---

2. Marshal Ney's father died a few years since, having lived almost a century. He loved his son with tenderness and respect. Though a man of great physical strength, taking long walks and violent exercise, it was feared that a knowledge of the events of 1815 might prove fatal to him. He was therefore kept in ignorance of them; but the mourning dress of his daughter with whom he lived, and of her children, convinced him that some great family misfortune had happened. He dared not ask what it was: but from that period he fell into a gloomy melancholy, and but seldom pronounced his son's name. His death occurred in 1826.

himself. When he commanded the vanguard of Collaud's division, a destructive action had just taken place. On his return, worn out with fatigue, he related the events of the day to a friend, who blamed what he termed Ney's imprudence.

"True," the latter replied, "I have had a narrow escape again today; for I was four times quite alone in the midst of the Austrians."—

"You have been more fortunate than your poor brother," his friend observed.—

"Good God!" said Ney in alarm, "What has happened? Is my brother dead? Oh! My poor mother!"

Ney's friend then informed him that his brother Peter Ney, officer in the 55th Demi-Brigade, had been killed in a sanguinary conflict which had just taken place in Italy. Ney was unable to restrain his tears at this afflicting intelligence; "What would have become of my poor mother and sister," he exclaimed, "If I had fallen today! Write to them, but conceal from them the risks I run, lest they should feel the alarm of losing me also."

War and the stagnation of trade had created a general distress throughout France, which more especially affected the operative classes. At that period, a general officer received only eight francs a month, and Ney was only a subaltern. His circumstances were therefore far from flourishing. Nevertheless, he submitted to the severest privations, and contrived out of his pittance to send pecuniary aid to his mother, then confined to her bed by a disorder which carried her off after four years of suffering.

Ney had just been made an officer. Poor, disinterested, and generous, the highest feelings of honour and delicacy had taken such deep root in his soul, that he would have scorned to acquire wealth at the expense of the enemy, by taking advantage of the chances of war. Some blamed him for not profiting by a chance which the following anecdote will explain, and punishing a base insult at the same time; others admired his inflexible rectitude of principle.

He was with the army of the North. Encounters with the British cavalry were frequent, and sometimes valuable captures were made. Ney had just been promoted to the rank of captain; ardent, daring, and eager to distinguish himself, he one day charged with such impetuosity, that with his small detachment he passed the British lines. A squadron of English cavalry appeared; having attacked and dispersed it, he eagerly pursued an English general officer,[3] whom it was escorting.

The latter, surprised at this determined pursuit, made no attempt to defend himself, but preferred treating: "Here," said he, "is a purse full of gold; take it and let me go."—

The French captain smiled at the proposal, and this encouraged the English general to press his offer.—"You are surrounded by our forces," he continued, "And must be taken prisoner. Do better; remain with us, and your fortune shall be made; your promotion shall be rapid, and you will serve your own princes."

"Really, this is going too far," Ney replied with indignation, placing his sword upon the other's breast; "You offer one money, and propose that I should desert my colours. Now, you shall desert, and that too in the presence of your own army. You must charge with me through your own ranks, and if you attempt to escape, that moment shall be your last. Follow me, my lads," said he, addressing his hussars; "forward!"

Then giving his horse the spur, he overthrew everyone who opposed him, and passed once more through the English ranks, amazed at seeing one of their own officers charging side by side with the French captain. Ney brought his prisoner in triumph to the head-quarters of the French army, and the captive general was quite confounded at his silly adventure. "Keep your money," said Ney to him; "I might perhaps be justified in taking it from you, but you will want it more than I shall. Another time, however, be more circumspect when you attempt to parley."

Ney, though submissive to those in command over him, was neither obsequious nor a flatterer. He did his duty with zeal and enthusiasm, because he loved his profession. Never did the idea enter his mind of pleasing his superiors or purchasing his

---

3. From delicacy, the name of this officer is withheld.—Ed.

promotion by meanly cringing. From his very entrance into the service, he had no feeling but that of the most entire devotion to his country, to which he had made an offering of his dearest affections, and even life itself. He knew how to elude too great severity, as well as to resist that which he considered unjust.

The character of Kléber is well known. It will be shown hereafter with what kindness and regard he treated Ney, from whom, however, neither the violence of Kléber's temper, nor his anger, nor even his friendship, could obtain any improper concessions.

Kléber was sometimes the slave of caprice. Having once taken a dislike to an officer to whom he had formerly been attached, he determined to get rid of him. He accordingly directed his *aide-de-camp*, Ney, to make a minute of an order to this effect;

"You are going to send him away," Ney observed, "because------"

"Because," replied Kléber with violence, "I don't like him."

"Well then," said Ney, "you may get somebody else to write the minute, for I would cut my arm off rather than be the instrument of recording such an order."

Kléber, speechless with astonishment, looked for a considerable time at the presumptuous *aide-de-camp* without speaking a word; then mildly said, "Well, let him remain! You wish it, and so let it be."

Though this was an open resistance to the will of his imperious commanding officer, yet it was the honest feeling of one brave soldier candidly expressed to another. There was much greater danger in braving the will of the representatives of the people, who had cemented their authority by blood, and could strike terror into the bravest men.

The emigrants having crucified some volunteers of the republican army, the latter had used reprisals; and as it always happens, one cruelty led to another, until the victims were allowed to choose the mode of their own death. Strict orders had been given to execute the decrees of the convention against the emigrants with the utmost rigour. Nevertheless, some of the latter had laid down their arms and called for quarter. Ney, then a general officer, would not injure those whom his soldiers had spared. He treated them with kindness, mixed them with the foreign prisoners, and sent them to the depots of the prisoners of war. The representatives were indignant at this; but as they had not full evidence of the fact, they were afraid to bring the matter forward in the shape of an accusation, and contented themselves with watching the offending General more narrowly. Ney, informed of the suspicion attached to him, became more circumspect.

His scouts, however, brought in, one evening, some priests whom they had found wandering through the country. The poor creatures were half dead with fright, hunger, and fatigue. Ney determined to save them. In the presence of those who captured them, he affected to speak with great violence, and to threaten the full penalty of the law; but having dismissed his men, under pretence of examining the prisoners in private, he altered his manner, gave them food and money, and sent them in disguise the same night to a town through which he knew the army would not pass.[4] Next morning, he affected violent anger at their escape, which was publicly announced to him. Though he endeavoured to keep as secret as possible his own share in this flight, it nevertheless became known to the representatives. But the measures of blood, so rife a short time before, were now beginning to be less frequent, and political hatred was rapidly subsiding. The representatives were therefore afraid to act against the kind-hearted general. One of them, however, loudly exclaimed against so flagrant a violation of the law; the other, more generous, admired Ney's magnanimity in risking his life to save his prisoners. "Your friend Ney," he observed to Kléber, "knows how to spare the blood of his countrymen."

---

4. One of these very priests was, a few years since, *curé* of the parish of St. Symphorien at Versailles.

Chapter 2

Ney's Character

Before we begin our recital of the Marshal's military deeds, let us pause an instant to complete the sketch we have already commenced of his personal character.

It is well known with what extraordinary energy and power he manoeuvred large masses of soldiers and brought them to act upon the enemy. Bold and impetuous when he led his troops to a charge, he at the same time evinced the most imperturbable coolness and presence of mind. Many persons, wonder-stricken at his extraordinary courage, have overlooked his other qualities as a commander; but the officers who have served under him, will relate other things of him than those mere bursts of enthusiastic valour by which the common soldiers were captivated, and made to brave the most appalling danger. Calm amid showers of grape-shot, unmoved by the most terrific discharges of artillery, by the missiles which dealt death and destruction around him, Ney appeared unconscious of the danger,—he seemed as if he bore a charmed life.

This calm rashness, which twenty years of peril did not overcome, gave to his mind that freedom of thought, that promptitude of decision and execution so necessary amid the complicated manoeuvres of war and battle. This surprised the officers under his command, still more than that courage of action in which they all shared. One of the latter, a man of tried valour, asked him one day if he had ever been afraid; thus summing up in a single word that profound indifference to danger, that forgetfulness of death, that tension of mind, and that mental labour, so necessary to a general-in-chief upon the field of battle.

"I have never had time," was the Marshal's reply.

This indifference, however, did not prevent him from noticing in others, those slight shades of weakness from which very few soldiers are wholly exempt An officer was one day making a report to him; a cannon ball passed so close to them, that the officer bent his head as if by instinct to avoid it: nevertheless, he continued his report without betraying any emotion. "Very well," said the marshal; "but another time don't make so low a bow."

Ney had a high respect for courage, and loved to bring forward those who displayed it. Whenever a man distinguished himself in the field of battle, and showed capacity and talent, the Marshal became his patron, and never ceased his good offices until his protegé had obtained the promotion to which his valour entitled him, or was placed in a situation to make his talents available.

We will not here name the individuals whose courage and abilities Ney was instrumental in bringing to light. They who owe their rise to him will do him justice;—they will acknowledge that he never failed to discover merit, and raise it from obscurity, even were it concealed in the lowest ranks of the army. Press of business at head quarters, was sometimes the cause of his recommendations being overlooked; but he always renewed them, for he was determined that reward should be bestowed upon such as deserved it. His division well knew the quarrels he had, in 1800, with Lahorie and Moreau, on account of a simple hussar who had not been duly promoted.

General B——, known by his courage and honourable services, as well as by the persecutions he endured in 1815, was captain of grenadiers in the 103rd Demi-Brigade. During the campaign of Hohenlinden, Moreau had himself appreciated the bravery and zeal of Captain B——. Nevertheless, others were rapidly promoted, whilst the captain was passed over. Ney attempted to overcome this injustice, which had its origin in secret enmity, and he recommended B—— to the general-in-chief, stating the services of this officer, and the necessity of giving the demi-brigade a commander who could restore its discipline. The recommendation was unsuccessful;—there was an evident repugnance to promote B——.

"I will get the better of it," said Ney, and he kept his word. He united the grenadier companies of the 103rd, and gave the command of them to B——, who performed so many brilliant feats that his enemies, so eager, before, to darken his prospects, were now forced to acknowledge his merits, and yield to Ney's determination to bring him forward.

Anxious as Ney was to make known the services of those especially under his command, he would also seek out and patronize men of superior talent not attached to his division, but whose power to render useful services exposed them to envy. The following is an instance of this:—to vast information, the author of the *Traité des grandes opérations militaires*, added the art of observing, and the power of putting his observations upon paper. His talents having become known to Ney, the marshal appointed him to his staff, and thus restored him to a profession from which the act of mediation in Switzerland had cut him off,—he being a Swiss by birth.

This officer turned his leisure hours to account; but the difficulties attendant upon the publication of military works are well known. Ney however came to his assistance, and not only overcame the obstacles to the publication, but promoted the sale of the work, and obtained a just reward for its author. Jealousy was again excited against this officer; again did Ney support him. In a word, from the day on which General Jomini, the officer alluded to, was admitted into the French army, until he quitted it to fight under another banner, Marshal Ney was his warmest friend, and supported him with all his influence. This was not forgotten by Jomini when adversity had stricken Ney, and he became the victim of a cruel and highly-excited faction, backed by foreign armies; for the then *aide-de-camp* of the Emperor Alexander took sundry steps in Ney's favour, and had the courage—for in those days it was an act of courage—to publish a pamphlet in favour of his old general.

We regret, however, that General Jomini seemed to think that his noble conduct on this occasion had relieved him from the burthen of gratitude towards his former patron and friend. His last works evince in general a wish to depreciate the character of Ney, which must surprise those who know the place which General Jomini held on the marshal's staff. Has the silence of the tomb encouraged this writer to raise accusations which he hopes no one will be able to refute? How is it that General Jomini, with his acuteness of intellect, does not feel that there is a want of delicacy in thus coming forward to denounce errors committed, as he dares to allege, in opposition to his prudent counsels, and in thus arrogating to himself, with the most singular assurance, the successes obtained by his general?

A foolish desire to increase Ney's celebrity, which required not such aid, has doubtless misled him, and he will probably be surprised to hear that he himself, the chief of Ney's staff, was ignorant of Ney's orders, and did not even comprehend military operations upon which he was never consulted. We might here begin to remark upon those narratives in which General Jomini tries to place himself in so advantageous a light; but we prefer keeping such observations for another part of these memoirs. General Jomini is an adversary of too great talents for his assertions to remain unnoticed. It is to be regretted, however, that it should be necessary to refute them in such a work as this.

> "It is to the sagacity with which he (Jomini) drew up in 1805, the orders for the movements of the 6th Corps, that the capture of Mack's army is to be attributed."
>
> "At Jena, Marshal Ney, impatient at being in the reserve, threw himself with his van guard, composed of three thousand picked men, into the village of Vierzenheiligen, where he was overpowered by the whole army of Prince Hohenlohe. Colonel Jomini, seeing the danger of his general, left the emperor and ran into the thickest part of the *mêlée* to defend with his own arm the audacious marshal,

who, after losing half his men, and three of his *aides-de-camp*, owed his victory to Jomini's opportune assistance.

"They were near undergoing, in the mud of Pultush, the fate anticipated in the contemned memoir (that of Jomini). They got out however; but the diverging road pursued by Marshal Ney, led them to the brink of a fresh abyss. Napoleon saw but one remedy, which was to send Colonel Jomini to look for the marshal. Although extremely unwell, he (Jomini) flew to the place where Ney's division was, and not only was the marshal's corps got out of danger, but likewise that of the Prince of Ponte-Corvo.

"At a later period in Spain, although he (Marshal Ney) had an exaggerated idea of the importance of Corunna and Ferrol, the chief of his staff persuaded him to evacuate Galicia."

(And in reference to the battle of Bautzen) "As he (Marshal Ney) could not comprehend this eccentric movement, the chief of his staff pointed out to him, that it was sufficient to show the head of a column," &c.

The above quotations from M. Jomini's article in *La Nouvelle Biographic des Contemporaires*, and which may be found in some of his other works, give an idea of the manner in which that officer speaks of his old commander, and of the personal share which he assumes of that commander's feats of arms. Perhaps M. Jomini had the modesty not to write these praises of himself; but in that case he certainly aided with his counsels" the person who did write them; for the same feelings and pretensions pervade the last of his works published by himself.

Far from allowing himself to be thus influenced by his officers, the marshal, on the contrary, never allowed any one to offer him unasked-for advice. He did not consider himself in need of them. Such a thing, in his view of the matter, would have impeached that belief in a superiority of talent which inspires an army with confidence in its commander. An officer of his staff presented to him, one day, a paper on the affairs of Switzerland, saying, "This, General, is what you should do." So disrespectful a pretension to superior wisdom was treated as a piece of impertinence, and the giver of advice dared not again, in the presence of his general, evince the faith he had in his own sagacity. The lesson was not lost upon others, and it imposed upon them a line of respectful deference, which none afterwards ventured to pass.

Nevertheless, Ney lived upon terms of great intimacy with his officers. He never made them feel his superiority of rank. He treated Lorcet like a brother—Ruffin like a valued friend; but in the course of time these were replaced by men less discreet. One of the new comers was once guilty of improper familiarity; Ney noticed it, and determined not to expose himself to such a thing in future; he therefore became more reserved and silent, limiting his confidential intercourse to those only with whose character and habits he was well acquainted. This resolution was strengthened by the following circumstance.

On his entrance into Switzerland, he had received with great kindness a colonel who had been dismissed from the service. This man had formerly distinguished himself as a soldier; he was, moreover, a pleasant companion, a man of talent, and every sentiment he uttered seemed to stamp him a man of honour. General Ney tried to get him restored to the army. The cantons were in violent agitation, and he sent this officer to inquire into its causes. Colonel C—— had great knowledge and address. He quieted the obstinate mountaineers, and drew up a very lucid report of their motives for being discontented with their new institutions, pointing out, at the same time, that which they regretted in their old. This able report confirmed Ney in his determination to serve the author, and he transmitted it with the colonel's name, to the minister, strongly recommending that C—— should be restored to his rank. But the minister had information with regard to this individual, of which Ney was ignorant, and the recommendation was not attended to.

But Ney always persevered in an act of kindness; and on his appointment to the command of the camp at Montreuil, he sent for C——, and strongly insisted upon his being reinstated.

In doing this, he at the same time energetically censured what he considered a great injustice. Though devotedly attached to the head of the state—though a strenuous supporter of a system which promised to protect the interests of all, and allay political excitements—he did not, however, consider himself bound to forego his personal opinions, which he continued freely to express. Unsuccessful in his application to the War Minister in favour of C——, he applied to the First Consul. Surprised at his request being coldly received, he urged it with some warmth. The First Consul listened to him with surprise, but refused to give him an answer.

Such conduct only rendered Ney more pressing. "There, read that paper," said at length General Buonaparte, "and you will then know in what kind of man you have placed your confidence." The paper was a denunciation by C—— against Ney. It gave an account of the private conversations of the latter, perverting every sentence he had uttered in confidential intercourse, and accusing him of being an enemy to the First Consul, a dangerous man, and one whose actions ought to be carefully watched. The treacherous C—— was disgracefully exposed; but the circumstance dwelt long upon Ney's mind, made him more reserved, and altered those habits of confidence which harmonised so well with his noble character and goodness of heart![1]

Ney was severe, but just. Being of an irritable temper, he sometimes gave way to anger, but as readily offered reparation to those he had offended. He was inspecting, in 1813, a regiment of heavy cavalry belonging to his division. Surprised at seeing a deficiency in the soldiers' fund called the *masse,* he was informed, by the men that they had not received their balances, which,

---

1. In 1815, when Marshal Ney was arrested, C——, who was likewise a prisoner, requested to see the *Procureur du Roi*, having, as he stated, an important revelation to make. The object of this request was to offer evidence against his former benefactor, and he actually made a deposition to this effect. Will it be believed that this very individual applied, a few years since, to Ney's family for pecuniary assistance upon the strength of the marshal's former regard for him? We withhold the name of this wretch for the sake of a member of his family, who has done great and brilliant services to his country.

however, had been entered in the pay-books as if issued to them. He sent for the colonel of the regiment, and reprimanded him severely. In vain did the officer attempt to justify himself by explaining that he had only obeyed superior orders: Ney, who saw in this circumstance an injustice to the men, would not listen to him.

The marshal had invited the field-officers of his corps to spend the evening with him; all were present but the colonel whom he had reprimanded in the morning. On perceiving his absence, Ney went to his quarters. "I was wrong this morning," said he, taking the colonel by the hand; "pray think no more of it, and come and join our party."

CHAPTER 3

Continuation of the Preceding

Prompt in the repression of excesses, Marshal Ney always exerted himself to prevent their occurrence. Having himself begun as a private, and being consequently well acquainted with the privations endured by the men, he was the better able to sympathise in their sufferings, which he did his utmost to alleviate. He knew that soldiers, though generally grateful to the officers who showed them kindness and paid attention to their personal wants, were nevertheless difficult to keep in subjection when those wants were not supplied, or when they perceived that their commanding officer did not share in their fatigues and privations. Ney loved those masses of men, composed of such a variety of minds, of elements so diversified, and which each day cooperated spontaneously in the same object, rushing upon danger as with one mind and with an equal contempt of death.

The French troops, inured at that period to the toils and perils of war, and accustomed to laugh at danger, were of ruder manners and sterner bearing than those of the present day, who lead a pacific life in their garrisons; and discipline, at times lost sight of for a moment, would afterwards resume its sway with more unbending rigour. Amid dangers constantly overcome and as constantly appearing in a new shape, obedience must be prompt, and command is sometimes unavoidably harsh. Bad weather, dearth, or reverses, affect the tempers of all; and as authority has always its engines of punishment—guard-mounting out of turn, arrest, and solitary confinement—the forgetfulness of a moment is often expiated by a lengthened severity in their application, which the ill-humour of an officer, nay, perhaps an injurious epithet, may have provoked.

Ney carefully strived to prevent such abuses of power, and convince the officers under his command, that by raising the soldier in his proper estimation, treating him as a rational being, and combining equitable firmness with kind and considerate attention to his wants, they would more easily obtain from him that blind obedience, and sacrifice of individual will, which form the great strength of military masses. He had always an exact report made to him of the moral state of his corps, and often when the generals and colonels under him least suspected it, would question them upon a case of individual punishment which they had long since forgotten.

Anxious to give his men as little useless labour as possible, he never loved, from vain ostentation, to be attended by brilliant escorts, or the mummeries of military pageantry. He always endeavoured to diminish, as much as possible, the soldier's fatiguing duties, and not weaken the strength of his regiments by sending detachments from them. This solicitude was remarked by the men, as were also the care and perseverance with which their general attended to their means of subsistence; and it secured their enthusiastic gratitude.

We shall hereafter show the wonders he effected in providing food for his forces during the Portuguese campaign, in a country ravaged by war, where by almost superhuman exertions he succeeded in meeting not only the consumption of the 6th corps which he commanded, but that of the whole army, during the six months it remained upon the banks of the Tagus. Constantly advancing towards the Mondego, and sending forward columns in every direction, he managed to obtain leather, cloth, and provisions sufficient for every demand. These recollections are indelibly imprinted on the minds of the soldiers who served under him; and when his quarrel with Marshal Masséna made him resign the command of the 6th Corps, the grief and murmurs of the men, and the first ferment of a mutiny, which a single word would have caused to burst forth with the utmost fury, proved to him that his services were appreciated, and had gained him the warm attachment of the troops he commanded.

Although so attentive to the least thing that concerned the comforts and welfare of his men, he nevertheless maintained the severest discipline, and punished every kind of excess.

A skirmish had taken place near Darmstadt. The Austrians having been repulsed, had formed again near Zwingemberg, where they were routed a second time. The action had been warm, and the French troops, excited by the resistance of their opponents, forcibly entered and pillaged some houses. Though circumstances might have excused this, it was considered an act of oppression, and an abuse of victory.

By it, the unfortunate peasants had been forced to pay for the acts of the government. Ney was not satisfied with inflicting military punishment upon the delinquents: he had an estimate made of the damage, and an adequate compensation given to the victims of this plunder; and in order that the estimate might be a just one, he directed that it should be made by the *Landgrave* himself.

"I am grieved to learn," he wrote to that Prince, "that excesses have been committed at Zwingemberg by some of the troops under ray command. The village was carried by main force, a circumstance which no doubt led to the disasters which its inhabitants have experienced. Nevertheless, I neither will, nor ought I to tolerate such things. My soldiers have disobeyed the orders they received; the cottages of unfortunate villagers have been plundered; and it behoves me, not only to punish the perpetrators of this outrage, but to repair the damage they have caused. Let the village magistrate draw up an estimate of the losses incurred, and I will take measures for its amount being paid."

Both soldiers and villagers had reason to remember this action. The former were taught by it what they had to expect from their general's severity, and the latter, the confidence they might place in his honour. The inhabitants of the banks of the

Necker, who had taken up arms to resist pillage, again resumed their usual avocations, and the approach of the French troops no longer inspired the same dread as before. Other acts of justice strengthened this confidence. Heavy contributions had been imposed, and the local administrations, eager to elude the payment of them, had thrown the burthen almost wholly upon Eberfeld.

This town, which had been almost wholly destroyed by fire during the preceding campaign, was unable to meet so heavy a charge, and sent a remonstrance to the States, who, notwithstanding, persisted in imposing upon it a burthen which ought to have been borne in equal shares throughout the country. Ney was more equitable than the States. He remembered the misfortunes of this little town, and felt for the situation of its active and industrious inhabitants; and he notified to the commissaries of his army, who were taxing it without mercy, that having been twice laid waste by war, it had already paid its share of war contributions, and should therefore, in the present instance, be exempt from impost.

Warring only with armies, and respecting the inhabitants of the countries through which he passed, and whom he considered already unfortunate enough from the territories they inhabited being made the seat of war, the marshal defended such countries against the wants of his soldiers, and the injustice of their own rulers. Inexorable towards those who took advantage of the disorder of conquest to oppress the natives, he was more than once obliged to exercise the utmost vigilance, and display a wholesome severity in repressing such abuses. Not that they were of frequent occurrence. Honour and delicacy generally accompanied the French armies; and if complaints were sometimes made, it was because they who bear the burthens of war are apt to exaggerate their sufferings, often increased by the avidity and selfishness of their own rulers.

Doubtless there are many extortions which cannot be avoided. The soldier is a burthen to the individual upon whom he is billeted; detachments sometimes pilfer rations from the villages in which they are quartered; and vanguards now and then make free with a few heads of cattle. But this is merely striking the surface of the water; the rulers of these countries alone draw it off;—war offers them none but lucky chances. They impose contributions, and shamelessly rob those whose interests they are bound to defend. If complaints are made—if there is any deficiency in the supplies, the enemy is there to bear the blame;— the enemy has given orders which must be obeyed. It is still worse, when a country passes under a new domination. Some of the former rulers cloak their own robberies under an exaggeration of the burthens they have borne; others magnify these burthens in order to obtain indemnities. And in justice we must add, that if exactions which the French officers had not made, were sometimes imputed to them, they were, on the other hand, often taxed with spoliations of which they were really guilty. But in such cases, punishment never failed to overtake the offending parties, no matter who they were.

A general officer, whose opinions on the rights of conquest were such as to remove more than ordinary scruples, had appropriated to his own use, two horses which had struck his fancy. The peasant to whom they belonged, and whose whole fortune they constituted, complained to Ney. The marshal, in a severe and peremptory written order, commanded that they should forthwith be returned to the owner.

The officer at first refused. He next endeavoured to substitute a couple of bad horses for the valuable ones he had taken; then altering his mind, complained of the harshness of the marshal's order.

"If my order appears strange to you," wrote Ney, "what must I think of your obstinacy in keeping that which does not belong to you? Your mode of acting does not suit me, and I have applied for your recall. You will no doubt be soon removed to another division; but in the mean time, you must restore the horses."

The following will give an idea of the severity with which the marshal visited these shameful robberies. It is a letter which he addressed to another general, who was apt to forget the difference between that which did, and that which did not belong to him, but who in other respects was an able and valuable officer.

January 4th, 18—

I cannot but express to you, my dear General, my surprise at your now stating that it was only at St. John's, on your march to Salzburg, that your secretary left you to negotiate the Botzen bills; whereas at Greusbranth you pledged your word of honour to me that you would remit seventy-five thousand *francs* to the paymaster (being the amount of these bills, together with the sums you received in cash,) the moment your *aide-de-camp* returned, who had left Botzen for Basle.

You have not answered the letter which I requested General Dutaillis to write to you on this subject; and you avoided seeing me when you passed through Clagenfurt. All this justifies my suspecting your good faith, until I am certain that you have fulfilled that which is most sacred to a military man— I mean his word of honour.

I have hitherto deferred laying the matter before the Emperor, in consideration of the services you have rendered during the present campaign; and in the hope that you would not—to use your own expression—destroy, for the sake of money, the good opinion which people ought to entertain of your delicacy. But I now declare to you, General that I will lay the whole affair before his Majesty, unless, in six days from the present date, you fulfil your promise, either by paying in the sum, or by sending to the *caisse* your acknowledgement for the amount.

I beg also to inform you, that your name is upon the list of gratuities granted by the Emperor; that your gratuity amounts to eight thousand florins; and that this sum shall be carried to your account as part of the payment which you are bound to make.

These two generals were thus forced to restore their plunder; and neither forgot nor forgave Ney's share in the transaction. The one showed his recollection of it in the field of battle; the other during the marshal's trial. By these severe measures, Ney made himself many enemies; for he spared no plunderers: he exposed them to shame, and at the same time forced them to disgorge their ill-gotten wealth. No personal considerations could deter him from the performance of what he considered a sacred duty. With this severity for others, it is needless to state that he never reaped any personal advantages from his commands in foreign countries. All his actions were guided by the principles which he had imbibed in his infancy; and he persevered throughout his life, in the same line of conduct he had adopted at the outset of his career.

General Ney having taken Eberfeld, whose manufactures of steel had rendered it opulent, the magistrates, dreading the occupation of the town, offered him a large sum of money if he would maintain the strictest discipline among his soldiers. "Yes," he replied, "I thankfully accept the conditions you offer; not, however, for myself, for I require not your money—but for my men, who are in want of everything. They are destitute of clothing and shoes. Employ the money you offer me in providing them with these necessaries, and I promise you they shall give you no reason to complain."

The magistrates, in surprise, readily subscribed to the terms. Under similar circumstances, Turenne evinced the same disinterestedness. But Turenne belonged to a rich and noble family, and Ney was very poor; nevertheless, the action of the former is trumpeted forth by everyone,—that of the latter, forgotten. Such is worldly justice—such the even-handed distribution of fame.

Galicia, and Salamanca, provinces particularly hostile to the French, have, nevertheless, preserved the recollection of Ney's integrity whilst governor of them. One only spoil of a conquered country did Ney bequeath to his descendants: this is a relic of St. James of Compostello, with which the monks of St. Jago presented him, in testimony of his humanity towards them.

Marshal Ney was tall, athletic, well made, and broad-chested. Each attitude and motion denoted health and strength of muscle. A soul of fire seemed contained in a frame of iron. His rather pale complexion, large forehead, under lip and chin rather prominent, and his strongly marked, though not harsh features, gave a manly and severe character to a countenance strongly depicting the workings of his mind, and the rapid impressions it received. The play of his features strongly expressed the feelings by which he was excited.

The fatigues of his profession during the last years of his life, had made him almost bald. His hair, of a fiery auburn, had caused the soldiers to give him the nicknames of Peter the Red, and the Red Lion, as they gave the Emperor that of the Little Corporal. And when from afar off they heard the thunder of his cannon, they would exclaim among themselves, "Courage! the Red Lion is roaring;—All will soon be right, for Peter the Red is coming."

Having given these personal details of the marshal, we shall now proceed to narrate the events of his life.

CHAPTER 4

Ney's First Feat of Arms

Equality of rights had been proclaimed; privileges and exclusion no longer existed. Each from that time was what his own deeds made him; no man could acquire any other importance than that which resulted from courage and talents, neither of which are confined to gentle lineage. Men, however, of high descent, refused, from one end of Europe to the other, to acknowledge such pretensions in the plebeian race. Those beyond the Rhine prepared to combat them by war; and in France, a portion of the aristocracy joined in this unholy crusade against the people, whilst the remainder sought refuge in their feudal residences.

The officers of noble birth having abandoned their colours, the vacancies which they left were filled up by men of ability from among the plebeians. Ney was appointed sub-lieutenant, then lieutenant, and soon after placed upon the staff of the veteran General Lamarche, a good and respectable officer, who had spent a great portion of his life in the subaltern grades of the army. The revolution raised him to the rank which his talents merited. He had appreciated Ney, whose activity and courage he admired, and he appointed him his *aide-de-camp*.

Thus Ney, almost at the outset of his military career, found himself in a situation to study the art of war, without being subjected to the painful drudgery of the lower grades. Being placed upon an eminence, whence his eye could embrace the whole field of military tactics, he was thus initiated into the secret of great movements, which he was in a situation not only to study and comprehend, but at times to direct in person; and he soon proved that the lessons he received were not thrown away.

War having been declared, Ney, who accompanied General Lamarche into Belgium, shared with that officer the glory and perils of the brilliant début of the French army in that country. But unhappily the reverses of the French troops were as sudden as their success had been rapid. They were beaten at Aldenhoven, and at Nerwinde, and defection having cooperated with the disasters of their defeat, they were near being annihilated ere the acclamations on their victory had well ceased. Mayenne had opened its gates, Valenciennes had surrendered, Condé was beleaguered; and the Departments, in a state of insurrection in consequence of the violent acts of the 31st of May, were on the point of overthrowing the power that governed them.

The situation of the country was critical, but never did it display greater energy, Kings were preparing to stifle the revolution, which, nevertheless, assembled its forces, and went forth to do battle with kings. Men and materials had been placed at the disposal of the revolutionary general, whilst armed masses were inundating the frontier. Nevertheless, this prodigious armament was far from being so formidable as it appeared. These general risings, these levies *en masse*, had undergone the common fate of things, which become less effective in proportion as they are multiplied, and degenerate with each repetition.

Experience proved this in the present instance. Three great levies had taken place, the first of which was incontestably superior to the second, as the second was to the third; and the latter, it cannot be denied, was much more effective than the corps raised by the decrees of the National Assembly, and ordered to the frontier.

Nor could it be otherwise. The first battalions of volunteers had almost all been commanded by officers whom the love of their country, an abhorrence of slavery, and, no doubt, the illusions of military glory also, had collected round the national standard. Disciplined and led on by commanders of experience, they did not strive in the field of battle without reaping some laurels. But their career was as short as it was brilliant. They were swept from the face of the earth, and recourse was had to new levies—composed, it is true, of young men full of valour;—strong, robust, and devoted, like those who had fallen, but who had not experience for their loadstar—no veteran and tried courage to direct and render their ardour available. And what is a body without a point of impulse— what power has a mass, when deprived of simultaneous action?

We must not imagine that patriotism alone, whatever be its intensity, can overcome fatigue, and obviate the disgust attendant upon warfare. War is marked with sufferings too acute, with privations too great, for the soldier to endure, were he not fettered by habits of discipline. These, however, were easily given to the recruits by incorporating them with old soldiers.

By so doing, the energy of the young troops, which the want of good officers had for a moment paralysed, was again excited at the same time that the thousand battalions of which the army was composed, were reduced to six hundred. This was still a great number; for men able properly to command a battalion, are not so numerous as people suppose. But at all events, the army now formed a flexible and compact mass; and if, as Feuquières alleges, God is always on the side of great squadrons and numerous battalions, then might the army of the French people have reasonably calculated upon Divine aid.

These changes left thirty thousand officers without employment; and it must be confessed that many of them were men of great talents. But if the measure was attended with some evils, it obviated others much more dangerous. For whatever is done by popular choice, is always carried to extremes; in such cases a certain exaggeration always accompanies the most prudent measures. Doubts having been raised concerning the opinions and talents of officers belonging to the aristocracy, the people seemed suddenly convinced that to lead the French armies to victory, it required only to be a *sans-culotte*. Neither the science nor the practice of war seemed worthy of a moment's consideration; and it was asserted from the tribune, that if Duguay-Trouin had not been an ignorant man, he never would have proved victorious.

This idea was embellished and adorned like an embroidered garment, and a swarm of patriots left the desk to buzz forth their pretensions in the army, which they filled with trouble and confusion. The incorporation of the battalions was a favourable opportunity to get rid of them, and it was taken advantage of. This was doing a great deal, no doubt; but it was now necessary to replace these would-be commanders with real warriors, most of whom had been either dismissed or suspended. Brilliant as were the services of General Barthélemi, that officer had been sent to the Abbaye for his independent principles; and the brave and devoted Tharrau was expiating his noble moderation in another prison.

The latter general had been convicted of an act of humanity. Some disturbances having taken place in the vicinity of Chimey, neither the troops nor the *gendarmerie* had succeeded in apprehending the authors of them. This was sufficient for Saint-Just to raise the cry of connivance and want of energy; and in his anger he issued the following strange order:—

> Generals Balland and Desjardins are hereby enjoined to kill, within three days, all the brigands in the country of Chimey. They shall answer with their lives for the execution of the present order.

The wording of this sanguinary order being vague, Tharrau took advantage of that circumstance to elude its execution. He knew that reflection often calms the workings of anger; and he endeavoured to provoke reflection, by writing to know whether the order included women and children. But this, instead of softening, only increased the fury of the ferocious representative, who sent back Tharrau's letter with the following words written under it:—

> A stupid question requires no answer.

Notwithstanding this harshness, Tharrau, to avoid spilling innocent blood, determined that the question should be repeated; but this time he made Desjardins write. Saint-Just was furious at this resistance to his order; and being aware that Tharrau directed everything, dismissed him from the service, and had him imprisoned. Some officers were also dismissed for having served under Houchard; others for having been appreciated by Custine; and all were replaced by men who had never seen a shot fired. Fortunately Pichegru was sent to assume the command of this new and unorganised army.

Not that he was himself very able; for he had been promoted to the rank of lieutenant-colonel only six months before, and possessed no very clear notions on the art of war. But he had tact and discernment, and, moreover, a decided aversion to those saturnalia which demoralized the army, from which he now expelled luxury and effeminacy, and allayed the uneasiness that pervaded its ranks.

His intimacy with Saint-Just enabled him to overcome all opposition; and he exercised over the representatives the same influence which they had before exercised over the generals of the army. He was thus enabled to remove such individuals as were useless, and appoint those whom public opinion pointed out as most worthy of command. His first choice fell upon Scherer, a veteran officer, well versed in the art of war, but who being of plebeian extraction, had been obliged to seek in foreign countries the reputation which his humble birth had prevented him from acquiring in his own.

He had served in Hungary and in Holland—had bled in the cause of freedom and civilization, and having learnt the art of war in the field of battle, had also written upon it. In a clever work, he had pointed out and examined the faults and manoeuvres which led to the reverses of the Austrians and the successes of the Turks. Entrusted with the defence of the Upper Rhine, he had kept a very considerable force in check with only a few battalions, and had evinced much talent in his instructions to the troops sent against Landau. With such claims, Pichegru was delighted to attach this able officer to the army he commanded.

Men experienced in practical warfare were scarce at this period. Pichegru was sensible of his own deficiencies: he knew that he wanted counsel and support, and he sought out those who were able to afford them. Friant, though still a novice, was a man of mind and action;—having evinced talent at the battle of Kayserslautern, he was appointed to the command of a brigade. Kussell, equally distinguished by talent and courage, was put at the head of another.

Thus, if the subordinate generals were not men of great military reputation, they were likely soon to earn renown. Providence, moreover, supplied the army of the North with what was still wanting, by giving it two officers of surpassing merit. These were Marceau and Kléber;—the one short, delicately formed, and in the spring of life; the other tall, strong, and of heroic stature.

Both under this contrast of form and appearance, displayed equal ardour and ability; both had won laurels in the field of battle, and both had already given proofs of those great military talents which they afterwards more fully developed. But if the composition of the army was such as to afford reasonable hopes, the state of the military stores, provisions, and artillery, were little calculated to inspire it.

There was a lamentable scarcity of powder, muskets were also scarce, and the issuing of rations was always uncertain. Measures were never taken to secure provisions for even a fortnight together; and often it was not known at night how the wants of the following day were to be supplied. Such a state of things cramped the energies of the army; no movement could be undertaken, no attack conducted with a prospect of success. The want of bread and of ammunition disconcerted the best combined operations; and if the soldiers yielded to a rash and thoughtless courage, hunger and famine soon avenged the attempt.

It was for want of powder that the French had lost the battle of Arlon during the preceding year; and at the beginning of the present campaign the want of provisions delayed for the space of two whole days the bold march so ably conducted through the Ardennes, and caused the loss of the battle fought on the 3rd of June, under the walls of Charleroy. It is true that this scarcity was not always attended with such deplorable results, but want is never felt in an army without producing murmurs and insubordination. Even the most simple measures often failed for want of provisions.

Nevertheless, battles were fought and victories gained. The enemy was defeated, because valour supplied the place of all that was wanting. Such success seemed the precursor of plenty. But two armies had penetrated into Belgium; the civil administrations which they dragged in their train seemed to vie with each other in adding to the privations which the soldiers were forced to endure.

They disputed the territory with each other, laid villages under contribution, and opposed force and violence to each other's exactions. A line was attempted to be drawn to limit their several pretensions; but it was respected by neither.

At length the two administrations were united into one, for the general provisioning of both armies. But this change proved by no means advantageous. The agents no longer appeared in behalf of such and such an army; but some acted in the name of one *ordonnateur,* others in the name of another. One would have orders to carry into effect a partial, another a general requisition; and each, exclusively occupied in the execution of his separate instructions, would embarrass the proceedings of the others.

Sometimes these men would even stop the delivery of provisions to their colleagues, forbidding the inhabitants to supply them with anything. Such unworthy dissensions ruined the country, and kept the army in a state of painful excitement. The cavalry were in want of forage, the infantry of rations.

Each corps was obliged to supply its own wants, and do for itself that which the administration did not do. Horses were turned into meadows, and the little which had been left to the inhabitants was taken from them. The soldiers lived by violence, and were worn down with privations.

To the Representatives of the People, at Brussels.

Cologne, 17th of *Vendemiaire* (Oct. 8th.)

My Dear Colleagues,

The agents sent to issue requisitions, have proceeded in a manner revolting to everybody. On entering a town, they put everything in requisition—everything, absolutely everything. From that moment no inhabitant can either buy or sell. All trade is suspended; and that for an indefinite lapse of time: some requisitions having been made for more than a month, whilst nothing is wanted, and in the mean time the inhabitants are unable to purchase the very necessaries of life. If such measures be not counter-revolutionary—if they be not vexatious and likely to raise the whole country against us, I should be glad to know what they are.

Unfortunately the whole territory is subjected to similar requisitions; they succeed each other rapidly, and blow upon blow is struck.

Let the articles we want be put in requisition—nothing is more proper; and this I direct to be done by the commissaries of the army, when there are no other agents. But let the quantity of each article be specified, and the inhabitants have the faculty of disposing of the remainder. No inhabitant will find fault with such an arrangement, provided the articles are paid for.

But that all should be put in requisition, and for months together, without stating what is really wanted, and without even paying for what is taken, is absurd and disgraceful, Citizens Colleagues. The agents caused Belgium to rise in the time of Dumourier, and alienated from us the love of its inhabitants. If we do not take good care, the same thing will again occur, and we shall have to wage war with the Belgians, as well as with the Austrians.

You are on the spot, and the principal agency is under your control. Institute then a rigorous inquiry into these measures, and endeavour to apply a prompt remedy to acts which may otherwise be attended with fatal consequences.

What is necessary must be obtained; at the same time sufficient must be left for the wants of the inhabitants. Every article put in requisition, must be immediately paid for and taken away. With regard to issuing requisitions that are not executed, it is unnecessarily vexatious.

Health and fraternity.

Gillet.

This state of things lasted during the whole campaign. It must, however, be stated, that the blame did not wholly attach to the administration; for many of its agents were incompetent, dissipated, avaricious, or more attentive to their pleasure than to their public duties. Besides this, the resources of the country had been greatly over-rated.

It was firmly believed that they would prove sufficient for the support of the two armies which had entered it, over and above the consumption of its inhabitants. But Luxemburg and Campen do not produce much; Guelderland, the Duchy of Cleves, and the County of Meurs, are not very fertile; and the resources of the Duchy of Juliers, as well as those of the Electorate of Cologne, had been exhausted by the Austrians.

Thus Hainault, Brabant, West Flanders, and that part of the territory of Liege which is situated on the left bank of the Meuse, were the only parts of the country which offered the least appearance of plenty; but these places had their centres of consumption, and were unable to provide food for so sudden an increase of population.

It was the same with regard to forage. Brabant, Juliers, and Cologne had only artificial meadows; Limburg, whose crops are more considerable, had been partly drained of its supplies; whilst the army of Sambre-et-Meuse had seventy thousand horses, and that of the North thirty thousand. Thus both infantry and cavalry were forced to suffer the most trying privations.

Such were the difficulties against which the republican troops had to contend;—such were the first obstacles they had to overcome.

At the end of July 1794, soon after the battle of Fleurus and the taking of Mons, Kléber, still excited by his victory, was preparing to follow it up. The Austrian army was at some distance from him. Anxious to reconnoitre its position, he set out with an escort picket, and on the road entered into conversation with the officer who commanded it. He was so pleased with the clear and judicious observations of the commander of the picket that he determined to appoint him to his staff. Pajol, *aide-de-camp* to Kléber, delivered the order of appointment to this officer, who turned out to be Ney.

He had just joined the 4th Regiment of hussars. Promoted to the rank of captain after the affair of Famars, which proved fatal to the respectable Lamarche, he had returned to his regiment with the intention of not again leaving it. He therefore declined the General's offer. But Kléber had appreciated his talents, and was anxious to have him. Detachments of Austrian troops overran the country; the inhabitants were in a state of increasing agitation, and Kléber resolved to organize a band of partisans, who might dislodge the Austrian detachments, keep the population in awe, secure a regular supply of provisions, and open safe communications throughout the territory.

The service required to be conducted by a man of superior talent and tried valour, and Ney was selected. Meantime, the army was debouching on Pellemberg. The Austrian forces were numerous; and the French vanguard, which followed them close, was by no means strong. An action had begun, and the hostile forces soon became warmly engaged. Ney, on hearing the report of the artillery, changed his route, and proceeded in haste to the scene of action. Adjutant-General Bouquet had just given way before a squadron of Austrian cavalry: his ranks were broken, and he was covered with wounds.

Ney came up, but the detachment under his command, worn out with their march, were unable to follow him. He however put himself at the head of a few dragoons, rushed on the Imperialists, and succeeded in routing them. Kléber, who was an eye-witness to this daring act, mentioned it in his despatch to the representative, in the following terms:—

> Captain Ney, acting adjutant-general, performed prodigies of valour. At the head of thirty dragoons, and a few *chasseurs* acting as orderlies, he charged two hundred of the Blanckestein hussars, and threw them into the greatest disorder.

Gillet, delighted with this act of heroism, appointed Ney to the rank of which he was provisionally performing the duties: that of adjutant-general.[2]

---

2. Gillet, Representative of the people attached to the army of Sambre-et-Meuse. In consequence of the report made to him of the military talents and patriotism of citizen Ney, captain in the 4th Regiment of hussars, hereby appoints the said citizen Ney to hold the rank of adjutant-general, and *chef de bataillon,* the duties of which grade he is already performing under General Kléber, commanding the left wing of the army. 14th *Thermidor,* Year 2. (August 1st, 1794.) Gillet.

CHAPTER 5

Battle of the Roer

The vanguard had recrossed the Meuse, and Jourdan was endeavouring to protect his rear, and render his position more secure. Landrecy had surrendered, but Quesnoy seemed determined to hold out. Kléber also had advanced and invested Maestricht; but this place was difficult of approach, and provisions were daily becoming scarcer. Ney resumed his excursions, and extended his detachments towards Peer. He left Diest on the 26th of August 1794, reached Peer on the same day, and captured a convoy of twenty-three wagons, which were immediately directed towards the French army.

The following day was not attended with the same good fortune. A French trooper who had deserted, gave the enemy information regarding the strength and position of the detachment which was harassing their rear. Ney, who from some neglect had not been made acquainted with this circumstance, was quietly pursuing his march. He surprised the village of Achel, carried off the stores which the Austrians had collected there, but lost them immediately after. The hussars of Blanckestein and the dragoons of Latour suddenly appeared, recaptured the convoy, and made the escort prisoners, who were conveying it to the army.

Ney knew nothing of the imperial cavalry being on the alert; totally ignorant of what had passed, he was quietly proceeding towards Werdt. But before he reached Hamont, he perceived the imperialists threatening his flanks and rear, and preparing to make a charge upon his detachment. His situation, and the desertion of the trooper, of which he had just received notice, showed him the perils that surrounded him, and he began to retreat towards Eyndhoven; but his scouts soon reported to him that this road was also beset—that the enemy's cavalry flanked it right and left, and it was impossible to pass.

"Impossible!" Ney exclaimed; "sound the charge!" And he attacked the Austrian squadrons sword in hand with such impetuosity, that he broke their ranks; then pursuing his march with rapidity, and avoiding the villages, he gained the woods, and escaped from the detachments of the enemy stationed to cut him off.

But the plain was covered with the Austrian forces. At almost every step he was forced to halt, and either receive or head a charge. At one place he was under the necessity of forcing a bridge, at another of making a long circuit, further on of storming a post—everywhere he was beset with dangers and difficulties. He at length came in sight of Eyndhoven. His flankers had sent a patrol in advance, which had cleared the approaches.

The prisoners which they brought in, as well as the inhabitants he met, having informed him that the place had but a feeble garrison, he hoped to surprise and carry it by a *coup-de-main*; and with this expectation he rapidly advanced. Unfortunately a body of cavalry, which had come to its assistance, debouched as Ney appeared with his little army. The surprise at this unexpected obstacle was great, but the French soldiers were as determined as their leader. They charged the Austrians without considering their numbers; threw themselves headlong into the midst of the enemy's ranks, broke and dispersed them, took their commander, the Baron Homspech, prisoner, and returned with him to Diest.

Jourdan was not less pleased with the manner in which this expedition had been conducted, than with the capture of the Austrian commander. He knew the noble baron well, and strongly suspected him of having exercised some influence over the determinations of the old French generals, and mixed himself up with various untoward negotiations. He therefore advised the committee to have the baron sent to Paris. With regard to Ney, the representative Gillet appointed him *chef-de-brigade*, in which capacity, "he purposed employing him with great advantage."

Towards the end of September, the column which had reduced Condé and Valenciennes prepared for the pursuit of fresh victories, and began a general movement. Meantime the enemy, beaten at Sprimont on the 18th, and defeated at Clermont on the 20th, were endeavouring to rally behind the Roer. A sad reverse of fortune had now dissipated their illusion. The French army, which at the beginning of the campaign was entrenched, in almost hopeless despair, behind the Scarpe, was now on the eve of reaching the Rhine. The Northern army had penetrated into the heart of Holland; the English had disappeared, and on all sides victory had crowned the French arms.

Clairfayt was not discouraged by these reverses. He retreated, but without ceasing to fight; and he ably availed himself of the advantages which the nature of the ground offered him. Neither the rugged banks of the Ourthe, nor those of the Ayvaille, had been able to shelter him from the attacks of the republicans; but the Roer was in a deeper bed, and more rapid; it had also higher and more rugged and precipitous banks than the former rivers. He therefore took advantage of these obstacles, and fell back upon the Roer.

The French army pursued him with all the ardour inspired by victory. Scherer commanded the right, Jourdan the centre, and Kléber the left. Each pressed forward upon the retreating enemy, each emulous to out vie the others. Divers encounters took place, all of which turned out in favour of the French, and the Austrians were in full retreat. But Kléber was not yet satisfied.

Bernadotte commanded the van. This officer, who had recently been promoted to the rank of general, combined with the courage characterizing the army of Sambre-et-Meuse an experience seldom found at that period in the French ranks. He had been a Soldier from the age of fourteen; had seen service in

America as well as in Europe; and had displayed on the banks of the Delaware, as he then did on the Sambre, that eagle eye, and velocity of manoeuvre, which few of his colleagues then possessed.

He added to the ascendancy which the habit of warfare had given him, many qualities not less precious in a soldier. He was enterprising, intrepid, and as ardent in action as in the expression of his opinions. His enthusiasm delighted the men under his command; his fine, soldier-like appearance, and his confidence, heated their imaginations. There was nothing too difficult for them when led on by him—nothing they would not undertake at his bidding. But everything has its limits; even valour meets with obstacles which it cannot overcome.

Bernadotte pushed on towards Heinsberg. He was desirous of attacking the enemy's rear-guard without allowing it time to breathe; but the hostile forces were numerous, and being favoured by the nature of the ground, made an obstinate stand.

Kléber had already sent reinforcements; but as the battle seemed to last much too long, he became impatient, and dispatched Ney to Bernadotte's assistance. Ney advanced with rapidity towards Stockheim, but had scarcely got half way ere he perceived a number of boats making the most strenuous exertions to reach Maestricht in as short a time as possible. In these boats he could discern wheels and gun-carriages, and he had no doubt that they contained guns and stores for the defence of that place. He therefore wheeled round, and gained the banks of the river, for the purpose of intercepting them. His half-naked *chasseurs* prepared to swim towards the boats and attack them; but the boatmen not daring to run the risk of such a conflict, sank their boats, and with them the guns and ammunition which they contained.

This incident was fortunate in itself, but it soon became still more so. Ney had resumed his march; his men were congratulating each other on having destroyed a part of the means intended to be employed against them in the defence of Maestricht, when a flotilla appeared at a distance. Ney ordered them to press forward, and seize a prey which could not escape them. A body of them soon reached the banks of the river, threw themselves into it, and swam to the boats, on board of which they succeeded in getting, in spite of the determined resistance of the crews.

Here a desperate conflict ensued. Ney, anxious to take a share in it, pressed hastily forward, and soon reached the banks of the river; but his appearance put an end to the action, and the crews of the boats instantly submitted. Having continued his march, he joined Bernadotte at Tranquemont, which the news of this double encounter had already reached. It was also known that Maestricht, deprived in the morning of part of the supplies intended for its defence, had in the last capture lost a portion of the provisions intended for the subsistence of its garrison; and this raised a hope that, being disappointed in these means of prolonging its defence, it would the more readily surrender on reasonable terms.

Bernadotte had likewise obtained some advantages; his troops were proud of his success, and he determined to push forward. Nuth was not far distant; and as the enemy seemed resolved to defend it, he purposed to meet them there. But the Austrians had already betaken themselves to flight; and as the French came in sight of the place, their last patrols could just be perceived gaining the woods.

Bernadotte did not think proper to pursue them in person, but ordered Ney upon this service. "See," said he to the latter, "they are proceeding towards Gangelt, where they probably hope to pass the night in peace; do you overtake and harass them; let them fall before you like corn before the reaper's sickle."

Ney did overtake them, but they were numerous and resolute, and he was obliged to send for reinforcements. An officer who has since highly distinguished himself, Maurin, then assistant adjutant-general, came to his assistance at the head of the 2nd Hussars. The pursuit was hot, skirmishes frequent, and at length Ney, accompanied only by his *chasseurs* and a few companies of light infantry, reached Heinsberg. The enemy occupied it with a strong force; the town was barricaded, and embrasures appeared on all sides, ready to pour death upon its assailants. But Ney had communicated his own impatient ardour to the troops who had kept up with him. The infantry scaled the walls, the sappers broke open the gates, and in a moment every point was carried. The Austrians, thus driven from the place, made an attempt to form under shelter of the wood; but with no better success. Ney's troops pursued them closely, and forced them to throw themselves in the greatest disorder into Wassemberg.

The Austrians were thus driven to their last resources. The French army debouched upon the Roer, and were already in front of the formidable obstacles raised to oppose them.

The main body had taken up its position between Heinsberg and Drumen. Bernadotte pushed forward towards Rutten at the head of the vanguard. Rutten is a village situated on the left bank of the Roer; it stands upon an eminence, from which might be fully seen all the obstacles which the army had to encounter.

There was in view a long line of redoubts, bristling with *chevaux-de-frise*, and broad entrenchments defended by deep ditches. In one place, a *batterie rasante* appeared; at another guns of large calibre, and behind these formidable works a numerous infantry drawn up, motionless, and waiting only for the appearance of the French forces to open a destructive fire. These works, and this attitude of defence, were calculated to inspire caution. But for six months past the Austrians had in vain attempted to regain their lost ground. Beaten in every action, they were constantly compelled to retreat, and as constantly driven from the positions which were to have stopped the progress of the republican armies.

The French troops could now perceive them entrenched and fortified in the midst of rocks, and behind ravines and coppices. Such obstacles only increased the audacity of the republican soldiers, eager to advance, cross the river, and encounter hand to hand the troops they had so often put to flight, and who now dared to face them only because they were protected by their position and works. Bernadotte excited, like his men, by a series of victories, participated in their enthusiasm. But the Roer was deep and rapid, and the rain, which fell in torrents, increased every hour the impetuosity of its waters. Unwilling to expose his troops to the torrent and to the enemy's grape-shot, without first ascertaining the precise difficulties they would have to overcome, he sent forward the light infantry to reconnoitre; but scarcely had they appeared in front of the river ere the Austrian batteries began to play. The fire was returned from the other bank, and in a moment the two armies were engaged. It was however impossible to meet hand to hand, and neither would retire.

For a long time death was dealt out unflinchingly on either side, and the hostile forces moved not from their positions. At length a fresh battery being unmasked, and the Austrians exposed to a murderous cross fire, they began to give way. The 71st seized the opportunity, and rushing into the river, succeeded in gaining the opposite bank. Bernadotte immediately reported this success to Kléber. "Great praise," he wrote, "is due to the brave Ney. He seconded me with the ability which you know he possesses, and I am bound to add, in strict justice, that he greatly contributed to the success we have obtained."

By the time the French troops had crossed the river, it was dark, and no bridges could be constructed till the next day, or other necessary preparations made to follow up this victory. The enemy withdrew during the night, and nothing remained next morning but the marks of their defeat.

Similar operations, attended with similar results, took place along the rest of the line. On this occasion the following report was addressed by Gillet to the Committee of Public Safety:

> I have delayed until now giving you an account of the most recent successes of the army of Sambre-et-Meuse, in order to be able at the same time to announce to you a victory, together with the capture of a fortified town, a citadel, sixty pieces of cannon, and a great quantity of stores and ammunition.
>
> The Austrian army, beaten in detail at Sprimont, and Cl-

ermont, on the 2nd and 3rd *sans-culottides*, had entrenched themselves upon the banks of the Roer, where they still formed a force of from sixty to eighty thousand men. On the 1st instant, we took Aix-la-Chapelle, and our army encamped on the plains of Aldenhoven, the left close to Worms, and the right towards Scherweiller upon the Dinse.

The enemy intending to defend the passage of the Roer, and keep open a communication with Maestricht, a considerable portion of their army was stationed on the right bank of that river, in a position just behind Aldenhoven, and in front of Juliers. This position, naturally strong, was moreover fortified with lines and redoubts which defended it on all sides.

Jourdan, determined to follow up our successes, resolved to force the enemy in their last entrenchments. To succeed, it was necessary to attempt one of those bold manoeuvres which render the most difficult enterprises possible when executed by able officers and intrepid soldiers; for the Roer, though fordable in many places, was swollen by the rain which had fallen during the last ten days. The fords, in themselves difficult, were covered with *chevaux-de-frise*, the bridges were destroyed, and the heights which extend along the right bank of the Roer, from its source to Buremonde, were covered with lines and redoubts, and defended by a formidable artillery.

Jourdan divided his army into four corps. Scherer commanded the right wing, General Kléber the left, and General Lefebvre the van. Jourdan retained the command of the centre, forming the *corps-de-bataille*, having under him Generals of Division, Hatry, Morlot, Championnet, and Dubois. Scherer was directed to force the passage of Dueren; Kléber to attack on the left at Heinsberg, and the vanguard, at Limnich, whilst the *corps-de-bataille* was to attack the camp in front of Juliers.

Yesterday, at five o'clock in the morning, every column

was in motion, and all commenced the attack with equal bravery. In less than two hours, the camp in front of Juliers was forced, and the redoubts carried with unexampled intrepidity. The enemy's cavalry appeared to cover the retreat of their army. Ours charged and routed it, pursuing it even to the glacis of Juliers; and it owed its safety, as did the whole Austrian army, solely to the guns of that place, which prevented our troops from continuing the pursuit. The other columns were equally successful, but they met with difficulties of another kind.

When the vanguard reached Limnich, they found that the enemy had destroyed the bridge, and set fire to the town. Every point of approach having been rendered impracticable, it became necessary to construct bridges under a dreadful fire of artillery and musketry. This was however executed under the protection of our artillery, which on this occasion, as on every other, showed its great superiority over that of the enemy, who were obliged to withdraw and abandon their redoubts. The bridges, however, could not be constructed before night, so that it was impossible to complete the passage of the river. Everything was ready to execute it this morning, when the clearing up of the fog showed us the enemy in full flight.

Several redoubts had been raised in front of Juliers, and a battery of mortars erected to bombard the place. This battery had already begun to produce great effect, when a white flag appeared on the citadel, and a deputation of magistrates came to deliver up the keys of the town, which had been evacuated by the enemy during the night, and now surrendered at discretion.

This battle must form a memorable epoch in the arms of the republic. An army of from sixty to eighty thousand men defeated under the shelter of a most formidable position; a place stronger than Landrecy—with a good citadel, fosses full of water, and in the best possible state of defence —with an arsenal full of stores, and containing more than fifty thousand pounds of powder—evacuated, taken without a struggle. Such, my dear colleagues, are the fruits of this brilliant day.

The enemy's loss is immense. On the other side of the Roer the ground is covered with slain, even within the Austrian lines. This we were able to verify this morning, and it proves the precipitancy of their retreat. everything denotes the most complete rout. Several columns of cavalry, light artillery, and grenadiers, are in pursuit of them; and I have just learned that General Dubois, at the head of six regiments of cavalry, has overtaken their baggage wagons, to the right of Cologne. We have made upwards of six hundred prisoners.

It would be out of my power to notice every act of heroism by which this day is honoured; for I should have to mention by name every corps, every general, every officer, and every soldier, because all have shown themselves heroes: I shall therefore designate only two.

The first relates to the vanguard of the divisions under the command of General Kléber. The brave soldiers who composed it, impatient at the delay which the construction of a bridge would cause, threw themselves into the river, swam across it, attacked the enemy's works, and carried them at the point of the bayonet.

The second relates to two squadrons of chasseurs, commanded by General d'Hautpoul. These brave men, having met four squadrons of the enemy's hussars, charged them without counting their numbers, and drove them into the river. Almost the whole were either killed, drowned, or taken.

Health and Fraternity.
Gillet.
Head Quarters, Juliers, 12th *Vendemiaire*, Year 3 (October 3rd, 1794.)

Chapter 6

Siege of Maestricht

The Austrian army was in a deplorable condition. Both generals and soldiers, struck with consternation at their successive defeats, were now only desirous of recrossing the Rhine. The courage of Werneck himself was at length shaken. This general, habitually so firm and decided, had now lost all confidence. Having made arrangements for the supplying of Maestricht with provisions, he left upon his table a duplicate of the orders he had issued. Bernadotte having come upon him unawares, found this document, and perceiving in an instant the full importance of the information it afforded him, despatched Ney to take the best advantage of it.

> The general who commands an army in which you are employed," he wrote to the latter, "is a fortunate man. I have that good luck, and I fully appreciate it. Continue to pursue and hussar the enemy, and I will second you to the utmost of my means. You shall have by tomorrow the 4th Hussars and the 16th Chasseurs. I will likewise send you a body of infantry, and will ride over and consult with you on the best means of supporting you with the dragoons.
> I must inform you, my dear friend, that there is something of great importance to be attempted. The honour of the attempt is reserved for you, and to you shall be attributed all the merit of its success. You must, if possible, obtain possession of the flour which Field Marshal Werneck is sending, under an escort, along the heights on the other

side of Vegong, whence it is to enter the high road, and proceed to Neuss and Dusseldorf. The undertaking will be, perhaps, hazardous—but no matter; the convoy is not far off, and we can make the attempt.

I am going to take a few hours' rest; I advise you to do the same, for I fancy we shall have no time for sleep tomorrow.

Bernadotte."

Guerack, 12th *Vendemiaire*, Year 3. (Oct. 3rd, 1794.)

Ney set out to intercept the escort, which had already arrived at Neuss, but which the report of his approach had prevented from leaving that town. He therefore resolved to make himself master not only of the provisions, but of the town which contained them. From a thousand to twelve hundred horse defended the approaches to the place. He braved and endeavoured to provoke them to an action, but the greater his ardour, the more determined were they to avoid a conflict; and every effort to bring them to battle was unavailing. Under these circumstances he came to the resolution of storming the town forthwith.

This bold resolve was singular, inasmuch as he had not with him a single foot soldier, and the ramparts of Neuss were covered with a numerous body of infantry. Nevertheless the *coup-de-main* succeeded. He had scarcely fired ten shots, when the garrison set fire to the storehouses, and escaped in great disorder with the flour wagons, which they still attempted to save. Ney pursued them closely, and seized a number of the wagons, dispersing the remainder, and driving them beyond Dusseldorf, which they had not time to enter. The night was however very dark, and his hussars being overcome with fatigue, he was obliged to halt, and allow the men and horses a few hours' rest.

The silence of the bivouac, which was on the banks of the Rhine, having succeeded the tumult of the pursuit, an indistinct sound was shortly after heard, then a confused noise of human voices and oars.

Ney's men now saw that they were about to effect the object

for which they had been striving, and this idea inspired them with fresh vigour. They ran to their arms, and resumed their march; but Dusseldorf sided with the Austrians, and no sooner did the French hussars appear before it than it thundered its artillery at them. Ney took no notice of this aggression, but continued his route, overtook the portion of the escort which had escaped from him under cover of the darkness of the preceding night, and after dispersing it, took possession of the wagons. Nor was this all. He knew that the diplomatists of the river were sending away their treasure; this he intercepted, and with the riches he expected, some valuable dispatches which he certainly did not expect, fell into his hands.

Kléber, greatly irritated at the aggression of Dusseldorf, determined to avenge both the insult offered to his vanguard, and the partiality which the citizens seemed to entertain towards the French emigrants. But this was by no means easy. His soldiers were without clothing, his wagons without cattle, and the season was becoming more unfavourable every day. He was not, however, to be turned from his purpose; and that which he needed, he purposed making the enemy supply him with. This was perhaps the first time that an army wanting the means of taking a fortified town, had attempted to force that town to supply such means against itself. But Kléber had resolved upon it: the attack therefore began, and the batteries of the French army soon set the town on fire. The general then sent for Ney.

"Do you see," he said, "the ravages made by our shells? Well, take a trumpeter, proceed to Dusseldorf, and tell the magistrates, that if I am not put in possession of the place forthwith, together with a million of francs, I will destroy everything in it."

Ney went, threatened, intimidated, and executed his mission so well that Dusseldorf opened its gates. It contained an immense quantity of artillery, stores, and provisions.

Ney having resumed his excursions, pushed on towards Cleves, at the head of four hundred horse, defeated the enemy, carried the place, and immediately advancing upon Nimeguen, carried that also. Meantime Kléber had resumed the siege of Maestricht.

The waters of the Sambre being low, he had been unable to receive the artillery and ammunition necessary for his operations; and the garrison, emboldened by the failure of former attempts, feared not to attack the besiegers in their trenches. Kléber, irritated at this, urgently demanded Ney; whilst Jourdan, who had employed him elsewhere, was in no haste to comply with the demand. But Gillet, having approached the place at the head of a reconnoitring party, put Ney's services in requisition. He kept him, as he stated in his despatch[1], to the commander-in-chief, "at the request of General Kléber, who was anxious to brink the besieged to reason, and sicken them of making sorties." And in truth they were soon confined within their walls.

The artillery at length came down the Sambre, and the siege commenced under the direction of General Bollemont, a brave and able officer, who though advanced in years, had preserved all the fire and energy of youth. He ordered the engineers to erect nothing but incendiary batteries upon the first parallel, reserving the siege batteries for the second. Such a thing had never been heard of before; but General Bollemont having directed that it should be done, the body of engineers determined to do their best to reach the second parallel without the support of artillery. In carrying their works along the right flank of Mont St. Pierre, they discovered the mouth of a deep cavern, which, according to the information given by the country people, had branches extending under the fortress.

In verifying this fact, a subterraneous city was discovered, which proved the exact counterpart of the city above. The circumstance was a singular one; the dark city became the sole topic of conversation, and inquiries were set on foot to ascertain the cause of its existence, and the use to which it was applied.

All this gave great uneasiness to the besieged, who sprang a mine in order to encumber the principal entrance, and prevent the besiegers from satisfying their curiosity. The explosion, though dreadful, did not produce the effect intended. It occasioned only the fall of a great quantity of earth, leaving an

---

1. Dated 22nd *Vendemiaire*, Year 3. (Oct. 13th, 1794.)

opening like a vast funnel, into which about sixty of the French soldiers immediately rushed. Considering, from what had just taken place, that there existed a passage communicating with the fortress, they resolved to ascertain the fact. They therefore advanced to a considerable distance within the cavern; but all was silent as the grave; nothing interrupted the sepulchral stillness of the place. Nevertheless they continued to advance, until at length a strange noise struck their ears.

They now fancied they had discovered the passage. Under the excitement of this pretended discovery, they made a vow never to see the light again except through the opening which led to the town. But what was their surprise, on advancing, to find that the enemy, whom they expected to encounter hand to hand—the foes whose voices they fancied they heard, were nothing but a flock of sheep which the inhabitants had concealed in the cavern. The adventure ended in their finding abundance of food, but no communication with the fortress.

As the place could not be carried but by a regular siege, an attempt was made to obtain its surrender by negotiation. The governor was summoned, pressed to this effect, and the reverses which the Austrians had encountered were very forcibly urged to induce his compliance. Although his courage was shaken by such a train of disasters, he would come to no decision until he had first communicated with the Hague, and received instructions from his masters. Kléber replied that the governor would soon have no master but him, and pushed on his works with vigour. The allies having, at Lille, Thionville, Valenciennes, and Landrecy, added the horrors of fire by bombshells to the ravages of their artillery, it was resolved to use reprisals on this occasion. Three mortar batteries were accordingly erected, and a considerable number of shells thrown into the place.

Still the governor persisted in his resistance. His fortifications were injured, his parapets and covered ways a mass of ruins; still he remained firm. The citizens were less determined, and Kléber was anxious to open a communication with the magistrates. Ney suggested a very simple plan: it was to summon the Austrian commander to allow the French to negotiate with the citizens, threatening him with the displeasure of the whole army if he refused. The expedient seemed good; and Ney being despatched to the gates with a flag of truce, displayed such confidence, and managed matters so well, that he intimidated the Austrian general into compliance. He was accordingly conducted to the Town Hall, where the City Council were sitting. The latter, however, pretended that the constitution deprived them of all right of interference in the defence of the place.

It therefore became necessary, after all, to batter in breach: and the works of the besiegers were continued with great vigour. Nevertheless, Kléber felt considerable repugnance to destroy this noble fortress, and determined on making a fresh attempt at negotiation. He again directed his adjutant-general to offer new matter for consideration to these haughty magistrates. Ney again appeared before them, and a discussion commenced which soon became animated. The governor exaggerated his resources; the council relied upon the strength of their ramparts; and all were bent upon running the chances of their resistance.

"If this be your ultimatum," said the adjutant-general, "I am bound to accept it. Your city will be destroyed, but the people you govern shall know to whom they are indebted for this cruel treatment. History will say that it was caused by your indifference to their interests, and your blind devotion to Austria. It will also say that a generous enemy wished to save your citizens and their property; but that you, their natural protectors—you, who are bound to defend them, sacrificed them without remorse to the pride of a government deaf to the voice of humanity, and which only seeks the vain glory of making a good but useless defence."

This speech produced an excellent effect. The governor himself was moved; he protested that so far from desiring to build his military reputation upon the misfortunes of the citizens, he would readily yield the place the instant he had proof that further resistance was useless.

"And have you not that proof?" replied Ney, with vivacity. "Can your armies, defeated at Aldenhoven, at Juliers, and at La Chartreuse, and whom the terror of our arms is now driving upon the Upper as upon the Lower Rhine, come to your assistance? And will the Dutch or the English effect that which is beyond the power of your own forces? Defeated on the Wahl, overthrown on the Scheldt, they have been unable to defend either Grave or Venloo. Bois-le-Duc and Crévecœur have just opened their gates to us, and neither the Austrians nor the English can henceforward do anything for you."

Ney spoke with vehemence, and the governor and magistrates forcibly admitting the truth of his account of the campaign, assumed a milder tone; the negotiations were resumed, and that which force had been unable to effect was obtained by address.

This was a noble termination to a campaign already unequalled in the annals of warfare. The French army had assembled on the 3rd of June 1794. Though deficient in artillery, and almost without stores, it had marched against the hostile forces which covered the frontiers of France and occupied many strong-holds; it had beaten and driven them from the French territory, and having pursued them across the Sambre, had defeated them in seven pitched battles. On the 16th and 26th of June they were beaten at Fleurus; on the 1st of July at Mont Palissel, in front of Mons, and at the camp of Rœulx; on the 6th at Waterloo; on the 7th at Sombref; on the 18th of September at the passage of the Ourthe; and on the 2nd of October at Juliers.

During these operations the French army had not received a single check, nor lost a single piece of ordnance; on the contrary, it had begun the campaign with a park of only sixteen guns, with which it had taken Charleroy, Landrecy, Quesnoy, Valenciennes, Condé, Namur, Juliers, Maestricht, Mons, Ath, Hall, Brussels, Louvain, Tirlemont, Tongres, St. Trond, Liège, Aix-la-

Chapelle, Cologne, Bonn, Coblentz, Creveldt, Gueldres, and Stephenwerth. It had captured nine hundred and ninety-five pieces of cannon, a hundred and five howitzers, and a hundred and fifty-eight mortars. At the end of the campaign it possessed four hundred and fifty field-pieces, stores for a whole year, besides twenty millions of cartridges; and its parks contained one thousand three hundred and sixty-eight pieces of ordnance. Such were the fruits of six months of peril and fatigue.

It might have been expected that labours of such magnitude would have insured quiet winter-quarters: no such thing. The Austrians still kept open their outlets upon the Rhine, and had, consequently, the power of again spreading over the Palatinate, and repossessing themselves, perhaps, of the rich plains from which the republican army had driven them; it was therefore deemed expedient to prevent the possibility of such an irruption, by laying siege to Mayence. Kléber, who commanded this expedition, selected the corps and officers he wished to have with him.

Ney was not forgotten; but the general-in-chief also claimed his services, and to elude the orders of the latter, it was deemed necessary again to have recourse to Gillet. Kléber thus driven to invoke the good offices of the representative, did not confine his demand to Ney, but requested also to have Marescot, Chasseloup, Duclos, Floyes, and the whole of the *bande joyeuse* who had assisted at the siege of Maestricht. Gillet felt a delicacy in deciding the question between the commander of the left wing and the general-in-chief, and referred it to the Committee of Public Safety; but he took advantage of his despatch to this body to say a word in favour of the brave men whose services the two commanders were so anxious to secure.

> "I know them all extremely well," he wrote to his colleagues, "and have seen them in actual service. They belong to a good and energetic school, by whose lessons they have profited. They display great zeal, and I urgently recommend them to your notice. It is but justice to these brave young men. As for Ney, you will determine whether

or not he is to remain with Kléber. For my own part, I think he would be very useful in the army before Mayence. He is a distinguished officer; and is necessary to our large body of cavalry. Men of his stamp are not common."

The question which Gillet dared not decide was already settled. Ney had seen with indignation the enemy sally forth from their ramparts, crown a redoubt erected in haste, and brave the efforts of the French soldiers. The *corps-de-siége* was composed of troops partly from the army of the Rhine and partly from that of Sambre-et-Meuse. Anxious to show the former how to fight, he assembled a few dragoons, saw that the horses were rough-shod, so that they could not slide upon the ice, and begged a few voltigeurs from *Chef-de-bataillon* Molitor. "I am going," he said, "to show you a trick after the manner of Sambre-et-Meuse."

Having put his *voltigeurs* in motion, they attacked the redoubt in front, whilst he got on the other side and brought up his dragoons against the pass it defended; but the men hesitated and dared not follow him, so that he penetrated alone into the redoubt. Surrounded by the enemy, he cut his way through them, single-handed, recrossed the ditch, and escaped under a shower of balls; but he received a wound in his arm, the pain of which was increased by the motion of his horse.

A species of lock-jaw ensued, and he became restless and desponding; at one moment under the excitement of burning fever, at the next weakened by the sufferings he endured, he refused all surgical aid.

His friends, uneasy at the strange turn his disorder had taken, hit upon an expedient to bring him to himself. Having assembled the musicians and young girls of the village, with Kléber and the representative Merlin at their head, they all went in procession to Ney's quarters, and danced the *farandolle* round his bed. The noise was at first unpleasant to him, but by degrees he joined in the hilarity it occasioned.

He then laughed at his gloomy thoughts and gave up his arm to the surgeons; his only uneasiness being now about the length of time his cure would take,—his only anxiety that of knowing how soon he should be able to return and face the enemy. Being informed that he had been appointed general of brigade, this promotion was only a source of uneasiness to him. He did not think he had done enough to merit that rank; and wished to leave it to those who, as he said, had better claims than his. In vain were his scruples laughed at—in vain was he urged to accept the promotion; it was impossible to shake his resistance or overcome his modesty. The chief of the staff came to his assistance on the occasion.

> "If you persist," wrote the latter, "in refusing the rank of General of Brigade, to which you have been appointed by the representative Merlin, I think you had better write to the board of organisation of the land forces. This would be the more advisable, as the representative Merlin is not yet returned from his journey to Paris.
> "Health and Fraternity.
> "Bourcier, General of Division, and Chief of the General Staff.
> "Head-quarters, Gandowblam, the 13th of *Pluviose*, Year 3. (February 1st, 1795.)"

Ney acted upon this suggestion, wrote to the board, and by dint of entreaty succeeded in getting his excuses accepted. As his wound continued painful, the representative Merlin recommended him to try his native air.

> "My brave friend," he wrote, "go and complete your cure at Sarrelibre,[2] your birth-place. I have despatched an order to the surgeon of first class, Bonaventure, to send one of his pupils with you. Return soon, and lend us your powerful aid against the enemies of your country.
> "Health and Fraternity.
> "Merlin.
> "Head-quarters at Oberingelheim, the 18th *Nivose*, Year 3. (January 7th, 1795."

---
2. The name of Sarrelouis was changed by the Jacobins to that of Sarrelibre.—Ed.

Kléber, also desirous of giving Ney a proof of his regard, and the estimation in which he held his services, addressed him the following document:

> Head-quarters of Observation, Ingelheim, 22nd *Nivose*, Year 3. (February 10th, 1795.)
>
> The General of Division Kléber, commanding the Corps d'Armée before Mayence.
>
> Hereby certifies that Citizen Ney, adjutant-general, *chef-de-brigade,* commanded with distinction various bodies of cavalry during the campaign of the army of Sambre-et-Meuse; that in every operation entrusted to him, he displayed the most consummate skill and bravery, particularly at the siege of Maestricht, where by his valour he did eminent service to the commonwealth; that having volunteered his services to the army before Mayence, in co-operating towards the capture of that place, he received, in a sortie, a gun-shot wound which has suspended his activity of service until his perfect cure.
>
> Kléber.

CHAPTER 7

Passage of the Rhine

The spring was advancing, active operations were about to be resumed, and Ney's wound was not yet healed. With anxiety, though resigned, he watched the slow progress of his convalescence. His hopes were still buoyant, and he trusted that his youth and the approaching season would speedily restore him to health, and that, in the mean time, the want of necessaries, unforeseen military combinations, or some other circumstances, might for a short time delay the passage of the Rhine.

A note from Kléber, however, put these notions to flight. The general ordered him to join the army the moment his wound would allow of his doing so; and Ney, supposing that the campaign was immediately to commence, set out for head-quarters, without regard to the state of his wound, and in spite of the remonstrances of his surgeon.

The month of May had already commenced. It had been intended to send detachments to many parts of the Duchy of Berg, invest Mayence, force Ehrenbreitstein, and by occupying the rich valley of the Maine, make the war feed itself;—the ultimate object being to impose terms of peace upon the enemy. But the troubles in France became daily more serious.

The faction, defeated on the 9th of *Thermidor*, attempted to excite fresh insurrections. Beaten on the 12th of *Germinal*, it had risen on the 1st of *Prairial*, more formidable and more violent than ever; and the Government, in open rupture with the Jacobins as well as with the companies of Jesus, and embarrassed besides by domestic troubles, had scarcely leisure to bestow its attention upon dangers threatened from abroad. Weariness and disgust had likewise crept into all ranks; and the people would have no more contests, no more battles, and, above all, no more sacrifices.

The Committee of Public Safety would willingly have yielded to the general wish, for nothing could be more pacific than the feelings of the men who composed it; but peace was a blessing which the "kings of the earth" would not suffer the French people to enjoy. The governors of the republic were therefore compelled to push on the war; and Richard, the representative attached to the army of the North, was directed to collect the means of constructing bridges, in order that the army of Sambre-et-Meuse might cross the Rhine.

Meantime, Luxemburg had surrendered; an event which, though it ought to have given fresh activity to these preparations, only served to delay them. No sooner was the garrison of that city freed from the iron discipline which had ruled it, than the licentiousness of the Austrian soldiery burst forth. Clairfayt's battalion immediately disbanded itself; the men indignantly pulled the metal plates from their caps, trod the imperial insignia under foot, and ran tumultuously through the streets, crying, "*Vive la France!*"—"*Vive la liberté!*"

This unexpected explosion, attended with such a profession of principles, created no little surprise. It led to the supposition that the Austrians were impatient under the yoke of despotism; and the republican government flattered itself that the Aulic council, too prudent to prolong a crisis which might prove fatal to itself, would at length submit to put an end to a contest, the dangers of which were not wholly confined to cannon-balls. This supposition was plausible enough, and a whimsical incident occurred to give it some appearance of . consistency.

Luxemburg, as we have just stated, had opened its gates. The representatives, persuaded that henceforward it would continue to belong to France, ordered a fête "in honour of the marriage of this place to the French republic." Field Marshal Bender, who had surrendered it, was invited to the fête. He was an old soldier, of a lively and amiable disposition. The ceremony seemed to him a good joke, and he attended it at the head of his staff. Jourdan was also present with his.

This was the first time any of the hostile forces had met in amity, and such a meeting seemed to afford pleasure to both parties. The conversation soon became confidential; no one on either side disguised his opinions or antipathies. The Austrians, full of esteem for the French, looked upon the Prussians with an aversion which existing circumstances had tended to increase; and they were impatient to put an end to hostilities with a nation who had fought them nobly, in order to call an unworthy ally to account for the reverses caused by his defection.

The representative Talot, struck with the sentiments of his guests, reported them to the Committee of Public Safety. A French agent at Vienna also reported, as the sentiments of the Aulic Council, some confidential sayings which had escaped certain Austrian generals. The committee took fire at these vague communications, and persuaded themselves that the war with the Empire was on the eve of termination. The preparations for the campaign were therefore suspended, the transmission of supplies stopped, and the government, without calculating the distance, now thought only of transferring the armies of the Rhine, to the Pyrenees; and as an imprudent measure always requires a pretence or excuse, the want of means, and the deficiency of arms and ammunition were put forward on this occasion.

Thus were the preparations in the North entirely stopped. In vain did Pichegru complain of want of supplies in all the fortified towns—in vain did Jourdan urge the weakness of his muster-rolls: the former received no supplies, the latter no recruits. The armies destined to cross the Rhine were on the eve of dissolution on the left bank of that river. Nothing was doing, nothing in progress; and to fill the measure of evil, the remainder of the season was about to be employed in useless marches. The hue and cry raised against such an error in judgement produced no good effect:—the committee had all the sensitiveness attached to power, and would not change their measures. Much time was lost in hesitation, in discussion, and in again mooting a question already disposed of Gillet, who deplored this cruel uncertainty, succeeded at length in putting an end to it.

He had long remained, as we have already shown, with the army of Sambre-et-Meuse, and was well acquainted with its feelings, opinions, and wants. He also knew what there was to expect and what to fear from the Austrians. He pointed out to the committee the fallacy of the hopes they nurtured, and the danger of the measures they seemed resolved to adopt in consequence. If the army, he observed, wanted means of conveyance or stores, the enemy must be made to supply them. The Rhine must be crossed, horses obtained, and the service of the army organized at the expense of the riverain princes. In short, that which had been done during the preceding campaign, must be repeated, and the enemy forced to pay the expenses of the war which they had declared.

But to withdraw from the Rhine when all was ready to cross it—when two hundred thousand imperialists were pressing towards its banks, was at once to decline a battle, and expose the French provinces to the chance of an invasion. Besides, what an unfavourable impression would such a resolution make upon the army, whose battalions loudly demanded and fully expected to be led against the Austrians! Indeed, this expectation alone had prevented the soldiers from deserting, like those of the army in the South. Surely such a consequence was not to be risked; for, if even a defensive warfare were adopted, it would infallibly lead to the immediate dissolution of the army.

> "Our armies," Gillet continued, "bear no resemblance to mercenary troops. Each individual composing them, fights to obtain peace. This is the reason why, with soldiers like ours, the enemy must often be attacked. The more numerous the battles, the greater is the satisfaction of the men; because, being excited by the hope of peace, they can better ascertain the precise period at which it will reach them, and when they shall be able, in consequence,

to return to their families. If you keep them unoccupied, each individual soldier will think that, if he is to remain idle, you can have no occasion for him, and this will induce him to desert.

Our intestine commotions are greatly exaggerated; but admitting them to exist to the extent alleged, do you think to appease them by exposing yourselves to reverses on the frontiers? Gain victories over the foreigners who attack you, and you will deprive our factions at home of all hope of support. Would you acquire respect at home and abroad?—strike terror into your enemies by the splendour of your victories.

I have, I confess, no particular attachment to the principle that the Rhine should form our limits; but I should consider it an act of high treason to restore the Austrian provinces on this side of that river. There are likewise portions of territory and electorates, which must be ceded to us under any circumstances. Should this question be debated some day, I will lay before the committee a paper upon the new frontiers which would suit France, and the points on which they should be defended."

These reasons were unanswerable, and the government yielded to them. The project was abandoned of sending to the Pyrenees, the troops collected on the Rhine, whilst that of passing this river and carrying on the sieges of the fortresses beyond it was resumed. Richard had yielded to the same illusions which had seduced the Committee of Public Safety: like them, he had relied too implicitly upon confidential communications made to mislead him. He also had suffered himself to be deceived by false overtures, and now that the construction of bridges was to be resumed, he demanded six weeks to get everything ready.

This was too serious a delay; and as there were numerous boats on the Meuse and the Moselle, it was agreed that they should be used for the passage of the Rhine. But this was attended with no little difficulty:—for how were the boats to be conveyed from one of those rivers to the Rhine?—and how were they to be lowered into it from the other, and brought to the point where they were to be used? The project was beset with difficulties; nevertheless there was good hope of its success. The work was begun; trucks served for one operation and an inclined moveable bridge for the other;—the rest was left to Providence. Everything succeeded without accident, and the boats reached the river for which they were destined. But here the danger began.

The fort of Ehrenbreitstein commands the mouth of the Moselle, and batteries had been erected all along the right bank of the Rhine. It was a fine moonlight night, not a breath of air was stirring, and the enemy were anxiously watching for the boats to come Within the range of their guns. The danger was certainly great, but there was still greater in hesitation, and the boats, trusting to Providence, dashed on towards Neuwied. The enemy's forts and works along the river thundered a shower of grape shot at the little vessels, as they passed. But in a moment of peril there is something that elevates the soul.

The French mariners braved death with as much coolness as if they were exposed to no danger whatever. Each successive battery, as they appeared before it, took up and continued the fire which those already passed had discontinued, causing considerable damage to the boats. The brave crews, however, uniting their exertions to the force of the current which carried them along, at length peaceably anchored behind the dikes. Neuwied then opened its fire. That beautiful city, so highly embellished by art, and lately enjoying all the blessings of peace, was now transformed into a fortress, raining its murderous projectiles upon the French boats.

This aggression was vigorously answered; but long did the French carefully abstain from injuring the city; they even exposed themselves to great risk with this kindly feeling. But the greater their forbearance, the hotter was the fire from the fortress. Their patience was at length exhausted; they threw shells into the town, and in a few hours reduced it to ashes.

Everything being now ready, and the boats assembled, the

republicans were enabled to land on the opposite bank, reach the enemy, and force them back. But this was not enough for Kléber, whose plan was not merely to beat them, but to dislodge them from the positions they had so long occupied. He proposed turning them with his right, cutting off their retreat with his left, routing them, and depriving them of every other means of escape except across the mountains.

This was a great undertaking; for it was necessary to force a line of redoubts which, being connected with each other, and palisaded and protected by covered ways, left but little chance of attacking them with success. Dusseldorf must likewise be again taken, and the Count of Erbach defeated, who was waiting for the republicans at the head of twenty thousand picked men. But Kléber had confidence in his plans; he had already erected batteries on the left bank, and his men were eager to come to blows. His preparations were soon made. Lefebvre led the left, Championnet the centre, and Grenier, who commanded the right, was sent to force Dusseldorf. These commanders were calculated to inspire their corps with courage; officers and men threw themselves into the boats, braved the Austrian grape-shot, and landed on the opposite bank. On the 5th of September, at daybreak, the republicans occupied the approaches to the river on both sides.

The Rhine once passed, the two wings of the army began offensive operations. The town of Dusseldorf and the line of redoubts, being battered by a formidable artillery, seemed to totter. Legrand advanced upon Dusseldorf, and Lefebvre pushed on to Portz, encroaching a little, as he proceeded, upon a neck of land confided to the charge of King William. The Palatine forces endeavoured to make head against the former, whilst the Prussians attempted to stop the latter; but Lefebvre was not a man to lose time in discussion. He allowed Hohenlohe's officer to say what he pleased, and pushed on towards Opladen, which the enemy occupied in great force. Lefebvre charged and drove them in great disorder into Eberfeldt. Ney, pursuing them with ardour, soon appeared before that place.

The town was opulent; its riches had awakened the cupidity of the retreating Austrians, and it had undergone every act of violence that a routed army could attempt. The French forces were however at the heels of their defeated opponents. Naked, hungry, and in the excitement of victory, they were expected to commit much greater excesses—at least so the Austrians had said. They had stated that a French army of a hundred and fifty thousand men was in pursuit of them; and that the republicans spared neither women nor children, but ravaged every place they reached with fire and sword. The alarmed inhabitants therefore feared that their total destruction was at hand.

Although the republicans had been represented as insatiable, the magistrates did not despair of averting the storm which threatened them. They went out to meet the French columns, and endeavoured to conciliate their kindness by the most lowly supplications and the most splendid offers. Ney, ignorant of the cause of their terror, was as surprised at their abject bearing as at the means they employed to obtain his good will.

"Money!" said he, "I did not expect such a proposal; but since you have more than you require, employ it in relieving my men, who are in want of everything. You cannot make a better use of it. The soldier is never unruly but when his wants are not satisfied."

The dread of the magistrates gave way to astonishment. They had expected to see the town pillaged by a swarm of barbarians, and, instead of the acts of violence announced by the Austrians, they found disinterestedness in the commander, and amenity and moderation in his men. The French soldiers were relieved; they obtained clothing and shoes. Meantime, the imperialists were precipitating their retreat, and Ney resumed his pursuit. Leaving the town, he again followed them into the mountains.

The ravines were deep; whilst rocks and trees thrown across the road continually impeded his progress. But success doubles a man's power; and Ney's corps, after crossing torrents and climbing precipices, overtook the enemy, and was on the point of forcing them to lay down their arms. But the French forces had been unable to attack them on the left, in consequence of the line of neutrality; and the Austrians, less scrupulous than the French, threw themselves into the county of La Marche and escaped.

Ney might have followed them; but he considered himself bound to respect a solemn convention, although the Austrians had violated it, and he took the road to Sollingen, an immense manufactory of arms, which in time of peace rivalled with those of France. In time of war Sollingen supplied arms to the enemies of this country. It was important to obtain possession of the place, and to apply to the use of the republicans that which was intended to effect their defeat. But Ney had scarcely occupied Sollingen ere the Austrians again appeared.

The Prussians having loudly complained of the violation of their territory, the Count of Erbach dared not persevere, and returned to the point whence he entered it. Ney, informed of his motions, joined him behind Lenap. Each was soon ready for action. The Austrians were six thousand strong; but Ney having only a few hundred men with him, could not with such numerical inferiority risk an engagement. He extended the heads of his columns in one direction, sent patrols in another, and managed his manoeuvres so well, that Erbach dared not attack him.

But such circumspection nearly proved fatal to him, and only rendered his situation more distressing. The Count being intimidated, had rallied all the forces he could dispose of, and General Rise had brought him considerable reinforcements. General Fink was also about to debouch, and the situation of the French was becoming very critical; for the Austrians might force them, reach Mulheim, and again open the line of communication which the republican troops had intercepted.

From the offensive, Ney was obliged to assume the defensive; his forces were so out of proportion with those of the enemy, that he was obliged to find, in the quickness of his manoeuvres and the difficulties of the ground, a substitute for the reinforcements he wanted. He destroyed the bridges, cut up the roads, and, sometimes giving way, sometimes fighting—employing by turns prudence and the most daring courage—succeeded in foiling his numerous foes, and in preventing the defeat of the plan of operations laid down by the commander of the French army.

The Count of Erbach, despairing of being able to force Ney's small body, again crossed the neutral territory, and reached Frankfort. Ney was less scrupulous this time, and prepared to follow him; but Jourdan still considering himself bound to respect a neutrality of which the Austrians seemed to take so little account, sent him orders to discontinue the pursuit.

CHAPTER 8

Battle of Altenkirchen

The right wing and centre having crossed the Rhine, the different corps of the army being united, orders were given to advance. The Prince of Wirtemberg, Wartensleben, and Erbach, had reached the mountains, where they were occupied in rallying their men and taking up positions. They placed detachments in advance of the republican forces to impede their progress, but did not succeed in their object: the only effect they produced was to make the French columns press forward, towards the Sieg, and debouch upon the points they were to occupy. The Austrians dispersed everywhere at the approach of the republican troops. But the heights being still crowned by a body of French emigrants, Ney attacked and drove them from their positions; after which, nothing farther opposed the passage of the French army.

The Sieg being crossed, the ground was found extremely bad; nevertheless the republicans continued to push forward. Whilst they were taking up their positions, the Austrians rallied, and concentrated their forces in front of Hennef. Being attacked on the following day by the whole of the French vanguard, under the command of Lefebvre, they received the shock unmoved, and, notwithstanding all the exertions of the French general, more than two hours elapsed before he could break them. Even then, these valiant soldiers gave way only to rally upon the neighbouring heights, where, having formed under the protection of a redoubt, they opposed the most determined and intrepid resistance. Ney arrived in the midst of the action, stormed the work which covered them, and artillerymen, infantry, emigrants, and Austrians, were all trampled under the horses' feet.

As the French army advanced, they found that the country became more rugged and impracticable. Here was a dark forest, there a deep glen; a torrent roared in one direction, a mountain crossed their path in another. They found an obstacle at every step they took: at one place they had to cut a passage through a wood, at another to construct a bridge, at a third to attack and carry a defile. They, however, triumphed over all difficulties, and at length came within sight of Altenkirchen.

The Austrians having employed, in re-forming their columns, the time which their opponents had occupied in overcoming the difficulties of the ground, had taken up a strong position upon the heights, where they were drawn up in line of battle, under cover of a formidable artillery. An open attack might therefore have been foiled, and recourse was had to stratagem. Ney took a demi-brigade of light infantry, with three squadrons of hussars, and, ascending the Sieg, advanced towards Ruppichterod. The time being calculated with precision, Lefebvre marched up to the enemy ere, according to his judgement, Ney could have reached the heights. The ground was cut up and extremely difficult, and he could use neither his cavalry nor his artillery, which reduced his forces to a few thousand men; he advanced nevertheless, and the action commenced. In a moment the troops were engaged all along the line, from right to left; but it was impossible to overpower a whole army with a handful of soldiers. These were repulsed, brought up again to the charge, and might perhaps have suffered severely, had not Ney fortunately succeeded in his movement: his appearance having thrown the Austrians into disorder, Lefebvre's men were again brought up, and the imperialists completely routed.

Fortune continued to crown the French arms with success. The republican forces were about to reach the Lahn, and perhaps cut off the retreat of the defeated Austrians; the army was in high spirits at this prospect, as well as at the idea of seeing the complete success of those combinations which had nearly been frustrated at the very outset. Mayence was about to be invested, and the Austrians could no longer maintain themselves upon the left bank of the Rhine. The French frontiers were settled, and the republican armies on the eve of reaping the fruits of their labours; but the advantages to be derived from the prodigies they had performed, were not to be enjoyed for a long time to come. The successes of armies, which on all other occasions produce abundance, far from relieving the wants of the French troops, tended only to increase them; for the Committee of Public Safety, in their wisdom, had imagined that the war was to pay its own expenses, and had confiscated to their own profit the provisions, cloth, iron, and horses, found in the conquered territories.

This measure, which, as they said, was "to provision their own forces, and disprovision those of the Austrians," but partially produced this effect. It ruined the Duchy of Berg, without benefiting the soldiers of the republic, or filling its warehouses. The feeble cattle, which had before dragged on the provision wagons, were now taken away under pretence of evacuations and transports, and sacrificed to the cupidity of that swarm of vampires which followed in the train of the French armies. The whole country was given up to plunder, and the rich booty which was to have insured success, served but to counteract it. No escort now brought to the soldier the humble ration which secured him from the horrors of famine; no wagon now appeared to receive the wounded.

Almost naked, without food, and barefooted, the French soldiers still held themselves in readiness to follow up their victories. But if courage is inexhaustible, physical want has likewise its limits of endurance. Condemned as the men were, in the midst of a country of abundance, to live upon a single ration of bread each, they had borne it without a complaint; but even this feeble subsistence was now taken away. At first the troops were reduced to half a ration, then to a quarter, and during the last ten days they had received none at all. Jourdan, cut to the soul at this cruel conduct, and deeply affected at the admirable fortitude of his men, dared not, under such circumstances, risk sending them in pursuit of the enemy. Nevertheless, it was necessary to commence a pursuit, in order to conceal the state of destitution to which the army was reduced; and the general selected for this service the men and horses least weakened by famine. All the provisions that remained were distributed among them; and one part of this body was directed towards Freysingen, the other towards Hachenburg.

At the same time, patrols were sent to the different villages, and flour and bread collected in sufficient quantity for a first consumption. But time had been lost; and in war, time is the most valuable of all things. Nevertheless, the troops advanced, and pushed on towards the Lahn, which they purposed crossing; but the bridges were either broken or barricaded, and the Austrians drawn up in an attitude of defence. To force the passage was a measure of some difficulty; but both soldiers and officers were animated with the most generous courage. Bernadotte carried Nassau, Championnet obtained possession of Limburg, and Poncet throwing himself into the river at the head of a small body of troops, swam across, and took Dietz.

On all sides the Austrians were broken, and thrown into the greatest confusion. Night came, and the French army halted. The republicans remained masters of the field of battle, and resolved on the morrow to renew their operations. Grenier occupied Weilburg, Lefebvre established his quarters at Wetzlar, and Ney, scouring the country according to custom, seized a convoy of provisions, and captured a considerable quantity of stores and clothing. Thus were the most pressing wants of the army met for a short time.

The enemy, beaten during the day, dared not renew the contest. They raised their camp and disappeared as soon as they saw the republicans take up their position for the night. The latter pursued them, pushed them upon Mayence, and themselves debouched upon Hochheim. Mayence was now on the point of being completely invested; and the French hoped ere long to see the whole of the left bank acknowledge no flag but theirs.

Whilst they were indulging in such hopes, the Austrians were taking means to disappoint them. The imperial forces had extended their line from Frankfort to Aschaffenburg. The river alone separated the two armies; but for want of provisions and ammunition the French were unable to go over and attack their adversaries. The Austrians being better provided, assumed the offensive in their turn, and crossed the river to attack the French, but were very cautious in their attempts! They imitated the very manoeuvre that their opponents had before used at Elkamp, requested the Prussian safeguards to shut their eyes, and directing towards Friedberg the masses which Pichegru's inaction allowed them to dispose of, threatened. to turn the left wing of the republican army.

The movement was well conceived, executed with courage, and the French were forced to make a retrograde movement, having advanced without marking their progress by any pitched battle, and now retiring without any serious engagement marking their retreat. They were unable to maintain their conquests, to repossess which seemed the only object of the Austrians; but scarcely any fighting had yet taken place. Nevertheless, as success engenders boldness, Clairfayt, who was in sight of the Hunsdruck hills, was anxious to occupy the mountain gorges.

The contest was accordingly renewed, and General Marceau carried it on with vigour. His attitude and manoeuvres soon showed the Austrians that they had a most formidable adversary in this officer. Admiration is expansive; they conveyed to him the expression of their sense of his talents, and he received the compliment with courtesy. Words of peace were then exchanged; nay more, proposals for an armistice were ventured upon. But we will extract Pichegru's account of the manner in which it was concluded, and under what feelings. The following is a letter which that general wrote to Moreau:

Herxheim, Jan. 10th, 1796.

You surpassed yourself in writing to me immediately on the 28th of *Frimaire* on the 4th of *Nivose*. At present you have a right to accuse me of idleness; but the public papers have amply made up for it with regard to ourselves, and if I do not say enough on the subject, it is because they have said too much, and even propagated some errors. I must in the first place offer a few words concerning our operations, in order that you may understand me.

The last actions in which both the army of Sambre-et-Meuse and this were engaged, took place during the last days of *Frimaire*. They were not very important; but the right wing of Sambre-et-Meuse, which had been defeated on the 21st, took its revenge by a marked success of from four to five hundred prisoners and two pieces of cannon. It then marched once more upon the Nahe, from which it had been forced to withdraw. Immediately after this action General Clairfayt proposed to General Jourdan a cessation of hostilities, in order to give the troops some rest. Jourdan replied that he would consent to suspend hostilities provisionally; but that he could make no definitive arrangement on the subject, without my concurrence. He then sent me an account of what had passed; and General Wurmser having likewise despatched to me an officer of his staff, we drew up together the document of which I enclose a copy. General Jourdan having done the same, we sent our act for the approval of government

The public papers have informed us that the government is not pleased with it; and without believing that it has called forth all the indignation which some pretend, I can see by the answer we have received that the act has not been approved of, because we had no right to make it. I think, however, I have read—perhaps in one of our preceding constitutions—that the general-in-chief of an army has the power of granting armistices.

However, whilst the form has been disapproved of, the matter has been ratified, and the armistice is maintained till further orders, according to the tenour of the enclosed paper. I am therefore about to enable the troops to take the rest that will be allowed them, by placing part of them in cantonments. I shall leave but a slight cordon upon our line, whose right is at Linguenfeldt beyond Germersheim, and its left at Homburg. The army of Sambre-et-Meuse will leave twenty thousand men in the Hunsdruck, and the remainder will occupy the cantonments in the territory of Juliers. The cordon in the Hunsdruck will support its left at Bacharach, its centre upon the Nahe at Kirn, and its right at St. Vendel, in ascending the same river.

I do not count upon being employed in the renewal of hostilities; for I have, six different times, demanded my recall. I desire it more and more, and shall not cease to urge it. The levity and injustice with which I have seen the commander treated who does not always succeed, have excited in me a feeling of disgust which it will be difficult to overcome. Be that however as it may, it shall never alter my friendship for you.

Pichegru.

Chapter 9

Capture of Dierdorf and Montabaur

Pichegru's resignation, so often tendered, was at last accepted, and Moreau, who had already succeeded him in his command in Holland, again succeeded him on the Rhine. This choice, judicious as it was, proved but an imperfect remedy for the evil: the troops still remained in the same state of destitution and the different branches of the service in the same disorder. The cavalry and artillery were without horses; and the provisions supplied by Belgium, which had obtained permission to pay its contributions in kind, could not be sent to the Moselle for want of the means of carriage. Ammunition was as scarce as food;—in short, there was a deficiency of everything, and the stores were completely exhausted.

The campaign in Italy was just opened, and Bonaparte had beaten the Austrians at Montenotte and Millesimo. His brethren in arms on the Rhine were impatient to share in his glorious undertakings; but it was necessary to reap the first-fruits of his victories, in order to procure the means of their doing so. The government had at last become more generous: provisions, horses, and clothing, formerly obtained with great difficulty, were freely granted at the present juncture.

The French forces now endeavoured to gain time, in order to collect these new resources; but Prince Charles, who had just assumed the command of the Austrian army, was not over anxious that his adversaries should increase their strength; he, therefore, on the 21st of May, gave notice of the rupture of the armistice.

Though too soon, this notification gave general satisfaction to the French army; the irritation produced by suffering was now added to its natural enthusiasm, and the close of its inaction was hailed with joy.

The Austrians had assembled the greatest part of their forces upon the Nahe. Their right wing commanded by the Prince of Wirtemberg, was distributed between the Lahn and the Sieg. The French prepared to meet them: Kléber occupied Dusseldorf with the divisions of Lefebvre and Collaud, and had concentrated his forces near Opladen. On the 31st of May 1796, at daybreak, he began his march. The Austrians were themselves preparing to commence operations; but Kléber wished to be beforehand with them. He advanced rapidly upon the Acher, a stream issuing from the Sieg, from which it is separated by a narrow strip of land interspersed with woods, ravines, and all the obstacles generally to be found in mountainous districts.

"Four battalions, with artillery and a few horse soldiers defended this neck of land, which was protected on the second line by a deep river, and a numerous army. The Prince of Wirtemberg came and strengthened the latter. Kléber having determined to force this point, crossed the Acher on the 1st of June, overthrew the troops he met on his way, and reached the Sieg. Here the danger began; and here indeed lay the whole difficulty of the undertaking,

The enemy in strong force occupied Siegburg; the columns which the Prince of Wirtemberg was bringing from Neuwied were beginning to debouch, and the situation of the French became very critical. Nevertheless, there was no alternative:—the passage must be surprised, and the troops dispersed who were preparing to defend it. Lefebvre was already before Siegburg; and Collaud, whose van was commanded by Ney, had reached Minden. They attacked the Austrians with irresistible impetuosity. On the right, the bridge, together with the artillery which defended it, was carried in a moment; on the left, the river was forded, its steep banks climbed, and the forces which guarded them separated into two parts, one of which Collaud drove upon the Rhine after dispersing and nearly destroying the other. Meantime, the fire was becoming brisk toward Siegburg, where Lefebvre's corps was warmly engaged. Collaud despatched two battalions in pursuit of the body of the enemy which he had cut off, and marched to the assistance of his colleague.

This act of foresight was most fortunate. The Prince of Wirtemberg had pressed his movement; his last columns had reached the field of battle, the action had become more desperate, and Lefebvre was in danger of being overpowered. D'Hautpoul, however, had just debouched. This officer had the eye of an eagle, and was endowed with an intrepidity which shrank before no obstacle. Everything therefore, might be expected from him: but his cavalry-was fatigued, the horses were out of breath, and two successive charges had scarcely been sufficient to stop the progress of the Hulans. Lefebvre's situation was therefore becoming more and more dangerous, when Collaud appeared. Ney commanded the hussars, and Ormansey, the *chasseurs*.

Their arrival seemed for an instant to surprise the enemy, who however soon recovered. The success which the Austrians had already obtained, and the laurels they still expected to reap, had wound up their courage to a high pitch of excitement, and they resisted for a considerable time without flinching, the shock of these fresh forces. But such violent exertion soon exhausts the bravest troops, and, if not successful, is followed by fatigue and discouragement.

The Austrians were tired of fighting without conquering, and were astonished at not being able to break the French ranks. The Barco hussars hesitated to make another charge, and there was some confusion in their ranks. Ney took advantage of this, and charging them with impetuosity, put them to rout; then despatching part of his force in pursuit of them, threw himself with the remainder upon the swarm of cavalry which the disaster of one of the wings of the Austrian army had just put into motion. But Ney had already changed the aspect of affairs.

Ormansey rushed with fury upon the squadrons that resisted him; Richepanse broke into the ranks opposed to him; and the *mêlée* became furious;—death was dealt on both sides with an unflinching hand, and its victims uttered not a cry. The Austrians, overpowered, sought in vain to evacuate the field of battle: flight was still more murderous than resistance. Driven in one direction, overwhelmed in another— wherever they appeared, and whatever obstacles they opposed to the French, they found nothing but shame and defeat.

Richepanse, following up the victory, spread death in the midst of their terror-stricken cavalry. A column of infantry attempting to stop him, he halted, exhausted his fire, then charging, overthrew and dispersed it even to the last man.

The main body of the Austrian army soon encountered a similar fate. Ney, Richepanse, and D'Hautpoul returned, and came upon it at the head of a body of cavalry, eager for fame, and elated by the day's victory. The Austrians dared not meet the attack, but retreated and gained Ukerath, leaving two thousand four hundred prisoners in the hands of the French.

Ukerath was an entrenched position covered with artillery, and could be attacked only in front; neither could it be turned except by a very long circuit. The men were worn out: the fatigue of the march, together with that of the battle, had exhausted their strength, and it was found necessary to halt. They however prepared to assail the Austrians in the rear no longer daring to attack them in front; but the imperial troops having no greater confidence in their means of resistance than the French had in their means of attack, began their retreat as soon as the night set in. At daybreak the French discovered that the enemy had decamped.

The republican forces forthwith crowned the heights, and advanced beyond Ukerath; but having left their quarters without provisions or stores, they had no supplies; and the convoys of provisions not appearing, they were forced to delay their pursuit. It being important, however, to ascertain not only the road the enemy had taken, but the position they occupied, reconnoitring parties were sent in the direction of Dierdorf, and detachments despatched to Altenkirchen. The country having been explored during the preceding campaign, it was presumed that the Austrians had divided their forces, and were occupying both these places in considerable numbers.

The conjecture was right: they had spread their light infantry along the banks of the Wittbach, and occupied the heights of Altenkirchen with from twenty to twenty-two thousand men. This position, naturally strong, became almost impregnable from the forces and artillery by which it was defended. Kléber had recourse to his usual manoeuvre on this occasion; he resolved to turn it and attack it in front at the same time. Ney was ordered to threaten it in the rear, Lefebvre to force it in front, and Collaud to station his men on the second line, ready to support either of the two that should require his assistance. Fortunately it was needed by neither.

Lefebvre had drawn up his forces in three columns; Soult led the left, Brunet, commanding the 25th Demi-Brigade, the right, and Leval the centre. The action began on the 4th of June. The French soldiers seemed to fear neither the grape-shot nor the obstacles arising from the nature of the ground, but rushed upon the batteries, and climbed the heights, deterred by neither the fire nor the steepness.

The Austrians, on the other hand, displayed the most admirable courage: attacking and attacked by turns, their resistance was most obstinate, and was overcome only with great difficulty. They were at length obliged to give way; and heavy charges of cavalry completed that which the bayonet had begun. Two hours sufficed to decide the contest—in that short period all was over. It is true that never did infantry display more order and method, or cavalry more fearlessness of death, than those of the French. Richepanse animated the cavalry with his own energy; covered with blood, and his arm in a sling, he constantly brought his men to the charge, and unceasingly stimulated their courage. This noble conduct led to an act which must have proved highly flattering to his feelings: promotion still depending upon the election of the soldiers, the army conferred upon him the rank of general, which was sanctioned by Kléber.

The French made three thousand prisoners, took twelve pieces of cannon and four stands of colours;—no victory could have been more splendid. Ney had also made his captures. Not satisfied with spreading confusion in the rear of the enemy, and facilitating the success of the troops who were attacking Altenkirchen, he had obtained advantages which belonged exclusively to himself. He defeated the columns that defended Schomberg, and overthrew those which covered Dierdorf; he also put to flight and pursued the enemy's flankers upon the Wittbach.

But the country was intersected, hilly, and covered with light troops, and for the space of two hours he had to encounter detachments constantly succeeding each other. During this time, his front, his flanks, and his rear, were successively attacked; but, firm as a rock, he succeeded in routing some, keeping others at bay, and, continuing steadily his march, fighting as he advanced, he thought he had at length reached the term of these annoyances.

A still more dangerous attack, however, awaited him. A column of infantry, supported by a body of hussars, had placed themselves on his passage, and, as soon as he appeared, poured their fire upon his troops. This sudden explosion, however, made no impression upon Ney's men, who rushed impetuously upon these new foes. The infantry fled to the woods, and the horse gained Dierdorf. Ney pursued them, took some of them prisoners, pressed closely upon the others, and entering the town with them, found it well stored with hay, oats, flour, and all kinds of supplies.

Meantime, Lefebvre was marching to Oberhadamar; the Prince of Wirtemberg had betaken himself to flight; General Finck was on the eve of being surrounded at Neuwied; and the French were about to reap the benefits of their labours and trials, and of the fatigues they had encountered in these bleak mountains.

Ney continued his movement. Montabaur, which served as a place of refuge for General Finck's retreating corps, contained provisions and noble warehouses full of supplies. Ney advanced towards it; the troops who covered the place endeavoured to stop him; but he soon routed them, and made a capture still richer than that at Dierdorf. Twelve hundred and forty quintals of flour, four hundred sacks of oats, and two hundred thousand rations of hay, were the fruits of this feat of arms.

The Austrians, ashamed of having been forced by a handful of men overcome with fatigue, determined to take advantage of the night to carry off, or at least destroy, the stores they had proved unable to defend. The night was dark, the French soldiers were plunged in a death-like sleep, and the garrison of Ehrenbreitstein was advancing to attempt this *coup-de-main*; but Ney, having penetrated their design, went out, charged them, and sent them back to their quarters in the greatest confusion.

Finck having reached Nassau, and the Prince of Wirtemberg crossed the Lahn at Limburg, the French lost the advantages which they had anticipated from their exertions. They had captured, it is true, abundance of stores, and were thus sure of supplies for some days to come; but they had no means of conveyance, for the peasantry, who had withdrawn to the mountains, had left neither cattle nor wagons. Thus they experienced a real famine in the midst of plenty, and were forced to undergo great hardships, though possessed of the means of comfort.

The republican soldiers, nevertheless, displayed all the enthusiasm which victory inspires. Jourdan had crossed the Rhine, Marceau was in observation before Mayence, Bonnard had surrounded Ehrenbreitstein, Grenier was coming up, and Bernadotte and Championnet were about to debouch. Such a state of things encouraged hope, and the French were justified in anticipating success. On the other hand, the aspect of affairs had sadly changed with the Austrians. Wartensleben had succeeded the Prince of Wirtemberg, and fresh troops from the left bank had come to encourage and support those which had been beaten.

These first reinforcements not being deemed sufficient, the archduke ordered part of the force commanded by Wurmser to join him; and putting himself at the head of the masses he had thus assembled round Blaumholder, advanced upon the Lahn.

He made his movement by Mayence, whilst Jourdan was accomplishing his by Neuwied. The archduke having sixty-four thousand rank and file, and the French only forty-eight thousand to oppose to them, resolved to bring the latter to action, and accordingly pushed on to Wetzlar. An engagement accordingly took place; it was warm, and obstinately contested by so inferior a force; but the archduke's columns continued to debouch, nightfall was approaching, and Lefebvre was severely bruised by a fall from his horse. The republicans were therefore obliged to fall back to their former position.

This check was of little consequence, and scarcely deserving of attention; for the archduke had been forced to evacuate the left bank, and Wurmser, deprived of part of his force, was not in a situation to oppose the passage of the Rhine. Thus the object of the movement of the French army was obtained, and its general-in-chief did not think proper to commit the result of his combinations to the hazard of a battle.

Chapter 4

Action at Herborn

Meantime, Kléber, who was not yet aware of this determination, nor of the check which had led to it, was preparing to cross the Lahn. He had sent for Ney, and was examining with him the approaches to this river, when the news reached him. Instantly perceiving the danger incurred by the troops he had despatched to the left, he ordered Ney to join them with a reinforcement of some hussars who happened to be at hand.

"Go," said he; "you cannot arrive too soon. Perhaps Soult has already a swarm of Austrians upon him."

He was not wrong in this conjecture. Scarcely was the vanguard in retreat ere the imperialists pushed forward to Herborn, and prepared to attack the feeble force that occupied it. The hussars of Caneville and the legion of Bussy were at the head of the assailants. Soult, in ignorance of what had occurred, boldly sallied forth to meet them; but large bodies of emigrants were collecting on the plain. Six thousand men had already debouched, fresh columns were still coming up, and Soult was soon surrounded, and summoned to lay down his arms.

Men, who once called themselves Frenchmen, were about to slaughter their own countrymen for the benefit of Austria. The French general and his soldiers were indignant at such conduct. The firing commenced, and caused great havoc among the emigrants; but no sooner was one squadron dispersed than another took its place, and the action became every instant more destructive. Seven charges made by the emigrants completely failed; but the ammunition of the republican troops was nearly expended, and the men exhausted with fatigue. The dragoons of Bussy and the emigrants were therefore preparing to make a last, and probably fatal charge, when a column of cavalry unexpectedly appeared in the field of battle. This was Ney and his detachment, who, guided by the firing, had reached the scene of action, where attacking and penetrating through the ranks which pressed upon Soult, they at length reached him and his handful of intrepid soldiers.

The Austrians soon formed again, and renewed the attack with fury; but in the mean time Ney and his men had taken breath. Their movements were calm and precise. They broke the shock of a tumultuous charge of the enemy's cavalry, and acting on the offensive in their turn, drove it back with great slaughter. But this was not sufficient: some squadrons still preserved their ranks, and Ney determined to attack and disperse them; but in coming up to the charge, a grape-shot struck his horse, and he was dismounted. Three emigrants immediately rushed upon him, and ordered him, as he valued his life, to cry "*Vive le Roi!*"

"*Vive la Republique!*" the general cried, and their intention of forcing the French to action was made manifest.

Kléber resolved to be beforehand with them, and strike the first blow. Having sent for Laval, Richepanse, Collaud, Ney, and Sorbier, he gave instructions to each. Sorbier was to bring the artillery as fast as possible to bear upon the Austrian columns; Ney was to attack their left with a demi-brigade and three hundred horse; Collaud was to take the command of the reserve, and remain in the camp ready to cover a retreat, should it become necessary; Richepanse was to put himself at the head of the 11th and 12th Dragoons, and the 6th and 7th Chasseurs, and rush upon the flank of the Austrians the instant it should be exposed; and Laval was impetuously to attack their right with the 105th Demi-Brigade and some cavalry. Lefebvre's battalion of grenadiers and the 96th were to remain in close columns ready to proceed wherever they might be wanted.

The parts thus distributed, each general took his station, and the action soon commenced.

Ney, with a body of dragoons, trotted down the ravine which separated the republican army from that of the imperialists, and ascended the height upon which the latter seemed to intend waiting for their opponents. As if from emulation, they pushed forward to meet him. The conflict was sanguinary and obstinate; the contending forces broke, formed again, and fought with fury. Richepanse reached the field of action with the remainder of the cavalry, and the Austrians likewise sent for reinforcements. The action became more extended, and the troops on both sides fought with fluctuating chances of success. By degrees the French gained a decided ascendency. Ney had already overthrown a squadron of hussars, and the Hulans were about to give way, when Kléber perceiving their indecision, took immediate measures to force them.

Adjutant-General Cayla formed the 96th; Laval led on the left wing, Bastout the right, and the general-in-chief put himself at the head of the 83rd. The action now became general from one extremity of the line to the other. The Austrians soon began to give way, and the French were about to snatch the victory from them. Unfortunately, the ground was so rugged and difficult that the cavalry could not follow up its advantages. The imperialists therefore regained confidence, and their battalions, which an instant before had betaken themselves to flight, now took up formidable positions, and waited without flinching for their opponents.

Nevertheless, the French had gained some advantages; their infantry were under cover in ravines and patches of wood, whence they supported the cavalry with their fire. Having attacked an Austrian battery, which spread destruction through their ranks, a large body of Hungarians was suddenly unmasked, and opposed a desperate resistance, which it took a considerable time to overcome. Kléber, tired of this ineffective musketry firing, brought up his artillery, and Sorbier, by turns commander, gunner, and grenadier, directed and animated all around him; but the enemy, whose numbers increased as they retreated, directed their cavalry upon the right of the French, and were about to break its line, when Ney, perceiving the movement, put himself at the head of the 14th Dragoons, and charged the hostile squadrons, without, however, being able to stop them.

His clothes were pierced with bullets, he was obliged to retreat, and it was a miracle that the flank of the French army was not turned. But the Austrians halted, being afraid to trust to fortune, and fearful of endangering their success. Kléber, on the other hand, who only wished to maintain his position, made no attempt to resume the attack, but continued his movement, and on the 21st entered Dusseldorf.

Chapter 11

The Army of the Rhine Begins Operations

Kléber's stay at Dusseldorf was but short. The Directory, to whom Jourdan had reported the enemy's proceedings, did not consider them so important as they really were, but imagined that the army of Sambre-et-Meuse, turned on its left wing, would at most have fallen back upon the Sieg. Meanwhile Bonaparte was pursuing the course of his unparalleled triumphs in Italy. Each day was marked by a fresh victory:—each day was some fortress carried, some river crossed, some position surprised, or some treaty concluded.

His army, constantly in action, marched, fought, and left the enemy not a moment to breathe. Victorious at Borghetto on the 30th of May, this extraordinary man carried Peschiera on the 1st of June, occupied Verona on the 3rd, and invested Mantua on the 4th. Seldom was his army found in the morning where it had taken up its quarters the night before. This continued series of movements—this succession of battles and manoeuvres produced the effect that might naturally be expected. The Aulic Council, which had a stronger partiality for Italy, where its power was established, than for the conquests that might eventually be made upon the Rhine, despatched Field-Marshal Wurmser to collect the scattered remnants of the Austrian forces, then wandering in the mountain passes of the Tyrol and of Carinthia.

Wurmser was an old warrior, whose career had been rendered illustrious by more than one act of prowess. Slow and methodical, but resolute, able, and fruitful in resources,—if he had not always commanded with success, he had at all events always evinced courage and talent. The undertaking now entrusted to him was one of great magnitude; but he began at the head of thirty thousand practised soldiers, accustomed, like himself, to all the chances of war, and encouraged, moreover, by their successes on the Rhine. They reached the Tyrol full of hope, which was, however, soon cruelly destroyed. On the other hand, Wurmser's departure with this force raised the confidence of the Directory; for a diminution of thirty thousand brave men in the enemy's force, offered many favourable chances.

General Bonaparte's victories had stimulated the courage of every French soldier: like him, all determined to conquer or perish. The Directory participated in the enthusiasm which his successes inspired, and Moreau was directed to press and harass the enemy, and imitate the rapid marches of his competitor.

> By transferring the seat of war to the further bank of the Rhine," said the Directory in one of its despatches to Moreau, "you must not expect to maintain yourself there except by the destruction of the enemy. Pursue and engage them therefore without intermission, and by rapid and unexpected marches, give them no time to look about and combine their movements. Endeavour on all occasions to give them battle, until they are not only broken and repulsed, but utterly defeated. It is to this wise policy that the glorious successes of the army of Italy are due. The example of preceding campaigns, and the impetuosity of republican courage, enable you to make a constant and energetic application of this principle to the decisive circumstances under which you are placed.
>
> The army of Sambre-et-Meuse acts upon the same plan of campaign as the troops under your command. Thus, after having beaten Wurmser, and dispersed the wreck of his army, threaten the rear of Prince Charles; you will thereby make General Jourdan resume the offensive, which he had

ceased to do only for a time, in consequence of having drawn upon himself forces which might have added to the difficulties of your glorious undertaking, with the success of which all Germany must resound. Affect to talk loudly of marching to Vienna, and let public report represent you at the head of a hundred thousand men, a portion of whom is on its march to take Beaulieu in the rear, whilst the other is proceeding to effect a junction with the army of Sambre-et-Meuse, towards Franconia, thence to proceed to the Danube.

The terror which always precedes a victorious army, is a powerful engine that must not be neglected, any more than all that can revive and stimulate the courage of the generous defenders of the republic. Above all, let discipline be attended to; for it is apt to become lax during success, particularly in conquered countries. Severe examples at first, and watchful care afterwards, are sufficient to maintain it.

The Directory, to whom Jourdan's retreat did not appear to lead to the serious consequences we have pointed out, was still more pressing with this general. According to the Directory, this retreat had only caused a removal of part of the forces which covered Brisgau. Moreau had crossed the river, and the army of Sambre-et-Meuse halted upon the Sieg. The offensive, they said, must now be resumed, the armies act in concert, and war without intermission until the enemy were annihilated. This project, though a good one, was built upon facts which had never occurred. Jourdan, far from having taken up a position upon the Sieg, had, as we have already shown, been obliged to recross the Rhine; while Moreau was far from being in a situation to cross it.

The French revolution had produced a profound sensation upon the inhabitants of the territories on the further side of that river. Every generous heart had been moved by the declaration of rights; all had felt a revival of that passion for equality which sometimes sleeps, but is never eradicated from the human heart; all accordingly wished to proclaim the principles of the republicans, and effect the same reforms that had been effected in France. They therefore applied to the French for assistance to obtain that which the latter had already succeeded in obtaining; but though they agreed upon the principle, they differed on the mode of proceeding. Some proposed to have recourse to arms; others fancied they had discovered means still more effective; each, in short, conspired according to his own views. The Directory resolved to let them do as they pleased, and accept the assistance of all parties. The French government had an agent in Switzerland—a doubtful one perhaps, but active and cunning—who represented an insurrection at Brisgau as infallible.

Orders were despatched to Moreau, to wait for and support it, and not to cross the Rhine until it had broken out.

Citizen Minister,

Since my return from Berne, I have not ceased my exertions in execution of the plan for the furtherance of which you sent me the necessary powers, and you may rely upon it that nothing shall be wanting on my part fully to realize the expectations of the Directory. Pray give this assurance to General Carnot.

General Laborde has communicated to me the letter he has received, acquainting him with the undertaking in contemplation. Hence, I have thought it right to enter with him into a confidential communication respecting the contents of the letter addressed, as I have before informed you, to the King of Verona, who first raised in my mind doubts with regard to that General. I am satisfied with the explanation which has taken place, and the General will derive this advantage from it, that it will lead him to examine with more attention the extremely suspicious individuals by whom he is surrounded, and to take care of himself.

I have already undertaken a journey with the General, to examine the course of the Rhine from New Brisach to this place, fix upon a spot to cross the river, and ascertain at the same time the feeling which exists among the soldiers. I think we have determined upon the passage at Huninguen, because the insurgent inhabitants, directed and seconded by us, will be in sufficient force to destroy at once the Austrian posts, put the men to death, and spike the guns. With regard to the troops I have seen, I am perfectly satisfied with the spirit existing among them, notwithstanding the hardships they still endure. It would be an easy matter to make them embrace our views in a very few days. I compare their moral situation to a loaded cannon, which I have no doubt with a little address it would be easy to fire.

I dined today with our conspirators of the Margravate. I am satisfied with their report, and the ardent zeal they display in the cause. I afterwards visited the right bank of the Rhine, and the enemy's batteries opposite Huninguen, accompanied by an adjutant-general, whom I intend to put at the head of the peasants, to command them during the commencement of the insurrection.

Tomorrow I have an appointment with General Laborde, to examine where we can place our bridge, and to have the cartridges and flints made, of which the inhabitants are in want, and which in a few days we shall be able to send to them. We are waiting for General Moreau to decide definitively upon our measures, and fix the day for the attack. I am desirous that it should take place as speedily as possible, for there is money in the Margrave's exchequer, and I am apprehensive it will be removed. If General Moreau can supply us with from five and twenty to thirty thousand men, there will be no limit to our success.

Assure the Directory of this fact; state also from me, that if I am left master of my actions, I will never importune it with details, nor tire it with calls for provisions or money. I can already perceive that from the very day of our passage, if I am not thwarted in my schemes, the army will be paid and fed by our friends, and supplied with horses by our enemies. There are ecclesiastical domains which will reimburse the former. We have already taken our measures for the formation of a provisional government. Whilst I am occupied with the means of execution, Bassal is busy about a plan of regulations, and his zeal is not inferior to my own.

We have already collected a portion of the necessary documents; and as soon as the troops arrive, and we have everything else we want, we shall begin to act, and in so rough a manner, I can assure you, that our enemies shall not easily forget it. If our beginning be serious, as I trust it will, and as indeed, from the precision of our calculations, we have a right to expect it will, every Austrian, from Fribourg in Brisgau, and Old Brisach, to Constance, will be exterminated, and all their guns and stores captured.

Next, according to the steps adopted by General Wurmser, we shall take measures either to enter Suabia by the valley of Keusch, and get there before him in the event of his retreat; or to harass his left wing to excess, whilst our new republic will be quietly forming, and we shall be revolutionizing on a grand scale in that portion of Germany which we are occupying.

May I beg, Citizen Minister, you will not forget that in my last I requested you would obtain for me from the Directory sufficient authority for my requisitions to be obeyed, and that you would also place some funds at my disposal, being unable at present to do without money. You must be aware that I have a great deal to lay out, not only for the travelling expenses of my agents, but in the necessary preparations for action. Once settled on the other side of the Rhine, if I have sufficient authority to give the impetus and personally to direct this great undertaking, I shall ask you for no further supplies; and if you hear of us, it will be only the recital of our success, which, when operations are once begun, will be rapid in spite of the efforts of the malignants, who overrun the country.

You will receive, by the next express, the first set of maps of Switzerland that has been found. A sheet is wanting to complete the collection, but it will arrive tomorrow. I will forward at the same time a more detailed account of the intrigues of our enemies. Switzerland is the principal seat of all their plots. Take care at Lyons and in the South. I expect to receive some valuable information respecting all these atrocities. I have gained an intimate friend at Wickam; and shall make good use of all this, at least I hope so. The second letter which you sent to the Canton has produced an admirable effect. All Switzerland trembles at it. Be firm, and above all things take advantage of this first moment of alarm to insist upon the removal far beyond the frontier, of all banished priests and emigrants, without exception. Fix the term of a week at the utmost, and I will answer for your obtaining all you ask.

Adieu, Citizen Minister; receive with your usual kindness the assurance of my fraternal and respectful attachment.
Poteratz.

P.S. Allow me to offer you a piece of good advice. Whilst the whole of Italy is in a state of alarm, why should you not signify officially to all neutral and allied powers, without exception, that not only they who admit English vessels into their ports, but also individuals of whatever nation coming from the ports of England, shall be treated as enemies? Such a measure would force the squadrons of that scoundrel nation to leave the Mediterranean, where they would no longer find a place to refit their ships. By attacking their commerce, you will soon reduce them to submission.

"The Directory is informed, Citizen General," wrote Carnot, "that an insurrection is preparing in the Margravate and at Brisgau. It is acquainted with the chiefs of the intended revolt, and has directed the minister for foreign affairs to entertain relations with them through the medium of Citizen Poteratz charged at Basle with this mission.

This circumstance seems to offer a great and favourable opportunity for introducing freedom into Germany, and making a powerful diversion upon the Rhine. This patriot party expect to raise twenty thousand men in the Margravate, and ten thousand in the Black Forest, with arms, provisions, and everything requisite for an army.

"The plan of operations laid down by the Directory for the forces under your command, is very proper to second the insurrectional explosion, and to impart to the operations of the patriots all the importance which they have a right to expect from us.

"General Laborde, who commands the Upper Rhine, must receive confidential instructions from you on this head, and be authorized to concert measures with Citizen Poteratz.

"The latter announces the certainty of making the passage of the Rhine easy by means of a rising which will break out on the other side of the river, and also of making it easy to force the enemy's batteries and works, which are but feebly guarded.

"You will easily perceive, Citizen General, the full importance of this undertaking. Its execution, like that of all great enterprises, requires secrecy, vigour, and despatch. The Directory, in which you have a just confidence, relies upon you for the prudence and activity of the means you will employ to carry its intentions into effect.

"Carnot, President."

"Paris, 14th *Prairial*, Year 4. (May 3rd, 1796.)"

Such were the instructions which kept Moreau upon the left bank, and such was the attempt he was to support. That preparing in central Germany was of another kind. The minds of the population in that part of the country were more cultivated, notions of justice and freedom more prevalent. The aim here was to proceed without violence, and to act in the name of the law. The movers of the intended revolution, uncertain at first what place to select as the seat of the insurrection, fixed at length upon Franconia. Almost touching the frontiers of the republic on the one hand, and on the other mixed up with all the dissensions which agitated Germany, this circle derived from its situation a high degree of importance, greatly increased by the good feelings of its inhabitants. Nor was this its only advantage: it possessed rich abbeys, and an assembly of the states, formerly holding sovereign power, but which no longer met nor was any longer consulted.

Franconia therefore had all the necessary elements for effecting a change in its form of government; they only required putting into action. The means of doing this were very simple. It was necessary to impose heavy contributions—which the Directory was always ready to do—and invest the states with the power which the law gave them. The latter would then distribute these charges, always attendant on war, among the inhabitants. They would fix with equity, and without respect of persons, the share which each individual was to pay.

The people, delighted at finding they were not to be utterly despoiled, would naturally support an order of things affording them protection. The nobles, on the other hand, could not dispute the power vested in the states without appearing to throw upon the inferior classes the full burthen of the impost: they would therefore be forced to bend their necks and assent to the change. They would also, no doubt, affect disinterestedness and patriotism, and being frightened into justice, would themselves ask to be taxed, and claim to bear their share of the common burthen.

The assembly would in this manner be acknowledged; and its legality once established, the sanction given to its proceedings on this one point, would soon extend to others, and thus the change of government be consummated.

The resources raised by the contribution would however prove insufficient, and other means must be devised to meet the expenses of the occupation. Neither nobles nor plebeians would like an additional impost, and the possessions of the clergy would naturally be thought of. The abbeys would consequently be secularized, the prebends alienated, and the priests, confined to their spiritual duties, would henceforward be without influence in public affairs, whilst their lands would once more become alienable. The *seigniories* would then be subject to imposts; and the people, freed from tithes and average,[2] would pay no further dues, and each would furnish his contingent of taxes in proportion only to the extent of his property.

Suabia, agitated by the same feelings and passions as Franconia, would naturally become a sharer in the destiny of the latter. Lower Saxony would follow the same example, and the Germans once in arms, would perhaps of themselves drive the Austrians beyond the Ems.

Such was the plan, and such the means of execution, intended to be adopted by the chiefs of the insurgents. But these magnificent views produced no alteration in the preparations already made; they required neither the movement of troops, nor a display of force: they merely formed, in the great drama that was preparing, an incident which was accepted with all its chances.

There was, however, some advantage in the project, for such enterprises always conciliate a portion of the inhabitants, and spread uneasiness in the enemy's rear. But this advantage, this uncertain co-operation, could not counterbalance the increase of force added to the enemy's ranks. Each day brought swarms of fresh recruits from the hereditary states; each day fresh columns came to occupy the place of those which Wurmser was leading towards the Brenta; and what was still more serious, the Archduke Charles was invested with the command of the whole of the Austrian forces.

Empowered to act as he thought proper, taking counsel from himself alone, and guided only by events, this prince was about to impress a uniform direction, and a simultaneous impulse upon the armies of the Upper and Lower Rhine; whilst the different bodies of troops opposed to him, carried on their operations independently of each other, and according to instructions from which they could not depart.

---

2. Labour due by the peasant to the lord.—Ed.

The French general-in-chief, unable to remedy this evil, had taken his measures against any attempts to harass his rear, and had secured his line from attacks by the garrisons of Mayence and Ehrenbreitstein. General Moreau, who had once before kept these places in check, was again sent upon the same service. But Jourdan was able to spare him, for this difficult undertaking, only twelve thousand eight hundred infantry, and fifteen hundred horse—a very inadequate force for the service required to be performed. But Moreau well knowing how to make up for the weakness of his means by the vivacity of his attacks, and the rapidity of his movements, the general-in-chief trusted therefore to his courage and well-tried talents.

Everything was ready, time sped on, and yet operations were not begun. Jourdan complained of this to the Directory, to whom he exposed the weakness of his force, and the danger which must inevitably result from delay. But appearances had already changed: ten battalions of infantry and eight squadrons of cavalry suddenly arrived from the army of the North. The conspiracy of Brisgau had been discovered, and Moreau, no longer detained by any of the causes which had stopped him so long, had begun the campaign. He had alarmed the enemy at Manheim, and scarcely were they grouped upon the Necker, ere, by a sudden and masterly manoeuvre, he surprised the passage below Strasburg. This skilful movement having succeeded, the army of Rhin-et-Moselle peaceably crossed the river, and on the 24th was engaged with the Austrians.

Chapter 12

Feats of Arms by General Ney

Moreau being now in line, the army of Sambre-et-Meuse had no longer to contend single-handed against the Archduke's forces, and the French generals began to execute their instructions. Kléber had been already seven days in the entrenched camp at Dusseldorf; his two divisions had rested themselves, and were once more eager for battle. He therefore began his march, rallied the troops under the command of Grenier, who had crossed the Rhine at Cologne, and proceeded towards the positions which the republicans had twice before taken and as often lost. Lefebvre was sent to occupy Siegen.

The country was wild, and intersected with lofty mountains, almost impracticable for artillery and cavalry; and this general had the greatest difficulty in executing his movement. He accomplished it nevertheless, and selecting the road which seemed the easiest, at length reached the river he was to cross. Collaud had arrived at Troisdorf, Grenier had advanced towards Minden, and the whole of the left wing was in position. But neither the Acher nor the Sieg could be forded on account of the floods, and the troops were impatient to encounter the enemy.

Ney took advantage of this impatience; and putting himself at the head of the 6th Hussars, attacked the Austrians, drove them from one river to the other, and pursued them fighting as far as Siegberg. The bridge still existed, and whilst the enemy were endeavouring to set fire to it, he charged and overthrew them, and succeeded in saving it from destruction.

The infantry having thus the means of crossing the river, continued its movement; but the Austrians rallied, and came boldly to meet it. Twelve hundred Austrian troopers prepared to charge the four hundred *chasseurs* by which it was accompanied. The chances were unequal; but, as usual, this disproportion of numbers was counterbalanced by superior ability. Ney ordered the charge to be sounded, and rushing upon this formidable body made it break ground.

The Austrian troopers immediately re-formed upon the heights, and prepared to resume the attack; but the fresh attempt was not more successful than the former. Nevertheless, there were dangers and difficulties attached to the situation in which Ney was placed: he had a river in his rear, and in front, forces which, by returning continually to the attack, must in the end overpower him. Obliged therefore to temper courage with prudence, and feeling the necessity of giving the infantry time to come up, he extended his front, paraded, and amused the Austrians with useless manoeuvres.

At length he contrived to take them in the rear, at the same time that the infantry appeared and formed in front of them. They perceived their error too late; for they were broken and completely overthrown. Such as escaped the edge of the sword were either dispersed or taken prisoners.

The imperialists being thus routed, and the French generals anxious to ascertain the numbers and positions of the forces which covered Ukerath, Kléber ordered the movement to be continued. The dragoons marched in front, and with such promptitude that they were enabled to seize upon the avenues leading to the place. But this rapidity had weakened them; the engagement, which had lasted three hours, the length of their march, and more particularly the obstinate resistance made by the enemy, had exhausted their remaining strength, and they were forced to halt.

The road was very narrow; for the space of a whole league it presented only wood and naked rocks, and there was not in the whole of this extent a single spot where a body of troops might be, drawn up in line. Ney advanced nevertheless at the head of his *chasseurs*, whom he excited, and made them forget their fatigue and danger.

They attacked the enemy with a vigour increased by the resistance offered, and drove them towards Ukerath. But the imperialists, who had been constantly defeated in the mountains, now sought their revenge upon the plain. The French horses were spent with fatigue; those of the Austrians were fresh, their forces numerous, and Ney tried to avoid an action which must prove fatal to him. He headed one charge, eluded another, and alarmed the enemy without committing himself. The French columns at length appeared, the Austrians withdrew, and the position was gained solely by skilful manoeuvring.

Jourdan had now crossed the Rhine, and the army was in line. The movement was continued, and the whole force directed upon Altenkirchen. Though the Austrians occupied it in strong force, they were wavering and undecided. It did not appear that they intended to defend those heights which during the preceding campaign had been so obstinately disputed. The position was soon carried, and the forces which attempted to cover it, put to the rout.

Jourdan had received instructions to keep as far from the Rhine as possible—reach the Upper Lahn— push towards the Kentzig, the Maine, and the Rednitz—harass Wartensleben's right without intermission, and if he could not beat him, drive him into Bohemia, or force him upon Ratisbon. The Austrian general, on the other hand, had orders to avoid coming to action, and to dispute the ground foot by foot, but without endangering his forces. To counteract the plan of his opponents and yet avoid a battle, was therefore the object he had in view.

Jourdan, thinking that the Austrian army was assembled at Limburg, advanced thither with his whole army, directing his left wing upon Wetzlar, in order to turn the enemy. Lefebvre debouched by Siegen; and Collaud having reached Dillenburg, advanced to meet him, but instead of his colleague, with whom he expected to effect a junction, he encountered the Austrians, whom he was certainly not seeking. This unexpected meeting might have proved fatal but for the intrepidity of the commander of the vanguard. The instant Ney perceived the enemy, the charge sounded. The action was hot and obstinate, and the victory long remained doubtful; but the skill and courage of Ney prevailed over a vastly superior force.

The French, about to consummate the victory, were already in pursuit of the flying enemy, when heavy columns again appeared to oppose them. It happened that Wartensleben was not at Limburg, but at Neukirchen, and his troops now made their appearance. The preparations for the attack were soon changed, and those for the defence not less rapidly made. The forces routed by Ney in front of Dillenburg were again overthrown by Lefebvre behind Wildendorf. They were beaten in front and in flank, and for fear of being surrounded precipitately recrossed the Lahn.

The republican troops were however worn out with fatigue; the weather was very unfavourable, for it had not ceased raining during a whole week; but as the Austrians were retreating it became necessary to pursue them, and the movement was continued. Lefebvre pushed on to Giessen, Bonnard to Lein, Collaud to Wetzlar, and Ney, advancing by the road to Frankfort, soon overtook the enemy's rear-guard.

This was now commanded by General Kray, one of the best officers in the Austrian army. It had halted in the plain of Butzbach; its infantry was placed between Obermarle and the Witter; its cavalry extended in front of Windermarle. It could not have chosen a more favourable position than this, which offered every advantage of ground.

Formidable as it was, Ney did not hesitate to approach, He attacked the enemy on the 9th of July, and obtained at first some advantage; but Kléber, who considered this action only a skirmish, did not support him. He had not one fifth of the numerical forces opposed to him, and he was therefore obliged to give way. The 20th Light Infantry appearing in the field, Ney again formed his men, once more attacked the Austrians with this reinforcement, and obliged them to abandon the position. They retired in confusion, and were eagerly pursued. They rallied, nevertheless, for they had reached a formidable esplanade, connected with the position occupied by the main body of the army, which now made an attempt to save its routed rear-guard. The action was renewed with increased vigour, and Kléber feared it would become general; he therefore directed Ney either to discontinue or slacken his fire. But Kray, indignant at the flight of his rear-guard, determined to avenge its defeat, and recover the ground it had lost. Every man in his camp accordingly prepared for action. Collaud, who perceived what was doing, also got ready for the contest, and in a very short time his arrangements were made.

Ney overthrew with the light cavalry the Hulans who covered the esplanade, and who soon after fell into an ambuscade, of which we shall give an account. On their being routed, the 6th Chasseurs, who had put them to flight, were sent in pursuit of them, and with the 11th Dragoons overtook their dense columns, now forming Kray's only hope. They attacked and threw them into confusion, then retreated as if seized by a sudden panic. The surprised Austrians uttered cries of triumph, and having formed again, eagerly and tumultuously pursued their assailants.

But the retreat of the French was only a feint, which was soon made manifest to their pursuers by dreadful explosions of artillery, which shewed them the snare into which they had fallen. A murderous fire of grape shot and musketry was opened upon them, and, to complete their misfortune, their mutilated squadrons were again beset by the intrepid dragoons, whom they fancied they had just conquered. The rout was complete, and the men who escaped death were dispersed in the woods.

From that period the left wing of the French army was more peaceable; but on the right the war became more and more animated. The republicans had taken the village of Obermarle, and thereby intercepted the high road. The Austrians, anxious again to open the communication, pushed both infantry and cavalry towards this point. The shock appeared irresistible. Unable to repulse them in front, Ney had recourse to stratagem: he allowed the enemy's masses to come in collision with a few battalions intended only to keep them in check, and attacking them in the rear as soon as he saw them engaged, he routed and dispersed them. Though the ground was covered with slain, and Kray's loss tremendous, he was irritated at his want of success, and urged his troops to fight to the death.

Scarcely had one attack failed, ere he headed another. Repulsed three times, he returned to the charge a fourth time without having any better success. He yielded not, however, to discouragement; but having again formed his men, brought them up against the village with such renewed energy and impetuosity, that he succeeded in carrying it. But Ney, throwing himself into the midst of the French infantry, rallied them, scolded the men, and succeeded in communicating to them their former impulse. They again attacked the enemy with all the fury arising from the shame of a defeat, overthrew the hostile forces, and drove them back to the heights. The conquerors, however, did not follow up this success as they might have done.

Kléber hoped that such a lesson as this would not be lost upon the Austrians; but they were little affected by it, and maintained their positions. Next morning it was perceived that if they were making no preparations for acting on the offensive, neither did they appear to avoid an engagement. Lefebvre, who was on the right bank of the Wipper, received orders to cross the Wetzlar and attack them on their flank and rear. Collaud was directed to engage them in front; but not to fire a shot nor make a single movement, until the firing announced to him that Lefebvre was first engaged. The Austrians, thus attacked in their communications, could not fail to move immediately; and Ney was then to harass them without intermission.

Everything occurred as Kléber had anticipated. As soon as the enemy perceived the French columns debouch, they fell back, and yielded two leagues of ground; but on reaching Rosbach, and finding the position good and well sheltered, they halted, determined once more to try their fortune. The French columns pressed hard upon them, and they exerted all their resources to prevent these from debouching. Charges of cavalry and the effect of artillery were both tried; but this display of force only tended to excite the French, who climbed the heights, carried the positions, overthrew the columns, and spread confusion and disorder through the Austrian ranks.

Taken in the rear by Lefebvre, they were still pressed in front by Ney, who had given no respite to the column opposed to him, and constantly attacking and attacked, had driven it as far as Hoostadt. Here the contest assumed a different aspect. Ney had only two pieces of artillery, and fifteen were opposed to him; he therefore thought it expedient to endeavour to gain time, until the arrival of some of the columns in his rear.

The Austrians, aware of his design, determined not to leave him this chance. But he charged, manoeuvred, gave way, and rallied by turns, and succeeded by his boldness and prudence in stopping the masses which were constantly debouching upon him. General Jacopin having at length arrived at the head of the 43rd Infantry and 11th Dragoons, the Austrians were driven back, and their assailants appeared before Friedberg. The gates of this town were closed, and the Hungarians, who defended it, opened a destructive fire upon the French, who advanced nevertheless, and, without summoning the garrison to surrender, broke and beat down the herses with cannon-balls, and hatchets, and crow-bars—with everything, in short, they could find. They succeeded at length in getting into the place, where their muskets and bayonets soon avenged the rash resistance they had encountered. Those of the garrison who were not put to the sword fled far away.

Ney pursued the fugitives, and was soon engaged in a fresh action. But his guns were dismounted, and his van, exhausted by marches and combats, and unable to head the storm about to burst upon it, was on the point of giving way, when Bonnard came up with the reserve. The men were again formed after they had taken a little rest, and the pursuit of the enemy was resumed. The movement of the columns, the impetuosity of the several attacks, and more especially the approach of the last corps, which threatened the Austrian line of battle, at length threw the imperial troops into dreadful confusion. They hesitated, gave way, and thought only of saving themselves.

Ney pressed them with vivacity, Richepanse harassed them without respite, and both, stimulated with the same ardour, drove them back, and did not stop till the darkness of the night and fatigue forced them to halt. The Austrians had two thousand killed; the French only six hundred *hors-de-combat*. The latter lost an officer of great promise, Captain Rouilly, one of General Lefebvre's *aides-de-camp*. This young officer had displayed the most daring intrepidity, and his zeal could be compared only to his modesty and military genius.

CHAPTER 13

Continuation of Ney's Feats

The retreating Austrians were driven to Frankfort, a place by no means prepared to sustain a siege, though its ditches, the artillery which covered its approaches, and the troops which had sought refuge within its walls, gave it some importance. Kléber, wishing to economize his resources as much as possible, appeared before it as if with the intention of immediately storming its ramparts. Having made a display of his mortars and scaling-ladders, he summoned the population, consisting chiefly of timid traders, to open their gates. The Austrians, whom they had received into the town, did not however allow them to comply with this demand, and a sort of bombardment was begun by the French. Adjutant-General Mortier followed up the effect produced by the shells; the place surrendered, and the French took possession of all the stores it contained.

The inhabitants of Frankfort had always evinced a feeling of aversion towards the republicans. In 1792 they had welcomed the emigrants with unusual kindness, and received the revolutionary troops with dislike, soon followed by the basest treachery. Whilst the latter were engaged with the Prussians, the citizens of Frankfort sallied forth and assailed them in the midst of the action with knives and hatchets,—an act of perfidy to which their defeat may be attributed. Again, in 1795, the French forces, obliged to retreat, had been several days without bread, or rations of any kind, when they arrived under the walls of Frankfort.

They applied to the merchants and magistrates of this city for sixty thousand rations. The application was favourably received, and the provisions ready for delivery; but as there were no funds in the military chest, and the rations could not be paid for in ready money, they were withheld. These same rations were afterwards sold to the Austrians. In vain did the French general remonstrate, state the wants of his men, and offer an undertaking to pay: the merchants and magistrates were inexorable, and the army was forced, for want of provisions, to cross over to the left bank of the Rhine. At the present juncture the French appeared as conquerors.

During the war, Frankfort had amassed immense wealth, and had not ceased to supply the Austrians with clothing, provisions, and ammunition. The French now thought that they also had won the right of sharing in that which was so prodigally lavished upon their enemies. Their soldiers were in rags; Frankfort possessed, in abundance, everything they stood in need of, and the inhabitants were called upon to supply it. Jourdan, however, was lenient towards the people of this city, although they had behaved so ill, and did not exact all that he was instructed to do; he even protected the inhabitants of Frankfort against the demands of the Directory, the turbulence of his own soldiers, and the industrious cupidity of the swarm of employees and speculators who always follow an army. These he did not allow to enter the place. He levied a contribution upon the city of eight millions of *francs*; upon the territory between the Sieg and the Lahn he levied one million, and three upon that extending from the Lahn to the Maine.

Instructions to General Jourdan

Frankfort has always been rich, and has increased its wealth by the present war. It has not ceased to assist our enemies, it ought therefore to make some exertions in our favour. The Directory leaves it nevertheless to your discretion to augment or diminish the amount of its contributions.

Frankfort contains immense stores of leather, cloth, provisions, and other objects necessary to an army. We naturally presume therefore that you will, at the expense of the city, supply the French troops with everything they are now in need of, or of which they may stand in need hereafter.

All the stores you do not want, you will immediately send to the left bank of the Rhine, where we shall find them when they are required.

For the due payment of the contributions which the Directory has just mentioned, and to put it out of the power of the malignants of the city of Frankfort to form a second plan for betraying us, you will demand and send to France a very considerable number of hostages. The Directory does not fix the number; but you cannot send too many, or select them with too great care from among the richest of the families most devoted to the Austrians.

The Directory, ever anxious to collect on the territory of the French Republic the most noble works of art, requests you will forward to the Minister of the Interior, the most celebrated pictures and every other object of art which may be worthy of a place either in our museum of arts, or in that of natural history. Among the pictures, the Directory deems it sufficient to mention only that by Piazzetta, representing the twelve apostles.

The Directory further directs that you will send to Paris such of the jewels used in crowning the emperors as may have been left at Frankfort, together with the original of the Pope's golden bull, and the register containing the names of the citizens of Frankfort.

You will entirely disarm the city of Frankfort and its inhabitants; and to this effect you will use the promptest, and, if need be, the most rigorous measures. You will send to France the powder, guns, and muskets you do not want.

You will give the command of the place to General Marceau, as also that of the blockading force at Mayence, Ehrenbreitstein, and Konigstein; and if the division now under the command of that general is not sufficient for this service as well as that he was before performing, you may increase its numbers to any extent you think proper.

He must have a sufficient force to keep the enemy's garrisons and the inhabitants themselves in awe, and establish a firm point of support for the army. Frankfort must, in some degree, become our central point.

Put no garrison into Frankfort; let there be no troops in the city but those which you send in, daily and successively, to guard the gates and prevent all individuals of the army from entering who are not bearers of a formal order from you. The troops composing these guards must be taken from a camp which you must form in the vicinity of Frankfort, and make of sufficient strength to keep the population of that city in awe.

No *employé* in the military administrations must be allowed to enter the city, with the exception of the chief-*commissaire-ordonnateur*, and any six or eight individuals he may select. You will give orders to the Jews of the city to behave with the greatest circumspection, on pain of severe punishment. They are not to be allowed to visit the camp.

The military chest was beginning to fill, and the troops thought they had reached the term of their privations; but the chest was always open to receive money, but never to pay any. The troops, who had filled it with the fruits of their victories, were left in the most deplorable state of destitution, and the officers were worse off even than the men. The administration issued no clothing to them, and the *assignats*, in which they received their pay, were of little value; so that they had neither food, clothes, nor pay, and were obliged to subsist upon a share of the plunder which they received from the privates. Their situation could not well be worse. They however, became resigned to it for a time longer, and the movement was resumed.

THE GOVERNMENT COMMISSARY OF THE ARMY OF SAMBRE-ET-MEUSE, TO THE DIRECTORY.

Neuwied, September 14th, 1795.

There is a point to which I cannot too strongly draw your

attention: namely, military discipline. Since I have been attached to this army, I have had too many opportunities of observing its extreme relaxation. Excesses of all kinds have been committed, and many corps have dishonoured themselves by pillage. It is true that the reprimands of the general officers, and the example of several battalions sent to the rear, have produced some effect; whilst a severe regulation of my colleague, Gillet, remedies the evil in part, and makes up in some degree for the insufficiency of the military laws during actual service. But these palliatives do not eradicate the cause of the evil, namely, the dependence in which the officers, from their wants, are placed with regard to the privates. The latter have resources arising from the portion of their pay which they receive in cash.

The officers have none whatever; for it cannot but be evident that their pay is of no value to them. They therefore deem themselves fortunate when the privates come to their assistance, admit them to their meals, and share with them the vegetables and other provisions which can be procured with ready money. The officers are consequently obliged to overlook the misdeeds of marauders, such as thefts of provisions, poultry, and other stock. Were they not to do so, they would be reduced to the most necessitous state and the most wretched existence.

Under circumstances such as I have described, the soldier shows no respect to the officer in distress, who lives in some measure at his expense, and is thereby driven to the necessity of tolerating the most monstrous abuses. No law that could be framed would prove any more than a weak palliative to this evil.

There is only one remedy for it, which is to relieve the officers from this dreadful state of destitution, which degrades them in the eyes of the soldiers, places them in the most humiliating dependence upon their subordinates, and forces them to take no notice of the disorders which occur even in their presence.

If an officer received at least eighteen *francs* a month in cash, he could live honourably without depending upon his men. He could, moreover, make a decent appearance, and resume, with a dignified demeanour, that ascendancy, without which all discipline is at an end. It would then be easy to repress the lamentable excesses which disgust the inhabitants, drive them from us, and deprive us of those means of subsistence which the country might otherwise supply.

I am aware how difficult of execution this plan is in the present state of the republic's finances; but I am positive—and such is the opinion of all the generals of the army—that it is the only means of restoring discipline, and preventing the disorganization of the army. If the state could support this increase of expense for two or three months, I have no hesitation in assuring you, that it would have the most happy influence upon the issue of the campaign. However brilliant our success, we have always reason to fear that disorder, pillage, and the disbanding of the troops—consequences attendant upon a want of discipline—will bring reverses upon us.

On the right bank of the Rhine we find the greatest difficulty in procuring supplies of provisions; for hitherto we have only passed through unfruitful and exhausted countries. I am about to employ all the means in my power to collect the few resources which the country affords. There is greater abundance on the banks of the Lahn.

Health and Fraternity.

Joubert.

Wartensleben, taking advantage of the halt which the French made at Frankfort, collected his forces, and established his position at Wurtzburg. The Maine, after running from the north, turns suddenly towards the south, and again alters its course at Schweinfurt; the French army would therefore have been obliged to appear before this river, without the means of constructing bridges to cross it. To avoid this obstacle, Jourdan marched towards Gemunden. As soon as Frankfort had opened its gates, Collaud and Lefebvre proceeded towards the Kentzig, where Grenier and Championnet effected a junction with them. Bernadotte likewise advanced to Aschaffenburg, and the French army was then in line.

All this was effected on the 20th of July. The heat of the weather was excessive, the country mountainous, and provisions had for some time been growing scarce; but the enemy were unable to make a formidable resistance on any point. The moment they perceived the French forces, they would take up a position, fire a few shots, and then run away. Their reverses had annihilated the courage and destroyed the confidence of the Austrian soldiers. The movements of Wartensleben now seemed nothing more than a prolonged defeat—one continued act of pusillanimity.

Fifteen hundred deserters joined the French in the space of three days; others were still coming over, when Ney, suddenly debouching upon a column, heard very unusual exclamations, and saw a number of the men composing it violently throw down their arms. These were Turks, formerly made prisoners of war; and having been forced to serve in the Austrian ranks, they took this opportunity of claiming to be sent back to their native country. Ney restored them to freedom; another French general afterwards liberated Austrians and Bavarians, whom a similar vicissitude had thrown among the militia of Mourad Bey.

The discouragement to which the Austrian army gave way, inspired the French troops with fresh confidence. On the 23rd of July they arrived at Arstein, and their position reached from Schweinfurt to Carlstadt. Bernadotte marched towards Wurtzburg; the hostile forces came in sight of each other, and both expected an engagement; but Wartensleben, little disposed to run such a risk, recrossed the Maine. Ney, unable to get at the imperialists, made an attack upon Wurtzburg. He had only a hundred horse with him; but his attitude was so threatening, and his movements so rapid, that the governor lost all confidence, and capitulated.

To General Clarke, *Directeur* of the Cabinet *Topographique*.
My dear General,

Wurtzburg is ours. It surrendered yesterday, the Austrians having evacuated it on the 5th. There only remained in the town, the prince's garrison, consisting of about two thousand infantry and three hundred horse. Adjutant-General Ney appeared before the place, and after driving back some detachments of the legion of Bussy, manoeuvred so well with a hundred cavalry, that his forces seemed doubled. His bold movements having intimidated the garrison, he advanced, and formally summoned the Governor to surrender. A capitulation was asked for; the general-in-chief sanctioned it, and today we took possession of the place. The appearance of Championnet's division, which arrived during the negotiation, assisted in hastening the Governor's decision.

The surrender of this place is of the greatest importance. It secures the right bank to the army, and affords facilities for marching to the Upper Rhine.

Ernouf.

Wurtzburg was certainly not a place of importance, but it contained ammunition and a great many pieces of ordnance; it was likewise well calculated for a depot, and could receive both stores and sick. All the advantages, however, which had been anticipated were not derived from it. Bernadotte had not finished his movement; he knew not where the army of Rhinet-Moselle then was, and the troops whom victory had led to the Maine, were disheartened at the prolonged distress in which the government left them. Jourdan was obliged to halt and endeavour to relieve the intolerable distress of his men.

Providence came to his assistance. The Austrians had then upon the Rhine, numerous convoys of provisions and stores, part of which Championnet captured, and Bernadotte the remainder. By such means the French forces obtained flour, forges, and bedding. They took all that was useful to them, but had unfortunately no means of conveyance; and, what was still worse,

General Ernouf had entered into an unaccountable convention with the deputies of the circle.

We have already stated the hopes in which the latter indulged, and the measures they purposed pursuing;—Ernouf adopted all their views, and entered into their combinations. Like them, he was desirous that the revolution should be legal, that it should break out on a fixed day, and not be disgraced by excess. To secure its marvellous results, he feared not to abandon the police of the army to the direction of the deputies, whom he authorized to apprehend and punish any soldiers who should stop their patrols; and to whom he even left it to fix the time and decide upon the mode of acting towards Prussia.

He thus sacrificed the interests of the army to chimerical schemes, and injudiciously raised state questions in a military convention. The general-in-chief was obliged to annul these untoward arrangements; but such an act, though necessary, was not the less attended with deplorable consequences. The people considered it a denial of justice; the magistrates, an act of servility towards the King of Prussia; and both became hostile to the French.

Meantime, stores and provisions had been collected to a certain extent, matters had assumed a new aspect, and the enemy bad provided the republican troops with the means of subsistence. The army of Rhin-et-Moselle, whose fate had remained so long unknown, was now about to debouch. The position of the French forces had therefore become free and secure, and their commander was preparing to advance in pursuit of Wartensleben. This latter general had established his quarters beyond Zeil; his reserve occupied Camburg, and his light troops extended along both banks of the Maine.

All seemed to indicate that he had made up his mind to encounter the republican forces. His position was difficult of access, and his cavalry numerous. The French therefore advanced towards him with circumspection; but this was a needless precaution, for before they had debouched, he broke up his camp and retired. They pursued, pressed him, and tried everything to induce him to give battle; but in vain did they force him to take up a position: his ground was always so well chosen, and his forces so well distributed, that he could not be got at without running too great a risk.

It being impossible to get at him in front, an attempt was made to attack his wings. Manoeuvres were tried on his right flank, and the left of the French advanced; but the mountain passes became more rugged and difficult of access, whilst, on the other hand, Wartensleben attempted to turn the left of his opponents. Thus it was found impossible to bring him to battle.

The French continued to harass his forces. Jourdan, attacked with a severe fit of illness, delivered over the command to Kléber, who pushed forward to the Rednitz. The fortress of Konigshofen was at a short distance. General Soult, taking with him a picket of hussars, and a company of carabineers, advanced and summoned the commandant to surrender.

This officer was far from desirous of gathering laurels in an honourable defence; but annoyed at its being supposed that he would yield to a single escort, he haughtily replied that he had provisions and ammunition, and would see what he should do when a larger force appeared; but until then he would keep the place. The fact is, he only wanted a pretence, which was immediately furnished him;—Lefebvre appeared with his division before the fortress; the gates were immediately opened, and all parties were satisfied—he at having saved appearances, and the French at being masters of the fort.

The left wing of the French army was now secure, and the Austrians could no longer surprise or injure it. Konigshofen being surrounded by marshes and extensive inundations, was, moreover, easy of defence. It was truly a valuable capture; but had it been less so, it was certainly worth what it cost.

Things were conducted less peaceably at Zeil. Collaud, who had advanced thither to support his colleague, as we have already stated, had no occasion to assist him. Ney was in front, and had brought the enemy to action, which was obstinate on both sides, without, for a long time, any decided advantage on either.

Ney was in very inferior force; he had only four hundred horse against double that number. He again availed himself of his superior talents, to give a new character to the engagement: he charged less, manoeuvred more, and taking advantage of every mistake of the enemy, at length succeeded in routing them.

This defeat did not, however, destroy the courage and resolution of the Austrians. Thrown into disorder upon Obelsbach, they had joined a body of infantry, and immediately rallied. But Ney was in close pursuit; and the 20th Light Infantry debouching, he formed them, and supporting them with his cavalry, made a furious attack upon the village, overthrowing all that opposed them. The imperialists again betook themselves to flight, and cavalry and infantry scrambled pell-mell, to the opposite bank of the Maine. Four boats, laden with corn and flour, were coming down the river; Ney sent some *chasseurs* after them, and they were captured.

The Austrians, beaten upon the right bank, still kept up a powerful resistance on the left, which Championnet's vanguard could not overcome. Adjutant-General Cacate, who commanded it, had in vain exhausted his means of attack: the Austrians, occupying a position defended by the river and mountains, counteracted all his efforts. Masters of Eltemann, and of the bridge across the Maine, they stationed on either bank dense masses of troops supported by artillery. Ney, informed of the dangerous situation in which his colleague was placed, hastened to his assistance, and by his presence restored the confidence of the exhausted troops. The action was then resumed, and the enemy completely overthrown.

At Burg-Eberach also, the Austrians were defeated. Unable, under such disasters, to maintain themselves at Bamberg, they crossed the Wiessent, and on the 6th of August took up a position at Aich. Their right was protected by the river, their left, at Rednitz, was covered by Forcheim. This place, situated at the conflux of the two rivers, derives further importance from its proximity to the mountains, which makes it both difficult of capture and easy to succour. Numerous bastions, half-moons, counter-guards, deep ditches, and the waters of the Rednitz, render it, if not a strong-hold of the first magnitude, at least a fortress of sufficient strength not to apprehend either a *coup-de-main*, or the attack of any number of troops unattended by a powerful artillery. In this position, protected by rivers, and by such advantages of ground, Kray seemed fearlessly to await Kléber's arrival. He had not to wait long: the French had crossed the Wiessent in the morning; before night Grenier, Bernadotte, and Championnet debouching upon the Reich-Eberach, drove in the Austrian light troops, whom Lefebvre and Collaud forced to fall back upon the left bank of the Wiessent.

Kray's field of operations was thus narrowed, and the French vanguard was about to reach him, when its commander received intelligence that Ebermanstadt was occupied by a column of the enemy, consisting of twelve hundred infantry, six hundred horse, and several pieces of artillery. Such a force seemed formidable, and Mortier was directed to march against it. This he did at the head of a battalion of infantry, four squadrons of horse, and two pieces of cannon. The action was hotly contested, but it lasted only two hours.

The French having remained masters of the field of battle, were now able to continue their operations on both banks of the river, prolong their patrols, and carry them even to the enemy's rear.

Whilst Mortier was forcing Ebermanstadt, Collaud was advancing to Forcheim. He had orders to drive back whatever forces appeared on the plain, and dislodge all that covered the place. This was a difficult undertaking; for all the approaches, the outlets, and the heights were carefully occupied, and Wartensleben exhorted his men not to suffer themselves to be driven from positions which ought to be impregnable. And, in truth, these positions were defended by all kinds of natural obstacles: the ground was precipitous, tortuous, covered with wood, and intersected with deep ravines.

To these natural defences were joined those of art;—masses of soldiers were placed upon one peak, batteries erected upon another; infantry was stationed at the bottom of the gorges, and cavalry at their entrance. But Ney was not intimidated by these formidable obstacles; and advancing at the head of a handful of men, he began the action. He had only two pieces of artillery; the enemy unmasked fourteen. Ney's men were broken for an instant, but being inured to all the mishaps of war, and undismayed at this check, they re-formed almost immediately, continued the attack, and after an obstinate contest, succeeded in throwing the Austrians' ranks into confusion. Meantime, reinforcements having successively arrived, the imperialists were at length driven from their strong-holds.

The imperial army having betaken itself to flight, the garrison were terror-stricken, and Ney, taking advantage of this feeling, summoned them to open their gates to the French. They hesitated to obey, and Ney getting angry, talked of bombarding the place if they did not comply. The commandant was an irresolute and pusillanimous man, who wished to avoid the consequences of an attack, and at the same time those of a too easy surrender. Intimidated by Ney's threats, he imagined a mode of reconciling these clashing interests.

He consented to surrender the fortress; but, as Wartensleben was still in sight, he wished to delay doing so until the imperial general was entirely gone. Ney refused to accede to any such arrangement; he knew the value of time, and was anxious to pursue the flying enemy. Bursting into a violent rage at such useless obstinacy, he swore he would put the whole garrison to the sword if the surrender were delayed another instant. This menace had the desired effect; the alarmed commandant capitulated, and delivered up the town and fortress of Forcheim to the French, together with arms, ammunition, and a considerable store of provisions.

Kléber, delighted with this display of energy, expressed his satisfaction to Ney in the highest terms. In the presence of his men, he said the most flattering things respecting his activity and courage; and suddenly interrupting himself, he added:—"But I shall not compliment you upon your modesty; because, when carried too far, it ceases to be a good quality. In sum, you may receive my declaration as you please, but my mind is made up, and I insist upon your being general of brigade."

The *chasseurs* clapped their hands in applause, and the officers warmly expressed their satisfaction at the general's determination. Ney alone remained thoughtful. He seemed still- in doubt whether he should accept a promotion which he had already declined, and he uttered not a word.

"Well!" said Kléber, in the kindest manner, "you appear very much grieved and confused; but the Austrians are there waiting for you; go and vent your ill-humour upon them. As for me, I shall acquaint the Directory with your promotion."

He kept his word in the following terms:

Adjutant-general Ney, in this and the preceding campaigns, has given numerous proofs of talent, zeal, and intrepidity; but he surpassed even himself in the battle which took place yesterday, and he had two horses killed under him.
I have thought myself justified in promoting him, upon the field of battle, to the rank of general of brigade. A commission of this grade was forwarded to him eighteen months ago, but his modesty did not then allow him to accept it. By confirming this promotion, Citizens Directors, you will perform a striking act of your justice.

Ney again set out in pursuit of the Austrians, as Kléber had directed him. Championnet and Grenier put their divisions in motion, and forming a junction, pressed the enemy on all sides, drove them from the heights, and pursued them down the hills. But still they kept possession of the villages, and poured upon the French a destructive fire from their batteries. Kray watched with anxiety the vicissitudes of the combat. He animated his men, led them in to the attack, boldly faced every danger, provided against every check, and displayed, in short, the great talents of which he had before given numerous proofs.

But whilst his attention was divided betwixt all these cares, Bernadotte debouched on the right, whilst Bonneau, at the head of his cavalry, turned the Austrians on the left. All this was executed with a precision seldom seen in the field of battle. Kray, disconcerted, no longer knew what manoeuvre to oppose to that of his skilful adversaries. He hesitated and wavered, and the French columns, stimulated by his indecision, of which they could perceive the effect, rushed upon his forces with irresistible impetuosity, overpowered, broke, and obliged them to retire with the utmost precipitation.

Chapter 14

Occupation of Nuremberg

Ney pursued them with equal rapidity, and drove them close to Nuremberg, a great and beautiful city, containing a noble-minded population, still smarting under recently inflicted injuries. Prussia, as heir to the power of the ancient *burgraves*, continued to exercise the rights which the latter had formerly enjoyed. Sometimes she would claim a toll, sometimes a portion of territory; and by successive pretensions and usurpations, she had extended her limits even to the gates of the town. As a free city, Nuremberg protested against these encroachments, and appealed to the Imperial Chamber at Wetzlar; but Prussia being strong, harassed the city, impeded its commerce, and did, in short, all that great powers are wont to do when they wish to force smaller ones to merge into them.

The daily vexations inflicted by Prussia not however producing the effect she anticipated, she had recourse to more decided measures. She seized upon the suburbs, levied tolls at the gates, and intercepted all communication with the neighbouring country. The inhabitants thus pent up within their walls, were obliged to call for mercy. In despair they entreated that they might negotiate with Prussia; but the haughty and harsh aristocracy which governed that kingdom, was insensible to the sufferings of the humble citizens of Nuremberg. They turned over to Austria those who had been the spokesmen in detailing the popular sufferings, and treated the proposals of the citizens with the greatest contempt.

Ney knew the feelings of the inhabitants of Nuremberg; and that the citizens were greatly irritated at the ambition of Prussia and the insensibility of their own magistrates. Desirous of profiting by these circumstances, he left the pursuit of the Austrians, and pushed on to that city. The place was open; and he took possession of it without opposition, but without any appearance of welcome from the inhabitants.

They had just been informed that General Ernouf's convention was nullified, and that instead of the eight millions of *francs* imposed upon the circle, Nuremberg alone was to pay two million five hundred thousand *francs* in money, and supply three hundred horses, fifty thousand pairs of shoes, ten thousand pairs of boots, fifty thousand pairs of gaiters, and fifty thousand shirts. Such a contribution was unreasonable, and the inhabitants were thinking how they should elude it. There was only one mode of doing so. The possessions of the King of Prussia being free from war contributions, they resolved to become Prussians, and raise the standard of Prussia.

Ney having assembled the deputies of the circle who took the lead in this project, endeavoured to bring them to more reasonable views; but he among them who had hitherto shown himself the most zealous and liberal in the cause of freedom, seemed now totally to have abjured his principles, and to be the most eager of all to submit to Prussia. Ney expressed his astonishment at so sudden a change.

"It is, however, very easy to conceive," the German replied; "I thought I was escaping from that most iniquitous constitution bequeathed to us by the middle ages—I mean that which now governs us; and I thought that the French, by grafting freedom upon their victories, would have saved us from a power about to put a yoke upon our necks; but as such expectations are not to be realized—as all my hopes are annihilated, and the indignant populace about to rally round the aristocracy whom I wished to destroy—I shall now give myself up to Prussia; for hitherto, at least, Prussia has protected freedom of thought. That she has her *obscurantins,* I am well aware; but they are about to give up the ghost; whereas in Austria, the taste for warped ideas and stupid measures still prevails."

"What cruel treachery!" cried another. "We were on the eve of conferring upon Germany the same institutions which govern France, and that without trouble or exertion. A simple operation of finance would have made the legislative power pass into the bands of the people;—a war contribution would have sufficed to overthrow feudality forever. But now, instead of a moderate tax that would have made Germany a confederation of free and independent states, an impost is laid which crushes the people, and places them once more in the hands of that proud aristocracy which ought to have been lopped off as a useless excrescence. How can men love an order of things that ruins them? How can they cherish reforms which inflict upon them charges beyond their means of endurance?"

Ney was obliged to dissolve this noisy meeting; but the people were in a still greater state of exasperation than the deputies. They knew that an offensive alliance was in agitation; and that the French were not insensible to the pleasure of seeing those who had fought against them, now arm in their favour. They trembled lest their territory should become the price of a useful co-operation, and in their blind fury seemed ready to commit every kind of excess. Another circumstance contributed to increase this feeling. The Prince of Hohenlohe commanded the Prussian forces in the territories of Anspach and Bareuth. This prince, being directed to protect the possessions of his master, and keep them free from the charges attendant upon war, pretended that the territory of Nuremberg formed part of those possessions, and claimed for it the benefit of the treaty of Basle.

This pretension threw the whole weight of the contribution upon the city, and raised the already irritated inhabitants to the highest pitch of excitement. Nor was this all. The reader may recollect the march of Clairfayt to Wetzlar, and the unfair manner in which the Prussians had lent themselves to his violation of the line of neutrality. Hohenlohe, who then commanded them, was still at their head. Fortune was now favourable to the

French, who were in the centre of that prince's possessions, and the Directory, still indignant at his base conduct, had transmitted orders to demolish his castles, and give up his domains to plunder.

Hitherto this order had not been acted upon; but Hohenlohe now came forward in an official capacity. He described the situation of his estates, claimed for them the Prussian "safeguard," and claimed an extensive territory for his liege lord. It was therefore no longer possible to elude the orders of the Directory; they must be executed, and the question decided between the King of Prussia and the Nurembergians. Ney was as little desirous of ministering to the vengeance of the latter, as of discussing the pretensions of the former.

Fortunately, the general-in-chief cut the matter short. "He had," he said, "personally to complain of Hohenlohe; for he thought that, during the last campaign, that general had not behaved towards him with the honourable feelings of a gallant soldier. Nevertheless, to demolish castles might indispose the King of Prussia, and could answer no good purposes." He therefore changed this measure to a war contribution, and would listen to no further remonstrances on the subject.

The population were thus freed from a part of their burthen; nevertheless they became not a whit more tractable. Ney was under the necessity of recurring to threats to keep them within bounds; but he soon after received orders to resume his pursuit of the Austrians, and, after delivering over the place to Bernadotte, set out upon this service[1].

1. Jourdan, General Commander-in-Chief of the Army of Sambre-et-Meuse, to General Collaud, Head-Quarters, Buchembach, 22nd *Thermidor*, Year 4. (*August 9th*, 1796.) I return you, Citizen General, the letter written to you by Adjutant-General Ney, to inform you that he is in possession of Nuremberg. General Bernadotte, as you may have perceived in the general orders for tomorrow, is to march to that city with the whole of his division; consequently, you must direct Adjutant-General Ney to remain at Nuremberg until relieved by the troops under the command of General Bernadotte, and then proceed upon the service which you shall direct him to undertake, in execution of my order of this evening, for the movement of tomorrow. Ney must reconnoitre Lauffen.
Health and Fraternity.
Jourdan.

Having pushed on beyond Lauffen, he found the enemy in the act of taking up their positions. Wartensleben had already extended his line on the one side to the river Pegnitz, and on the other to the fort of Rottenberg. This fort, situated upon a hill, commanded the plain, the high road to Bareuth, and that to Bamberg. It gave a sort of consistence to the Austrian columns. Wartensleben had concentrated all his forces, and united all his detachments. The French general-in-chief, who had just joined the army, fancying that his opponent wanted again to try his chance in a battle, took his measures accordingly; but the instant the Austrians perceived this, they acted precisely as they had done before at Zeil and Wurtzburg: they raised their camp during the night, and at daybreak their rear-guard only could be perceived pushing into Hersbruck.

Ney again set out in pursuit of them; but fearful of not overtaking them, he attacked the fort with his small body of cavalry. The approaches being rugged and precipitous, he had some difficulty in climbing them; but having at length surmounted the ascent, he was preparing to summon the commander, when he perceived a flock of sheep proceeding towards the place. An idea instantly entered his mind, and seizing the opportunity, the moment he saw the bridge encumbered, he sent his adjutant, at the head of a few hussars, among the sheep which were crossing it. The adjutant and his men passed through the gate, and boldly demanded the surrender of the fort. It contained a garrison of two hundred men, together with provisions and ammunition sufficient to enable it to hold out a long time. But so panic-stricken was the officer in command, that be opened the gates and surrendered.

Ney immediately resumed his pursuit of the Austrians. The country was hilly and difficult, and was intersected with deep ravines, narrow roads, and impenetrable forests. He had no map, neither could he obtain any useful information from the inhabitants. He proceeded onward nevertheless, and after exploring rugged mountains,—after surveying defiles, and glens, and gorges,—after leaving no wood unexplored, no path unexamined, he transmitted to head-quarters a report of his long excursion. The general-in-chief, much pleased with what Ney had done, forwarded to him, with the following flattering note, an enclosure contained in a despatch from the War Minister.

> I enclose you, General, your commission of general of brigade, which I have just received from the War minister. Government has thus discharged the debt which it owed to one of its worthiest and most zealous servants; and it has only done justice to the talents and courage of which you daily give fresh proofs. Accept my sincere congratulation. Health and Fraternity.
> Jourdan.
> Head-quarters, Hersbruck, 28th *Thermidor*,
> Year 4. (August 15th, 1796.)

Nothing could be kinder than this letter, and Ney determined in his next action with the enemy to prove the value he set upon the praises of his commander. He continued to command the van, and pushing forward came within sight of Sulzbach. The army followed the movement; Lefebvre was approaching Neukirchen, Collaud pursuing the road to Hohenstadt, Grenier advancing by Pachetzfeld, and Championnet marching towards Heinfeld, whilst Bernadotte, who had been directed to effect a junction with Moreau, and at the same time to keep in check the archduke's cavalry, which was beginning to bear upon the right flank of the French columns, was proceeding to Neumarck. The whole army was in march, and converging upon Sulzbach.

Ney in the van, debouched in front of a range of platforms and hills, strongly fortified and covered with numerous forces. The enemy's artillery commanded the road, ready to pour its thunders upon the French the moment they appeared; whilst the Austrian cavalry was likewise prepared to receive those who might penetrate within the line of fire, and attack and cut to pieces such of the French columns as might be thrown into confusion by their artillery. To reach the positions occupied by the main body, a swarm of sharp-shooters must first be driven in, and the light infantry overthrown which filled the larch groves spread along the foot of the hills. The fire of the latter must be braved, that also of the field-pieces which defended the road, that of the batteries protecting the plain, and lastly that of the troops formed along the skirts of the wood.

The obstacles were immense, but Ney hesitated not to attempt forcing the position. After halting and resting his men, he formed them; then making them a short but energetic address, he ordered the charge to be sounded. The light infantry advanced to the wood, the flankers towards the hill; and this mode of operation, by dividing the enemy's attention, rendered the chance less unfavourable. Hohenlohe, however, was at the head of his men, whom he stimulated by the most energetic appeals.

The French were received with a tremendous fire, which took them in front, in flank, on all sides in short, and made a dreadful havoc in their ranks. But they remained firm, and rushing impetuously towards the wood, at length reached the imperialists. The onslaught now became dreadful; the men fought hand to hand, and the earth was strewed with corpses. At last the Austrians fell back, and left the French masters of the field. The Prince of Hohenlohe attempted to rally his troops; but Ney came suddenly upon them, overthrew them, and galloped towards their commander, who was exhorting them to resistance, and who escaped only by the fleetness of his horse.

The French now prepared to follow up their success. Masters of the outer positions, and the enemy being in full flight, they were about to crown the heights; but Kray's columns were already in motion, and the ground becoming more and more rugged and difficult, they were forced to halt and prepare to receive the attack of that general. This was impetuous, and great courage was displayed on both sides.

The French at first obtained some advantage, forced back the Austrians on the left, and ably maintained their ground in the centre; but fresh forces were constantly coming up to the assistance of the imperialists, and the republicans were pressed on one side by General Fink, on the other by Montfort, whilst General Elsnitz, at the head of a heavy column, threatened to flank them. They could therefore no longer maintain their ground, and were forced to fall back.

The general-in-chief now reached the field of battle, and sent reinforcements to the troops engaged. The republicans again moved forward, manoeuvred on their wings, and changed the aspect of the battle. Lefebvre advanced by Neukirchen; Grenier penetrated into the wood which covered the opposite flank of the mountains; and whilst the one endeavoured to turn the right of the enemy, and the other the left, Ney, supported by troops withdrawn from the main body, attacked the centre.

Between the point of action and Sulzbach, the ground is covered with woods, intersected with small plains and furrowed with deep ravines; consequently no manoeuvre could be executed with rapidity, nor could the marching be simultaneous. Grenier drove back the enemy without being able either to shut them up in the gorges, or confine them within the passes they were defending;—so far from it, that they fell back from post to post, and from peak to peak, until they occupied the last and most formidable of the hills.

In front of Sulzbach is a rock covered with larch firs, the summit of which forms a platform upon which five or six hundred men may be drawn up. Inaccessible in front, it was defended on every other side by troops and artillery. The high road runs along its left flank, which forms an easy ascent, and is covered with fir trees. Further to the left is a little plain surrounded with wood, which could not be entered from the side on which the French forces were, except through a narrow defile. In the middle of the plain was a hamlet, with plantations containing trees and hedges. The enemy having no fear for their left, had neglected to occupy either this position, or that part of the wood which extended beyond the plain in the same direction.

This fault soon became fatal to them. General Olivier, an active officer, with an excellent eye and of tried valour, who commanded the van of Grenier's division, threw himself into the wood and occupied it. The enemy then perceiving the error they had committed, sent an overwhelming force to retake the position; but their efforts were vain: Olivier maintained himself in it, and assuming the offensive in his turn, drove his assailants back upon the rock. Nor was this the most serious of their checks: Ney, as well as Olivier, had taken advantage of their oversight, and whilst they were endeavouring to retake the road, he occupied the hamlet, and lined it with infantry. This movement had escaped them, and they fell into the snare so ably laid.

A few companies of chasseurs debouched from the hamlet, and the Latour Dragoons hastened to meet them; but perceiving that they hesitated and seemed little disposed to receive the charge, the dragoons charged full gallop upon the hamlet, where, instead of an easy victory, they found only confusion and death. The infantry allowed them to come within twenty paces, and did not fire until the horses were almost close to the bayonet-points. Men and horses bit the earth, and those who escaped reached in great disorder the rock whence they had set out.

It was now seven o'clock in the evening, and the combat had never ceased since the morning; it was, on the contrary, increasing in vehemence, and both parties redoubled their exertions. No artillery could approach to aid the republicans;—it might, it is true, have been brought up on the right flank; but on the left it was impossible, for the enemy occupied the heights commanding the road: the contest, therefore, remained to be settled at the point of the bayonet. The French grenadiers, tired of fighting without success, attempted to scale the rock. It was soft, its projecting parts gave way, and they got only scratches and contusions for their pains. At length General Lefebvre, having completed his movement, debouched and attacked the heights. The engagement now became an act of desperation on both sides. Night came on without ending the struggle; the firing continued, and the hostile forces sought each other in the dark.

At eleven o'clock, the French made a fresh charge; their opponents fell back upon the glacis of Sulzbach, and, covered by a ravine which separated them from the rock, took up a position still more formidable than that from which the French had found so much difficulty in dislodging them. At this unexpected movement, the republicans made a desperate charge, succeeded in breaking the Austrians, killed great numbers of them, drove the remainder among the precipices, and Ney accomplished his attempt to reach the road which leads to Sulzbach. Here he sent forward his *chasseurs*, who charged the flying enemy, and brought in a whole column of them prisoners. This was the end of French success on that memorable day. The night was dark; and General Championnet, engaged with the enemy on the heights, was unable to debouch.

The Austrians retreated; the French pursued them, and took possession of Amberg. This town, situated at the foot of a hill, on the right bank of the Wills, is surrounded by a beautiful plain, interspersed with gardens and orchards, and bounded by woods. The road from Amberg to Ratisbon leaves this plain on the left, runs through pines and larch firs, and then branches off into two parts, the one leading to Bohemia, the other to Ratisbon. Wartensleben followed the first of these branches, and took up his position with his left on the Naab, and his right against the wood-crowned heights behind Wolfering.

This latter wing and the centre were protected by morasses and felled trees. Numerous batteries commanded the openings of the wood, and covered the other wing. The position was formidable, and Collaud attempted to turn it. He despatched Ney to Nabburg, and proceeded in person against Wolfering, which Kray occupied with a considerable force. The action was long and obstinately contested; Grenier and Lefebvre were obliged to come up with their forces.

Ney, stationed in the rear, beheld with anxiety an engagement in which he could take no share. We have already stated that he occupied Nabburg, and the heights of Wolfering commanded a full view of the plain. In vain did he attempt several times to debouch upon Schwartzenfeldt; an overwhelming force always came to meet him, and obliged him to suspend his movement. One of his charges at length succeeded: the Austrian lines were broken, and he hoped to be able to reach the field of battle. But

Kray had taken precautions to foil this attempt, by placing troops at short distances; and the country was moreover covered with woods and ravines;—so that with all his exertions, Ney could not overcome the obstacles opposed to him. His attacks, however, gave the Austrians great uneasiness; and Wartensleben, already assailed in front, and anticipating an attack upon his flank, retreated, and the French army reached the Naab.

The republicans, now on the confines of Bohemia, and about to assail Austria in its very vitals, were sanguine in their hopes of soon bringing to a close the obstinate war which, during the last six years, had caused so immense a loss of human life. Their long and tedious march had hitherto procured them no decided advantage, the Austrians having always declined a battle; and their progress was marked by no brilliant victory, nor by any striking success. But fortune had not deserted them. They had entered upon their campaign without provisions, and almost without the means of carriage; and in their state of destitution, they showed what men can achieve under the inspiration of courage and patriotism.

They never received rations of food until they had first fought for them; they never obtained necessaries, such as shoes and clothing, until they had taken them from the enemy. Obliged to exist upon what the countries supplied through which they passed, they were often reduced to the most painful extremities; frequently in want of cattle for their wagons, they were even sometimes destitute of ammunition. Yet, notwithstanding these disadvantages, they attacked the enemy with the most admirable courage, and pursued them with an intrepidity which nothing could resist. In much less difficult situation, many celebrated armies had been on the point of dissolution.

The army of Sambre-et-Meuse displayed extraordinary firmness: it called the Austrians to account for the privations it endured, attacked them with the feelings of exasperation, roused by unmerited sufferings; and it never encountered them without achieving a victory. It defeated them on the 4th of July at Wildendorf, on the 9th at Butzbach, on the 10th at Friedberg, on the 5th of August at Zeil, on the 17th at Sulzbach, and on the 20th at Wolfering. It took Seigan, Frankfort, Friedberg, Wurtzburg, Schweinfurt, Konigshofen, Forcheim, and Rottenberg. It occupied Bamberg, Aschaffenburg, and Nuremberg. Although without the means of constructing bridges, it was never stopped by any of the numerous streams which intersect the difficult country in which the scene of its operations lay.

It crossed the Sieg, the Lahn, the Nidda, the Maine, the Kentzig, the Reich-Eberach, the Wiessent, the Rednitz, the Aurach, the Schwalbach, the Pegnitz, and the Wills. Always in pursuit of a retreating enemy, it may almost be said never to have beaten them, but with the produce of a former defeat. The ammunition found at Frankfort enabled it to conquer upon the Wiessent; that which it took at Nuremberg and at Forcheim, aided its triumph at Sulzbach and at Wolfering. It was supported by its conquests, which provided stores for its artillery, and funds for its military chest. It captured four thousand muskets, ten flags, nine hundred and thirty-three pieces of ordnance, and it had now ammunition sufficient for several battles.

These results were certainly not very great for six weeks of marches and warfare; but the Austrians had constantly declined giving battle, and the army could only seize such opportunities to distinguish itself as fortune offered.

CHAPTER 15

Death of Marceau

The Austrians retreated to the other side of the Naab, pursued by the French, who were on the point of reaching Ratisbon, when an untoward event completely altered the aspect of affairs. The archduke, keeping Moreau in check with a portion of his forces, unexpectedly debouched with the remainder upon the river Lahn. Bernadotte fought valiantly; but neither the resistance he made at Teining, nor the skill and bravery he displayed at Neumarkt, could stop the progress of the Austrian Prince.

The French army was threatened in its rear; and it became necessary to halt, make the advanced columns fall back, and keep the communication open. The artillery was immediately directed towards Sulzbach, and began the retreat on the morning of the 23rd of August. The troops followed at ten o'clock the same evening.

They were now pursued in their turn by Wartensleben; and the archduke was coming upon them by the road leading to Amberg. The former pressed upon their rear, the latter threatened their flank; but the movement, though in danger of being stopped, was nevertheless accomplished. The whole army had crossed the Wills, with the exception of Ney, who was alone with his brigade on the left bank, when the enemy came in sight.

For a long time he fought and manoeuvred to secure the retreat of the division to which he belonged. His men were worn out with fatigue, and his instructions not very pressing.¹ The Austrians, broken in three successive charges, did not seem disposed to renew the attack, and Ney thought he might give his men some rest. He accordingly halted amid the groves and gardens with which the plain, extending to the left of Amberg, is intersected; but scarcely had he quitted his stirrups, ere a host of Austrians poured upon his little band. Kray himself had come up to give a fresh stimulus to the exertions of the Austrian van; and infantry, cavalry, and artillery crowded in appalling numbers upon the French.

As there was nothing to be gained by a further contest, Ney wished to avoid coming to action, or at all events to circumscribe the attack of the Austrians. He had with him two battalions of the 23rd Light Infantry; these he ordered to retreat, whilst at the head of his hussars he advanced upon the debouching columns; but these were so numerous, and at the same time so impetuous, that he found it impossible to keep them back. They poured in, and spread like a torrent upon the plain, and in a short time surrounded the French force by which it was occupied. The contest was soon reduced to a handful of brave men contending for a passage through the ranks of their enemies, whose masses became every instant more dense.

Nevertheless, Ney did not lose confidence: his soldiers fully appreciated their very critical situation;—they were silent, attentive, prompt in obedience to the word of command,—in a word, they were such as French soldiers always are in the hour of imminent peril. Ney was obliged to defend himself on the one side, and attack on the other. He fought and manoeuvred with the most extraordinary presence of mind, and for an instant

---

1. "Collaud's division shall begin their march this evening at ten o'clock, follow the high road, and encamp upon the heights behind Amberg. The rear-guard of this division, commanded by General Ney, shall set out at midnight, and cover the march of this division, and also that of Grenier's division. General Ney shall halt at the extremity of the wood behind Freyholtz, to give the two divisions time to gain an advance upon him; he shall then continue his march, and take up his position upon the heights in front of Amberg, where, by posts and patrols, he shall keep open a communication with General Lefebvre. Collaud's division shall leave a battalion at Amberg for the defence of the town."—Order of the 23rd of August. The instructions for the following day were not more pressing.

succeeded in disengaging his cavalry; but a ball having killed his horse under him, his ranks were thrown into momentary confusion. The Austrians took immediate advantage of this circumstance, formed afresh, and ultimately surrounded the two battalions of retreating infantry. In vain did Ney attempt to extricate them: the hostile columns, by which they were assailed, rapidly increased in numbers, and he was forced to leave them to their fate. They were commanded by Dehay, an able and intrepid officer. As extreme courage sometimes commands fortune, Ney still hoped that they might be able to force their way. They attempted to do so by forming into a square and continuing their march.

The Austrian cavalry made a charge upon them; they received it with calm firmness; and having repulsed it, continued their movement. The imperialists charged again; Dehay and his little force halted and again drove them back. These repeated attacks exhausted the men; but Dehay encouraged them and raised their drooping spirits. Having, in front of the square, formed a rampart of the bodies of the slain and the carcases of horses, he boldly awaited the attack. The Austrians dared not approach this living citadel, and therefore, instead of men, determined to employ grape-shot for its destruction. They brought up their artillery to batter it in breach; they furrowed it with their missiles—they poured their projectiles upon its ranks;—and when those ranks were broken—when the brave men composing them were nearly swept away by the artillery, the Austrians rushed upon them. All who escaped the sword's edge, were trodden to death by the Austrian cavalry; but the rear-guard had, in the mean time, cut a passage through the enemy, and the honour of the French arms remained untarnished.

But the republican army was in a very critical situation. The inhabitants of countries forming the theatre of warfare, always wreak their revenge upon defeated armies for abuse of power when victorious. The French after raising the most flattering hopes in the territories which they had conquered, had, instead of giving them reform and freedom, oppressed them with intolerable burthens. There was, on this account, a general exasperation throughout the country. They, who had called for the French with the greatest impatience, were now the most incensed of their enemies. The Count of Sodres appealed to the mass of the population; and this titled *sans-culotte*, whose imagination had before run wild with the anticipated delights of revolution, now represented the French as ferocious invaders, who ought to be hunted down and exterminated—as a race of oppressors who deserved to be massacred without pity. Memorandes, on the other hand, had much less regard for the rights of man than for his own independence. He saw that Prussia was about to subdue his country; the French had refused either to interfere or to treat with the circle, and he could not forgive them for their conduct on this occasion. His reputation stood very high—he was extremely popular, and he used these advantages to the detriment of the French, with a vehemence which betrayed feelings of personal, not public interest.

"You see," he cried, in the midst of a multitude by wham the name of the King of Prussia was held in execration—"you see what we have to expect from the French. They promised assistance to nations, and support to freedom. Behold them now the obsequious courtiers of an insatiable despot, to whom they betray a generous people. They destroy the hopes which they themselves excited: they refuse to treat with the circle; and that tyrant who attempted to strangle French liberty in its birth—that tyrant who raised all Europe against them, who nearly destroyed their republic, exhausted its treasure, and shed the best blood of its youthful citizens, is now the object of their courtesy and predilection, to whom they would fain sacrifice and betray us."

Speeches like this, the exactions of the soldiery, and more especially the number of hostages carried off each day, awakened a lamentable spirit of hostility throughout the whole country; and a feeling of opposition and dislike to the French was everywhere manifested. A portion of Prince Charles's forces had continued to advance upon the Pegnitz, whilst the other pushed on towards the Naab. The communications of the French army were cut off; and it was forced to throw itself into the mountains, and trust solely to the information and indications furnished by the inhabitants. It could not, however, place much reliance upon the latter; still, as the country was difficult, and the gorges of the mountains deep and extensive, it was sometimes necessary to use the information given by these peasants; but whenever this was the case, the republicans had ample proofs to what excess of perfidy a people may be led by disappointment. At one time the French army was conducted into a defile, from which it had great difficulty in extricating itself; at another it was diverted from the only good road which the country afforded. It nevertheless continued to advance; but reverses and misfortune destroy the confidence of soldiers in their commanders, and some of the troops obeyed but imperfectly, others slowly marched on with listless apathy.

Jourdan, who was never influenced by personal motives, thought himself called upon to resign the command, and he did so with noble candour. He addressed the following despatch to the Directory.

> As, in accepting the chief command of an army, I was actuated by no other ambition than that of serving my country to the best of my humble abilities, and so long only as, in my own judgement, I could do it with advantage, it is my duty to make known to you, that the good of the service requires I should no longer retain the command of the army of Sambre-et-Meuse. I have lost the confidence of the generals under me, and have no doubt that they consider me unworthy of being at their head. Nevertheless I think they will do justice to my probity, zeal, and readiness in everything relating to the service, and that on these points I enjoy their esteem.
>
> You must feel, Citizens Directors, that as I have lost the confidence of the generals under my command, I shall soon lose that of the subordinate officers, and ultimately of the privates. My recall is therefore urgent, as well as the

appointment of a commander-in-chief whose military talents will give the confidence which I have no longer the power of inspiring. I think the generals would be pleased were they to see General Kléber at their head.

You will doubtless perceive, Citizens Directors, that in this step I am actuated solely by my devotion to the public weal, and the desire of being useful to my country, even when I quit her service.[2]

The army had struggled during seven days among rugged and barren mountains; both officers and men were worn out with fatigue and want; yet the privates had not, like the general officers, lost confidence in their leader. Still actuated by the same ardour and courage, they could not bear to be driven back by troops whom, during the last three years, they had been accustomed always to beat. On the other hand, Latour had been defeated on the banks of the Lech; the disproportion of the hostile forces might change from one instant to another; and a rapid march might carry back the French army to Nuremberg. Jourdan consequently halted. The archduke continued to follow the republican army with his whole force. The battle of Wurtzburg only aggravated the situation of the French, who were defeated; and all the peaceable inhabitants of the country took up arms, cut off the French detachments, and surprised their convoys.

The woods and defiles were equally fatal to the republicans, who never approached a glen without being assailed with a thunder of musketry and cannon. They nevertheless overcame every difficulty, crossed the Lahn, and debouched upon the Acher; but the rapidity of their march tended to increase the hostility evinced by the inhabitants of the country, who supposing the French completely lost, aimed only at securing the spoil of what they deemed a discomfited army. A detachment had nearly reached Attendorn. A report was spread that it escorted the military chest, and such was truly the case. The people ran

---

2. Schweinfurt, September 1st, 1796.

to arms; *bailies* and burgomasters co-operated in the attack, and the chest was captured. But the country authorities, though united for the attack, did not agree in dividing the spoil. One thought his share too small, another cried out with indignation at the portion assigned to a third. The public treasury interfered, the nobles set up claims, and the whole country was thrown into confusion. Ney, knowing the cause of this turmoil, took his measures for bringing the quarrel to an issue. He was aware that the burgomaster, who had led the attack, was an old miser, whom the hope of booty had alone rendered valiant; and that the principal accomplice in the feat was a manufacturer of steel, who likewise had become warlike upon speculation. Both were men of considerable property. He therefore turned back, routed the troops that covered Attendorn and succeeded in carrying off these two men, whom he forced to return to the military chest fourteen hundred thousand *francs*, which they had taken as their share of the booty.

Though the Austrians were but lukewarm in their pursuit of the columns they had defeated at Wurtzburg, they followed the chord of the arc they had been forced to describe in their progress, and proceeded to meet the French force under the command of Marceau. They hoped to beat the latter as they had done his colleague, and by interposing betwixt the two armies, and preventing their junction, either to annihilate the French entirely, or to drive them across the Rhine.

Marceau's situation was critical. With only an effective force of seventeen thousand men, he saw an immense army, flushed with victory, debouch before him. But he displayed equal talent and intrepidity. He raised the siege of such places as he could no longer expect to carry, concentrated his force, marched towards the Austrians, routed the first detachments he fell in with, fought, manoeuvred, and gained time. He at length effected a junction with Jourdan; and if the French army had undergone reverses, it nevertheless withdrew without having encountered any fatal defeat. But it met with an irreparable loss in the death of Marceau, who received a gun-shot wound, which in a short time assumed so dangerous an appearance that he could not be removed. A wounded enemy is however always treated as a friend by soldiers of honour. The Austrian generals showed how much they were touched at his misfortune: the archduke paid him a visit; and the brave and venerable Kray, much more affected than Marceau himself, did not quit him until he had breathed his last. Marceau expired amid the homage paid by his noble enemies to his great qualities as a man and a general. All commanders have not been equally fortunate.

The army had reached the Sieg when Bournonville, who had been appointed Jourdan's successor, joined it. He found the men almost naked, and in the disorder and discouragement attendant upon defeat. The task he had undertaken was one of alarming responsibility, and it quite appalled him. Brave, but without experience in war, he saw in the tumultuous state of the retreating columns nothing short of the most irremediable disorganization, and in the petty pilfering produced by starvation, nothing but the most profound immorality.

He treated the common soldiers like a mob of vandals, and included officers and generals in the same reprobation. Some of the latter, unable to repress the disgust excited by their long sufferings, resigned their commissions. He treated these in the most outrageous manner, threatened to have them led at the head of the army with their hands tied behind them, and then shot as cowards deserting their colours at the moment of danger.

Ernouf and Jourdan persisting in their resignation, his anger exceeded all bounds. Imagining that they wanted to make away with the papers they were to deliver up to him, he uttered the coarsest invectives against them, and in his despatches to the government, brought charges against both.

> "Not," he wrote, "that I attach great importance to the services of Ernouf; for what can be expected from a staff officer who always keeps himself at a distance of thirty leagues from the field of battle, mislays his correspondence, and loses even his orderly book? But I will not suffer him to retire from the service until he hands over to his

successor all the documents he possesses. Jourdan seems to participate in these criminal intentions, and I shall consequently adopt the same line of conduct towards him as towards Ernouf.

"I will not allow him to withdraw from the army until he has delivered up to me a true list of everything he leaves behind, and furnished authentic evidence of the state of the troops on my assuming the command. I must confess, Citizens Directors, that I expected better things from this general. I proposed to him to share with me the command of the two armies; he should have kept the right, and I would have taken the left. Not only has he declined this offer, but he will not even retain the command of the army of the North. Although he has not been quite candid in his communications to me since we have been brought into connexion with each other, I would nevertheless have made it my glory to preserve his reputation. But I cannot with decency ask of you anything for a general who forsakes his army at the period of a complete rout and total disorganization."[3]

Nor in truth could he ask for anything; for what could be offered to a man devoid of ambition, who had disinterestedly devoted his whole life to the service of his country, and who, raised by fortune to the command of an army, had accepted it only at the cost of his personal feelings?

"During five years," Jourdan wrote to the Directory, "I have served the republic in different ranks, and have neglected nothing in my power for the fulfilment of my duties. I know not by what chance I was raised to the rank of general of brigade, and successively to that of general-in-chief. I never solicited such promotion, and I always declared that I was not qualified for so important an office as the latter. Having, however, been forced, under peculiar circumstances, to accept it, I have worked day and night to

---

3. Bournonville's letter to the Directory, dated September 20th, 1796.

acquire military talent, and have endeavoured to make up for want of experience by the greatest activity.

"If my endeavours have not always been successful, I have at least done all in my power to make them so. I have been supported, in the toilsome career I have run, by my earnest love of freedom. I have ever proved myself a friend to order, and an obedient slave to the law. The feelings of my heart have led me to command by the confidence of friendship; and from the moment I perceived that these feelings were not reciprocal, I did not hesitate to sacrifice my military renown and my personal interest, by demanding my recall. I never belonged to any faction; and whenever internal commotion has occurred in the republic, being too far off to be able to appreciate its causes, I have always calmly awaited the result, occupying my mind solely with the means of defeating the foreign enemies of my country. Such, Citizens Directors, has been my military conduct; if you think it merits your approbation, I should be proud to receive an intimation of it.

"At all events I beg to assure you, that though I have returned to the rank of simple citizen, the republican government will ever find in me a sincere and zealous defender. I shall busy myself, in my retirement, with studying the art of war, and shall seek to acquire the knowledge necessary to a general who would perform his duties worthily; and if, when I have joined a careful study of the theory to the experience acquired during a practice of five extremely active campaigns, I could be usefully employed in the service of the republic, I would then with pleasure accept such employment.

"I have likewise the honour to inform you that Citizen Marceau has died of his wounds. The zeal, military talents, and bravery of this officer must make his loss severely felt by every true patriot, whilst the qualities of his heart must render him an object of true regret to his personal friends. The Austrian generals have done justice to his military merit. During the short time he lived after his wound, they showed him the most distinguished attention and kindness, and the Archduke Charles allowed his body to be brought back to the army by the officers I had left with him. He will be buried with military honours, of which he is in every respect worthy, at the camp of La Chartreuse near Coblentz.

"Health and Respect.

" Jourdan."

"Cologne, September 25th, 1796."

Chapter 16

Distress of the French Troops

Bournonville's début was not a happy one; but the enemy were at hand, and his conduct was overlooked in the occupation caused by their progress. The different corps were nearly assembled, and had been joined by fresh generals with reinforcements. The masses were organised anew, the different commands distributed, and each took possession of his post.

With the right wing, General Ligneville covered the Moselle and the Sarre; the centre, commanded by Kléber, formed a corps of observation along the Rhine from Bingen to Cologne; and Macdonald took up a position with the left upon the Strunderback. This is a torrent, which was each day swollen by the rain; but its volume not being considerable enough to stop an enterprising enemy, it was fortified and entrenched; and as it was intended to secure from incursions the plains of the Duchy of Berg, which still offered some resources, Ney was directed with a corps of flankers to keep the approaches clear and protect them against the enemy.

This corps, consisting of the 6th and 9th Chasseurs, the 20th Light Infantry, and a battalion of the 105th was assembled at Opladen. Ney assumed the command on the 25th of September, and on the following day began his march towards Sollingen. He immediately extended his patrols along the banks of the Sieg, thereby spreading uneasiness in the Austrian cantonments. His object was less to fight than to observe—less to join the enemy than to penetrate their intentions. He pushed his parties through their lines of posts, sent his agents among their rear, explored their works and establishments, and discovered at last that the earth which they were moving at Ukerath, and their pretended works at Neukirch, had no other object than that of keeping the French in a state of alarm; that the imperial army, also suffering from famine, was unable to attempt any offensive operation.

This was of some consequence, no doubt; but the enterprises and exertions of the enemy were matters of but secondary importance. That which rendered the situation of the French army more complicated was the irremediable want of the first necessaries of life—the cruel state of deprivation which accompanied it everywhere. The republicans had performed a march of three hundred leagues; men and horses, both equally exhausted with fatigue, required to have their strength recruited, and they found, upon the banks of the Acher, the same deplorable abandonment which they had encountered on those of the Wiessent. There were neither stores, nor provisions, nor pay; yet the enemy were at hand, and the cold weather was becoming daily more intense. The troops could not withstand this excess of wretchedness, and Ney was forced to come to their assistance.

He seized upon the forage still in the fields, and levied imposts upon the villages, demanding bread from some and cattle from others. In this manner he contrived to collect the provisions which ought to have been provided by the civil administration attached to the army. The latter was at this period under the charge of a man who pretended to principle, supplied the troops with nothing, and yet would not have them become a burthen to the country in which they were. He charged the men to exact nothing, and the natives to supply nothing. Strange as this may seem, it was nevertheless the plan he pursued.

The commanders of the army, persuaded that he had the means of providing necessaries for the troops, suspended their demands upon the inhabitants. For two days they expected that rations would be issued; but as none came, they had recourse to their former expedients. The burgomasters, however, had now a pretence for eluding the charges of the occupation, and availed themselves of it with the most inflexible cruelty. If a soldier invoked their humanity in his own behalf, they opposed to his solicitations the order of the government commissary; if he begged a handful of hay for the animal which had shared his dangers and often saved his life, they threatened to sound the alarm-bell. The men were reduced to live by their industry, and the horses either to feed upon rye straw, or browse in the woods. Dreadful as such a situation was, neither the commander of a wing nor any other general officer on duty dared to put an end to it. Each feared to commit himself with the stern proconsul, who, himself well sheltered and well fed, coldly condemned the poor soldiers to starvation.

Ney, less timid, allowed the government commissary to pursue his philanthropic course, and once more made his flankers live at the expense of the country. This the inhabitants most strenuously resisted;—both peasants and magistrates refused to bear the burthen; rigour became necessary to enforce it, and, thanks to the imprudent measure of the proconsul, the troops which had at first been well received in every village, were now in open hostility with the population. Ney persisted nevertheless, for the necessities of the army were imperious.

He assembled the burgomasters, laid before them the exact state of things, and persuaded them to grant with a good grace the supplies they could not ultimately avoid contributing. The meeting took place at Huckeswagen, and the magistrates immediately proceeded to fix the amount of contribution which each was to bear, assessing indiscriminately those who had suffered by the war and those whom it had not touched. This cold indifference roused the indignation of Ney, who, merciful even under the most trying circumstances, demanded that such as had been ruined by passing events, should be exempted. The magistrates of Wipperfurt seemed little disposed to yield to this demand; but Ney took a pen and wrote a few lines, which he handed to them, to the following effect.

> In consideration of the losses which a great portion of the citizens of Wipperfurt sustained at the period when

that commune was almost entirely destroyed by fire, the magistrates and burgomasters of the town are hereby enjoined not to include, under any pretence whatever, any inhabitant who suffered by the fire, either in the charges of provisions and forage to be supplied to the troops of the republic, or in the share of contributions imposed upon the said commune of Wipperfurt. The villages, farms, and hamlets shall alone support the expenses of the war."
Huckeswagen, 3rd *Frimaire*, Year 5.
(November 23rd, 1796.)

This lesson of humanity was not lost. The magistrates felt that the general who watched over the interests of those whom they governed, had a right to force them to provide the necessaries of life for his soldiers. They therefore collected cattle, bread, and forage; and if they did not supply all that circumstances required, they at least saved the troops from starvation.

On the other hand, Ney sought the means of indemnifying them for their supplies. Some of the inhabitants of Attendorn were still in possession of the funds of which they had robbed the military chest. This hostile population supplied the Austrians with provisions and forage; they were filling the storehouses which Elsnitz had built at Weyerbusch; and Ney thought it not impossible to recover from them what remained of their spoil, and to exact from their villages the provisions of which the French army was still in need.

The sky was clouded, and the rain fell without intermission. This appeared to him the most favourable moment, and he accordingly sent out parties and detachments in all directions. These glided through the woods, took advantage of the inequalities of the ground, and alternately prudent and daring, succeeded in debouching on the other side of Attendorn. They dispersed the guards, seized the provisions, and spread confusion and terror among the inhabitants.

Elsnitz, on receiving intelligence of this *coup-de-main*, ran to arms: withdrawing his forces from the pot where his forage was, in order to carry assistance to those who had supplied it, he advanced to Attendorn, accusing the French of having violated the line of neutrality; but this was not the case, for they had passed Attendorn under cover of the fog and rain. It was of some importance, however, to remove this imputation. As the French had been beaten, Prussia, always disposed to side with the strongest, only wanted a pretence for hostility, and Ney was anxious not to give her one. He therefore combated and discussed the complaints made to that power, and proved that he had neither violated its territory nor its rights.

In explaining away, however, a grievance of which the King of Prussia might take advantage, he did not neglect his own interests. The sudden movement made by General Elsnitz, and the rapidity with which he had brought his forces towards Attendorn, had revealed his weakness, and the indication was not lost. A blow, moreover, had been already struck; the Austrian cavalry had been driven back upon the rear, and the infantry was deserted in the midst of the mud. Ney prepared to attack and force it back upon the Sieg; but Bournonville being himself about to attempt a diversion for the purpose of relieving Moreau, who was still exposed to the brunt of Austrian masses, this operation was deferred. The general-in-chief exaggerated to himself the importance of his own undertaking, and in his despatches to Ney spoke of nothing but the difficulties which it presented.

> "They are less than you seem to think," Ney wrote to him; "and if I had notice in time of the movements you intend to make, I could render them still more easy. I could without trouble attempt a useful diversion, force the enemy upon Attendorn, and carry off, or at least destroy, the stores collected at Weyerbusch. This *coup-de-main* would render the passages of the Acher and the Sieg much easier, should the enemy attempt to defend them, and perhaps it would bring us by a single leap to the Maine."

Bournonville did not aspire to such high renown. Waiting or, planning was now impossible; it was necessary to act immediately. The enterprise was however beyond the strength of that general, and he thought only of resigning the command, or at all events of sharing it with some other officer. He now offered to Pichegru what he had formerly proposed to Jourdan; but Pichegru having become odious to the Directory, Bournonville was informed that such a thing was out of the question, and he must cross the Lahn and proceed to the Rednitz. This despatch threw him into a dreadful state of anxiety.

> "The Lahn!" he wrote in consternation; "I can doubtless reach it, provided I have bread to enable me to cross the desert which separates me from it, and wagons for my wounded, that I may not leave them to the ravens of the forest. But the Rednitz! No, Citizen Minister, that can never be. I have neither bread, hay, meat, nor oats, and I cannot push on to the Rednitz. Confide the enterprise to someone who fears not being beaten. Appoint Kléber, or Scherer, or Hoche. You will kill me if you insist upon my performing this painful pilgrimage.[1]"

The Directory gave the preference to Kléber; but this general, who enjoyed the embarrassment of his commander, and delighted in laughing at him, declined the proffered honour.

"I know," said he to Bournonville, "the influence you have had in this flattering appointment. But can I accept it?"

"Why not?" inquired Bournonville.

"I will tell you," Kléber replied, with his habitual irony. "To be a commander-in-chief requires qualifications which I am far from possessing; the leader of an army like ours must be able to unite to the talents required for the practice of war, those of administration; and I am a mere soldier."

The government commissary, who was present, uttered an eulogium upon Kléber's modesty, and called to mind the courage and ability of which he had given so many proofs.

"This is all very fine," said Kléber; "perhaps I might be able to command one or two divisions; nay more—perhaps with such a force I might obtain some success,—at least I have done

---

1. Letter dated October 4th.

so before." And looking hard at Bournonville, he added: "To carry on operations with the courage and audacity which lead to victory, is easy to one attentive to his duties; but to combine manoeuvres, and make all their different parts proceed simultaneously, it is necessary to be a great man,—one peculiarly gifted by nature."

Bournonville, at first disconcerted by these ironical remarks, soon recovered himself. He had the conviction of his own incapacity, and was particularly anxious to lighten the burthen under which he was sinking. Unable to shift it entirely from his own shoulders to those of Kléber, he endeavoured to make this officer share it with him. But in this he was not more successful, and all that he gained by the attempt was a fresh eulogium upon his talents as a commander. The commissary now thought proper to add his entreaties to those of Bournonville, but let slip some unhappy expressions relative to the perseverance and discipline of the army. Kléber stopped him at the very outset of his speech.

> "The army," said he, "has given proof that it can fight and suffer. I do not think that anyone can attribute its reverses to a want of either discipline or courage. If our troops have given way, it is because human suffering has its limits, and the bravest men cannot long contend against hunger. Make for the soldier but one half of the sacrifices which he daily makes for you; let him be sufficiently clad to brave the inclemency of the weather—let him have now and then wherewith to drag on his painful existence—let him see in his rear a wagon to carry him off the field when wounded, and you will then perceive what he is capable of doing, and to what a pitch of heroism he can elevate himself. The insubordination to which he has for an instant given way is the result of the culpable indifference with which he is treated, and the constant want in which he is kept. Obviate the dreadful penury which overcomes and exasperates him—force the people in your own department to perform their duties, and your contractors to ful-

fil their engagements, and you will then obtain victories, and no longer have to reproach the troops with defeats caused by your own negligence."

Kléber had waxed wroth. In vain did the commissary protest that he had collected a store of clothes and shoes, and that for the last three days there had been no want of bread. Kléber withdrew, censuring his culpable neglect of his duties, and Bournonville was obliged to retain a command in which he could find neither a successor nor a colleague. The time for action was thus consumed; Moreau reached the left bank, and there was no further necessity for pushing on towards the Lahn. But inaction was soon succeeded by disgust. Some of the generals retired from illness and disappointment, and for these it was necessary to find successors. Grenier and Championnet recommended some officers to fill up these vacancies, whom Bournonville proposed in the following despatch.

General Bournonville to the Minister at War,
Bonn, January 10th, 1797,
You inform me, Citizen Minister, in your letter of the 6th instant, that General Lefebvre, commanding the vanguard of the army of Sambre-et-Meuse, is to join the army on the coast under the command of General Hoche, and you direct me to transfer the force under his command to another officer.
General Kléber likewise quits this army the day after tomorrow, and General Bernadotte has already left it with the column proceeding to Italy. Lastly, General Ligneville, whose constitution is destroyed by a disorder of the chest and the fatigue of the service, has just been obliged to retire, for the recovery of his health, behind his line of cantonment.
The following, Citizen Minister, are the changes I beg to suggest to you under these circumstances, and I likewise beg leave to add my observations upon those who abandon me prior to the armistice, and whom, on my arrival at

Paris, I should have proposed to you to intersperse among the other armies.

General Kléber has real talent; but it would be difficult to find a vainer man, or one more susceptible of offence and fonder of domineering. I think him badly qualified for subordination; but as he knows how to enforce it, I proposed him to you as general-in-chief. Had he accepted this nomination, he would doubtless have performed brilliant feats. It is, however, bad policy to retain a man so disgusted with the service, and I protest that I have neglected nothing to raise his courage.

Generals Lefebvre and Bernadotte are entirely devoted to Kléber. They are two valiant soldiers who have been withdrawn from this army. It was perhaps necessary for us to separate, and I should have brought this about had I resumed offensive operations; but it is too bad at present to deprive of such men an army so deficient as this in able generals.

It is very probable that the delicate state of General Ligneville's health will henceforth prevent him from pursuing any very active mode of warfare. I consider this officer one of the best commanders of a column which the army contains. He is brave, prudent, and bold when requisite. He possesses real talent, is acquainted with the art of war, and well qualified to command a military division.

The following, Citizen Minister, are the appointments which I venture to suggest, in consequence of the changes that have taken place as above stated.

"I recommend your proposing to the Directory that Brigadier-General Ney be appointed general of division, to command the vanguard of the place of General Lefebvre. This officer, intrepid in action, has during the campaign, covered himself with glory. He has always commanded corps in the vanguard, and is the only one I know who could efficiently command that of the army of Sambre-et-Meuse.

I have provisionally appointed General Bonnard successor to General Bernadotte; but this officer, who has been taken from, the artillery, is better qualified to command a fortified place.

I would propose to you, as commander of a wing, General Souham, commanding the 24th Division. This officer, who has often asked to serve in line, greatly distinguished himself in the North; I can send General Ligneville to succeed him at Brussels.

By this arrangement Generals Souham, Ney, and Bonnard, would take the places of Generals Kléber, Lefebvre, and Bernadotte. General Moreau can determine, when he arrives, whether or not he will retain General Bonnard, who has also evinced military talent.

May I request, Citizen Minister, that you will propose the above promotions and changes to the executive Directory? I must observe that I remain alone with Generals Grenier and Championnet, and that, under the circumstance of the army being so weakened, it is indispensable that no vacancy should be left unfilled. It is moreover urgent that every General should be at his post to organize the several divisions, and put them in a fit state to enter upon the campaign.

Health and Fraternity.

Bournonville.

Such was the opinion which Ney had raised of his abilities and courage, and such the destiny allotted to him. But the Directory now felt how dangerous it would be to impose upon a commander a task which by his own confession was beyond his power; Bournonville was therefore recalled, but the appointments were made as he had recommended.

CHAPTER 17

Hoche Takes Command of the Army of Sambre-et-Meuse

The rigour of the season increased daily, and the consumption of each day rendered the supplies of the next more uncertain. The sensitiveness of the Directory was therefore unheeded, and the French commanders concluded a suspension of arms. The army, peaceably reposing in its cantonments, imposed no very arduous duties upon its general-in-chief, and Moreau was directed to add to the duties of his own command that of directing the several corps under the command of his colleague.

He accordingly set about making such changes in the latter army as accorded with his own views; organising it afresh, and giving it new commanders. He sent Ney from the left wing, which had now no active duty to perform, to the right, which was to be ready for sudden and energetic attack on the renewal of hostilities. But the Directory was too jealous to leave so large a force under the control of one man; and Hoche, who had just been prevented by contrary winds from landing in Ireland, was despatched to take the command of the army of Sambre-et-Meuse.

This general now appeared on the banks of the Rhine, after an absence of four years. He had, in this interval, overcome the emigrants, pacified La Vendée, and alarmed England: he was therefore received as a man ought to be, who united the genius of a statesman to his military talents. Lefebvre, Championnet, and Grenier, his lieutenants of the army of Moselle, were delighted to be under his command, and the veteran soldiers exclaimed, as when he first appeared upon the banks of the Sarre, "Courage and confidence, fellow-soldiers; we shall now awaken from our trance. Our new commander is young as the revolution, and robust as the people. He will lead us as Frenchmen ought to be led."[1]

On the 23rd of February, General Hoche arrived at Cologne, where he found Championnet and Moreau. Though attached to the former by ties of the closest friendship, he had never seen the latter; but both had entered the service at the same period, and both were among the most famed of the French generals. Their first interview was highly gratifying to both. Hoche was delighted, Moreau evinced real satisfaction, and each had no other wish than worthily to beat the enemy. The former, nevertheless, was anxious to ascertain the feelings of the troops, and the events which had led to so unaccountable a retreat. It appeared that all who composed the French forces were not particularly fond of the field of battle; but the real patriots had at length gained the upper hand, the disorganization had been checked, and, by the exertions of Championnet, the whole array had been preserved from ruin.

These details naturally led to other painful communications. The sources of the evils against which army was struggling, were pointed out, and all the frauds and artifices of the civil administration attached to the army, laid open to General Hoche, who resolved to reform all abuses. He had an explanatory correspondence with the Directory on the subject, whose attention he again called to the complaints which had already been made against the agents for provisioning the troops. He determined to do without those administrations which are always attached to the French armies, and seemed to consider it their duty to leave the men in want of the very necessaries of life. The complaints against them were general, and every one loudly exclaimed against the excesses in which they indulged.

---

1. *Journal of the Army of Moselle.*

Had such administrations been composed even of the most honest men, Hoche would still have considered that they ought to be suppressed. They were, in his opinion, very expensive without doing any real service. Most of the individuals employed in them were ignorant of the language of the country, and had no knowledge whatever of the productions of the soil or of the fortunes of the different inhabitants. They were moreover headstrong, unreasonable, and devoid of talent. Their false notions on politics and the art of administration, joined to their imprudent exaggerations, seemed, to the general, calculated to injure the cause of the revolution, and cast odium upon the republican government.

Instead of the multitude of rapacious men then employed, it appeared to Hoche much more advisable to restore to the inhabitants their natural administrators, the bailies, and place the church property once more in the hands of the chapters, by whom it had formerly been managed.

Economy, he observed to the Directory, seemed to dictate these measures, and he did not think that good policy would disavow them. Administration, he said, was a family matter; and no one could well administer that with which he was unacquainted. To distribute equitably the charges which each individual must bear, it is necessary to know the personal resources of each—to have an exact notion of what he possesses. The burthen is much lighter when its weight is properly distributed; the population remain peaceable, and the supplies derived from them are more abundant. The chapters had shown the superiority of a well understood management of property. Such among them—Closterbock[2] for instance—as could not provide food for seven or eight hundred men when their estates were in the hands of the French agents, fed ten thousand when the same estates were under the charge of the monks.

All this seemed so decisive to Hoche that he resolved to adopt a plan sanctioned by experience. He therefore purposed to restore to the inhabitants their own government, tribunals,

---

2. An abbey in the neighbourhood of Coblentz.

and magistrates, and direct the chief *commissaire-ordonnateur*, under his own inspection, to demand the supplies which the troops might require. This project seemed strange to many with whom the old system of French exaction was in especial favour, but it was a wise one.

Hoche, in his personal opinions, had already yielded to influence from which no one is exempt— that of time; he no longer displayed the tender solicitude which he had formerly shown in favour of the *sans-culottes*, whom he did not now think of clothing in "satin waistcoats and velvet breeches."[3] He had no longer "the mania of *municipalizing* Europe." Experience had corrected him; and he now scarcely thought that the Palatinate, the Archbishopric of Treves, and the Duchy of Berg, ought to enjoy the constitutional regime. He had discovered that men do not become republicans in a day; and that when despotism is without taxes, nations do not care to exchange it for an expensive freedom.[4]

Tired of war and insurrection, Hoche was anxious to settle the condition of his country, and crush the league of Kings which for five years past had forced its inhabitants to shed their best blood in battle. Prussia no longer inspired him with that sovereign contempt which he had formerly shown towards her generals; nor did he now feel any repugnance to correspond

---

3. Citizen Hoche, Commander of the Army of Moselle, to the Minister at War. Deux-Ponts, 1st *Frimaire*, Year 2.
(November 21st, 1793.)
I have to inform you that, unwilling to lose an instant, I employ the leisure moments which my military occupations allow me, in making requisitions.
 The consequence is, that horses, cattle, church plate, cloth, linen, leather, shoes, and a multitude of other objects, are all brought to the camp.
We have plenty of emigrants, and I think that, without inconvenience, we may despatch to the interior looking-glasses, clocks, bedding, and other pieces of furniture. The poor *sans-culottes* ought not always to work without profit. They will have freedom; and the velvet breeches, satin waistcoats, and coats with large sleeves, shall clothe them.
All the tailors and shoemakers are at work. Do you not approve of what I am doing?
                                        Hoche.
4. Letter from Hoche to the Directory, dated 14th of *Pluviose*, Year 5. (February 2nd, 1797.)

with Brunswick, or communicate with Kalkreuth.[5] The interests of Prussia and those of the republic were the same, and he proposed forming an alliance with that power. He was not however blind to the ambitious views of Prussia, whose government, he knew, was sedulously watching events, and would take advantage of every turn of fortune. But he thought that for some time to come, King William would not be able to resume his connexion with the Emperor, their differences being submitted to the Germanic confederation.

The French, he considered, might easily overcome the irresolution of the Prussian monarch, by making him a sharer in their successes—by giving up to him Wurtzburg, Bamberg, Nuremberg, and Schweinfurt, and thus forming a province for him of which Erlangen should be the centre, and which might even include Frankfort. King William, who had long coveted these territories, would not resist such an offer.

When once engaged, he would remain attached to France, and a continental peace would be secured; for if the Prussian eagles were but united to the tricolour standard of the French republic, all the other powers of Europe would lay down their arms. The only thing necessary was to strike the first blow with a firm hand, and commence hostilities with some great and brilliant feat of arms. Moreau was of the same opinion, but he hesitated as to the means to be employed, and the place where this first blow should be struck.

Before fixing upon any plan, Hoche was desirous of making

---

5. To General Vincent
.I am not sorry that you put the brigands before you on the alert. The day of vengeance is coming; and remember that it must be terrible. I forbid your corresponding with Kalkreuth, in any other way than with cannon balls and fixed bayonets. The object of the letter which you sent me yesterday is, to ascertain who commands this army.

I will make myself known to him in the field of battle. Would that vile slave of tyranny attempt to employ means which have been but too successful? Do not you condescend to reply to this Kalkreuth, who is every man's humble servant?

The moment you receive the order from me, pounce upon the enemy like the eagle upon its prey. Let us smite the satellites of kings so lustily that none who escape shall attempt to meet us again in the field. Take your measures accordingly.

Hoche.

himself well acquainted with the resources at his disposal; he therefore carefully inspected the army. In the infantry, the men were in good health, their arms in excellent order, and their clothing, without being good, still serviceable; all were eager for battle, and he was highly satisfied with their appearance and bearing.

The state of the cavalry was much less satisfactory. The horses were effective, able, and in excellent condition, it is true; but fatigue and the want of forage had destroyed a great number at the end of the preceding autumn, and the squadrons in effective force did not amount to a third of their complement. Ney explained to the general-in-chief the appalling privations they had undergone, and the means to which they had been obliged to resort, in order to alleviate their sufferings. Hoche listened to these details with emotion.

"Well," said he, "you have lightened sufferings which you could not possibly have foreseen, and as usual, you have deserved well of your country. But you have still much to do. We require horses, provisions, and money, which I shall not ask government to supply, but which we must find somewhere. You know to whom I must entrust the care of providing these things."

As Hoche was speaking, many of Ney's men appeared, some carrying branches of trees, others pushing before them rickety carts groaning under the weight of a few logs of wood. The general-in-chief stopped short in what he was saying, and seemed trying to guess the meaning of what he saw.

Ney explained it. The commissaries for providing fuel, who cost the country several millions of *francs* annually, had supplied none for several years past. He was therefore obliged to find his own fuel; and as on his arrival on the Rhine, his brigade had been deprived of the wagons which it had preserved during the retreat, he sent his hussars a league and half for the wood they wanted, rather than suffer the hedges in the neighbourhood to be destroyed,. and the trees cut down. The men generally carried the fuel on their shoulders; but they took it from the government forests; and if the duty was hard, it had at least the effect of diminishing the charges of the occupation.

This information, together with the complaints which Bournonville had not ceased making against the carriage agents, roused the anger of the general-in-chief. He desired to know the nature of this agency to which both the army and the inhabitants paid such deference; and the information he received was even worse than he had anticipated.

Three *chefs-de-service* had formed this establishment in the following manner:—Bournonville being in want of carriages to resume the offensive, a requisition was made for nine hundred carts, in the country between the Meuse and the Rhine. The peasants obeyed it, but had scarcely reached the place of rendezvous, when means were found to make them abandon their carts and teams. Thus nine hundred carts and eighteen hundred horses were obtained, and appropriated by these *chefs-de-service* to their own purposes.

They were let to the government on favourable terms, as may be easily supposed; and at a rate indeed which in a few days covered the first expenses in fitting them for immediate service. The profit, however, not appearing sufficient to these rapacious men, they resorted to means for further increasing its amount. Among the horses so easily procured, many were strong and serviceable; these were exchanged for worn-out and unserviceable jades, and the pretended damage carried to the account of government.

This seemed but fair to the commissary-general, who was ignorant of the trick; and it was agreed that Mullens, the individual put forward in this affair, should receive four hundred francs for every horse that died. The mortality after this arrangement was very rapid: three hundred horses expired in a few weeks; and the funds intended to provide subsistence were soon exhausted in these indemnities. The treasury of the conquered country was then resorted to, and thus the money which was to have supplied the wants of the army, was continually diverted to another channel.

General Hoche was indignant at such acts of dishonesty, and

Ney having informed him that there was a fresh interruption in the service of the forages, he sent for the contractor, whom he received very harshly. But this man, cold and unmoved, at first opposed the phlegm of a calculating speculator, to the general's impetuosity. To the harshest reproaches he only made this laconic reply: "I have no funds."

"What!" said Hoche, "have all been employed in paying for the supplies? You never furnish anything yourself, yet you constantly oblige the commanders of corps to make requisitions; and your sole employment seems to be to buy up their receipts. These you obtain from the unfortunate peasants at a discount of eighty *per cent*, and your worthy partners at home receive the full amount from the treasury. I shall know how to put an end to such disgraceful speculations."

The contractor now became alarmed, and altered his tone, protesting that he never participated in such culpable transactions, and that the want of funds alone prevented him from fulfilling his engagements.

"That is singular," said Hoche.

"And yet true," the contractor replied.

"Are you sure of it?" retorted the general, opening the lists before him, which showed him the strength of the army in Alsace and in Holland. He knew the amount of the advances made by the treasury, and also that of the proceeds of the requisitions issued on Belgium. He therefore took a pen, made out an account of receipts and disbursements, and found that this company, without funds when anything was to be supplied, had still in their hands a sum of two millions of *francs*, which was without employment.

It was easy to make the calculation. The company of contractors were to have commenced their supplies on the 1st *Pluviose*, (January 20th, 17970 and they had then reached the 15th *Ventose* (March 5th). Thus they were supposed to have met the consumption of forty-five days. The army of Sambre-et-Meuse contained 15,000 horses, and 55,369 men; but to cover losses and double rations, the number of men was taken at 65,000.

There were therefore of bread, *per diem*, 65,000 rations.
or 65,000 x 45   =2,925,000
of meat   do.   = 2,925,000
total   = 5,850,000
Forage, 15,000 rations *per diem*, or 15,000 x 45=675,000.

The army of Rhine and Moselle had 18,000 horses, and 75,193 men. Let it stand 80,000 men, to cover losses and double rations. Thus, there were
80,000 rations of bread, x 45   =3,600,000
Meat   ditto =3,600,000
total   = 7,200,000
Forage, 18,000 rations, x 45   =810,000.

The army of the North contained 12,000 horses, and 48,000 men; but part of this army was employed in garrisons in Holland, and consequently paid by that state. Another part had joined that of Sambre-et-Meuse; so that there only remained to provide for 15,000 men and 4,000 horses.
Thus 15,000 rat. of bread *per diem*, x 45   =675,000
     Ditto   meat   ditto   =675,000
total   = 7,200,000
Forage, 4000 x 45   =180,000

General Total of Rations:
Bread and meat:
5,850,000, 7,200,000, 1,350,000   = 14,400,000
Forage:
675,000, 810,000, 180,000   = 1,665,000

The company had received a considerable stock of provisions.

A cwt. of corn was considered to contain 75 rations of bread; and the same weight of meat, 50 rations. The consumption of a horse *per diem* was fixed at 10 lbs. of hay, 10 lbs. of straw, and three-quarters of a bushel of oats; or 30 lbs. of hay in lieu of all.

The price of the ration of bread was fixed at four *sous* ten *deniers*; which for the army of Sambre-et-Meuse made 15,708 *francs*, six *sous*, eight *deniers*, or in round numbers

15,708 x 45=706,860 *francs*

The ration of meat was fixed at the same price, thus making

706,860 *francs*

The ration of forage was fixed at one *franc*.

Thus, 15,000 x 45 = 675,000 *francs*

Total 2,088,720 *francs*

The expenses of the army of Rhine and Moselle during the same period amounted to

2,549,970 *francs*

Those of the army of the North were less considerable, amounting only to

506,250 *francs*

Total 3,056,220 *francs*

Which, together with the other total of   2,088,720 *francs*
Made a general total of   5,144,940 *francs*

Now, the company had received, the following advances:—
1st *Pluviose*, from the 4th quarter of the sale of national property   600,000 *francs*
24th *Pluviose*, from the arrears of contributions

4,500,000 *francs*

5th *Ventose*, from the customs   500,000 *francs*

When they began, they found in the warehouses of the Rousseau company, and in those of the republic, corn, flour, biscuit, and forage, valued according to estimate at   1,500,000 *francs*

They received from contributions in kind, and from the national domains, provisions, value   1,500,000 *francs*

On the 17th *Nivose* a requisition on Belgium produced—

Hay	1,060,000 cwt
Straw	60,000 *ditto*
Oats	410,000 *ditto*
Wheat	860,000 *ditto*
Rye	28,000 *ditto*

All had not yet come in, it is true; but several departments had supplied the wants of the troops, kept on the move. Thus the immediate consumption, and what was still to come, might be valued at 2,500,000 *francs*. Thus:—

	1,600,000
	4,500,000
	500,000
	1,500,000
	1,500,000
	2,500,000
Make the general total of receipts	12,100,000 *francs*
Total general of consumption	5,144,000 *francs*
Difference	6,956,000 *francs*

Hoche was indignant at the result of his investigation. Harshly dismissing the contractor, he immediately sent for the *chef-d'administration,* not doubting that the skill of the one fully corresponded with the industry of the other. His surmises were just, and he determined to unravel the tissue of fraud which had been so fatal to his unfortunate soldiers. His questions were concise, and positive, and he soon discovered that the administration yielded not the palm of roguery to the members of the agencies. It had not only issued illegal requisitions, and committed arbitrary acts, but appropriated to its own use the proceeds of the imposts. The contribution of the Archbishopric of Treves, for instance, amounting to 300,000 *francs* a month, was not sufficient to cover the emoluments of those who administered this archbishopric, and recourse was had to the public treasury.

"'Tis well!" said Hoche to the *chef-d'administration;* "but every dog has its day, and I am determined to do things at a much less expense. I will form a new administration, which, I warrant you, shall not cost 15,000 *francs* a-year, including everything. Nobody, indeed, shall make a fortune, on pain of being shot; but then the army will profit by the subsidies which the country supplies, and the inhabitants no longer be shamefully plundered."

General Hoche said this with emotion. The impunity with which this system of plunder had been carried on, and the long suffering of the soldiers, had roused his anger. The administrator had disappeared, long ere Hoche recovered from his astonishment at the soldiers not having risen and inflicted summary justice upon the herd of depredators who were fattening upon their misery. This feeling was manifested even in his despatches.

"I have read," he wrote to the Directory, "that the King of Prussia, of venerable memory, built palaces with the money gained by war; and I could not comprehend how, after so many conquests, we were obliged to sell our houses to cover the expenses necessary for the defence of freedom; but I am now better informed. What treasures, what mines of gold could suffice for the scandalous extravagance of some of our military officers, the splendid equipages of our army contractors, the magnificent houses of our commissaries of all classes, and *employés* of every rank! Is the luxurious opulence in which these men live, to be wondered at? The public fortune has passed into their hands, whilst our country's defenders go bare-footed, lie sick in the hospitals which are unprovided with the necessaries of life, and die for want of broth or *ptisan*. O virtue! how great is thy power over the heart of a French soldier!"

CHAPTER 18

Ney is Appointed to the Command of Hussars

It required time for the useful reforms of the general-in-chief to produce their full effect. The season was however advancing, the first days of March were already passed, the weather was mild, and the snow had disappeared; Hoche therefore took measures to open the campaign. He did not now pursue the method he had hitherto adopted in the distribution of his forces; he did not mix the divers corps, and associate horse and foot soldiers, but grouped together troops of the same arm, united men who had similar views and feelings, and thus formed distinct masses. His object was to try the effect of emulation. We give his views in his own words, in a letter addressed to General d'Hautpoul.

My dear General,
As you have accepted the command of the cavalry, permit me to make you a few necessary observations.
The cavalry generals, Ney, Richepanse, and Klein, have received their several instructions relative to the command of the divisions to which I have appointed them.
General Ney, with his hussars, will clear the march, cover the wings of the army, and perform the general reconnoitring service, in conjunction with the engineers and adjutants-general appointed to this duty. He will also levy contributions, and force the inhabitants of conquered countries to comply with the demands made upon them.

I shall habitually employ his corps when I myself reconnoitre.

The corps of chasseurs, quite unconnected with the hussars, will be attached to the vanguard of General Lefebvre's division, which, properly speaking, will, in the line of battle, form the right wing of the army. I deem it for the good of the service not to separate General Richepanse, commanding the division of *chasseurs-a-cheval*, from General Lefebvre, who esteems and honours him.

General Klein, in command of the dragoons, is attached to the service of the reserve, under General Championnet, whose friend he is; and as heretofore, this corps, in the present order of the army, will form its left wing.

The four divisions of infantry of the main body will each have only one regiment of horse; and these will be chasseurs. The division of cavalry will generally remain with the centre of the army, under the command of General Grenier. May I beg that you will place under the personal orders of that officer, either Brigadier-General Palmarole, or Brigadier-General Oswald. You will attach Adjutant-General Becker to the corps of hussars, and the corps of *chasseurs*; Becker (of the North) whose letters of service I enclose, you will attach to the division of dragoons, and Adjutant-General —— shall remain with the cavalry division.

From your command, my dear comrade, you will be the general commandant of all these corps. When in winter quarters, you will pay attention to their drilling, their appearance, their discipline, and to the goodness and salubrity of their cantonments. When in the field, you will station them, and give them such orders as you may think fit. If it be my intention when in the field to applaud deeds of valour, it is also my intention to reward such deeds.

If an officer loses his horse, it shall either be replaced or he shall receive its value in money. No man, whatever be his rank, shall take cannon, colours, or standards from the enemy, without receiving a reward in the field of battle. You cannot, my dear General, make these my intentions too public; they are engraven on my heart, and I will never depart from them.

The friendship you have shown me, and your attachment to the government, convince me that your constant exertions will tend to the good of the service. Believe me, my dear General, when I say that I shall neglect no opportunity of making known your own services to the French people, both in past and in future campaigns.

L. Hoche.

Head-quarters, Cologne, 18th *Ventose*, Year 5. (March 8th, 1797)

Ney had already received his instructions.[1] The general-in-chief concluded his despatch with some flattering expressions, and Ney professed equal confidence in the talents of his new commander. "I sincerely participate," he wrote to the latter, "in the delight of all my comrades at your arrival among us. The confidence with which your presence inspires the whole army, is a sure presage of your success. I shall be too happy if I can at all

---

1. Head-quarters, Cologne, 17th *Ventose*, Year 5. (March 7th, 1797)

General, I have to inform you, that it being my intention to form the different arms composing the cavalry of the army of Sambre-et-Meuse, into so many distinct divisions, I have given you the command of the division of hussars. Yon will accordingly organize it on the banks of the Simmern, and place the different corps which the head of the general staff has received directions to send you, in such cantonments as you may deem most eligible with regard to provisions and military order, and which offer the greatest facilities for effecting an immediate junction, whether for the purpose of encountering the enemy, or for the mere drilling and exercising of the different regiments.

The corps under your command will consist of the 2nd, 3rd, 4th, and 5th Regiments; and you will take from the depot of each, every serviceable man mounted and equipped for actual service, and give orders to the councils of administration to forward to the commissary-general an abstract of the articles the men are most in need of,—so that whatever is ready may be immediately issued from the stores.

You are to be attached to no particular division, and will receive orders either from General d'Hautpoul, who commands the cavalry of the army, or from myself. Allow me, general, to express my satisfaction at serving with you, whose military merit is so generally known and appreciated.

L. Hoche.

contribute in bringing your undertakings to a favourable issue, and thus deserve your esteem."

Ney proceeded to the Simmern, cantoned his hussars on both banks of this stream, and applied himself to giving them the necessary consistence. Most of them had seen service, but having been constantly engaged in contending either against the enemy or against famine, they had had neither time nor opportunity to become skilful in manoeuvring or in making evolutions in line. Another inconvenience of the long marches of the array, was the dispersion of the men, many of whom had been taken from their regiments.

One hussar had been forced into one direction, another into a different one; this man had served as orderly to a general officer, the other had been attached to the baggage trains, to the store wagons, or to the artillery. In this manner the privates had been dispersed, and the corps which ought to have had their full complement, were, in fact, mere skeletons.

Ney soon remedied this. He sought out and brought back the soldiers to their respective regiments, and began exercising them in manoeuvres. Personally inspecting, and often directing their evolutions, he soon imparted to his division the simultaneous action and suppleness which triumphs over superior masses deficient in the same discipline. Unfortunately there was something more to be done than to put his corps in a situation to appear with credit in the field: it was necessary to provide arms and provisions for the men, and forage for the horses; and the barren mountains around them, devastated by four years of war, could scarcely supply them with the most scanty fare. Unwilling to add to the already excessive distress of the inhabitants, he had tried to make his own resources suffice, by putting up to auction all that was unfit for service in his division. But the proceeds of sale of the unserviceable horses were not sufficient to pay even the expense of shoeing the horses of the war squadrons.

Necessity was therefore imperious, and he was forced to have recourse to the usual measures. He issued requisitions, levied imposts, and by patience and menaces succeeded, not only in obtaining from these barren mountains wherewith to feed his troops, but in forming reserves, and laying in provisions and forage to meet the consumption which must follow the breaking off the armistice.

The other generals followed Ney's example, and like him, assembled and disciplined their troops. Both officers and men were eager for battle. The imperialists however did not share in this impatience: they were tired of warfare and sighed for peace. The difficulty of proposing it when fortune is uncertain, and the political engagements into which they had entered, had long prevented them from making overtures; but at length the voice of reason and humanity was listened to. They applied to Marceau, and that ill-fated general was about to transmit their proposals to the Directory, when he was cut off by death.[2]

Hoche, like Marceau, was noble, generous, and magnanimous, and Kray did not despair of renewing with him the negotiations which had been broken off by the death of his predecessor, or at least of slackening the preparations of the French army, and thus gaining the time he wanted. Hoche had inspired him with real esteem; he had often manifested a wish to see the French general, and express to him in person the high estimation in which he held his activity and military talents. Kray, who had just arrived at Coblentz, proposed a meeting; Hoche acceded to the pro-

---

2. General Hoche to the Directory. Cologne,
March 15th, 1797,
Citizens Directors,
I am informed that the Austrians have long wished for peace. Their generals offered it confidentially to Marceau, who was about to apply for your orders on the subject when he was killed. Prince Charles has forced us to retreat in spite of himself, for he was in hopes of encountering greater resistance. He is furious against the Bourbons since the marriage of the daughter of Louis XVI. to the Duke of Angoulême; and he wishes for peace at any price. Nevertheless the preparations for war are great, and continue to be carried on with activity. I have these facts, Citizens Directors, from one who is well informed on the subject.
After this information, do you not think it necessary to instruct me as to the line of conduct I am to pursue, in the event of proposals being made to me? I have reason to expect that they will be made, as I march towards the Maine, which the enemy cannot defend against the army under my command. In a short time, Citizens Directors, we shall know what we are to expect on this head. L. Hoche.

posal, and set out for the place of appointment, accompanied by Lemoine, Lefebvre, and Championnet. The interview took place at Neuwied, and was pleasing to all parties. The conversation naturally turned upon the war, and upon those events in which each had been an actor. Kray, who was a profound admirer of daring acts of heroism, was loud in his praises of the undaunted valour displayed by the French troops. They had, he said, shown themselves ardent and intrepid in their successes, and had nobly borne their reverses.

They had won the glory attendant upon both good and evil fortune, and their names were now imperishable. But the glory in which they delighted, had not the same charms for him, because it reached him amid grief and mourning, and the vapour of blood tarnished its splendour. Hoche was much of the same way of thinking. Like Kray, he deplored the blindness of men in granting admiration only to those among their fellow-creatures who slaughter or betray them. He regretted that he had no authority to accept the overtures made to him; and contented himself with endeavouring to pave the way for their future success by ascertaining the real feelings of his adversary.

This was easy enough; for Kray was really anxious for peace, and could not understand why it should not be forthwith concluded. Was it, he asked, on account of the treaties which bound his government to Russia? Why, policy had made them, and policy could also annul them. Was it on account of Belgium? His cabinet cared little for the loss of those rebellious provinces; and the bishopric of Bamberg, or Saltzburgh, or some other, might form an equitable indemnity. The course of the conversation led them to mention Prussia. Kray became warm, and was very vehement against King William, whom he accused of endeavouring to destroy the Germanic confederation. Hoche now interrupted him.

"Where would be the evil," he said, "if it were made advantageous to the Emperor;—if you obtained Bavaria, and Belgium were given in exchange to the Elector?"

"Then," replied Kray in the same tone, "matters would be

bearable;—we would suffer violence, and say nothing."

The conversation again reverted to the Prussians, and Kray resumed his invectives against them.

"They are deceiving you," he repeated several times; "they are deceiving you. The day is at hand when you will rue the weakness you are showing in their favour. Things have already come to such a pass, that we cannot conclude a peace with you without immediately declaring war against them."

Hoche had nothing to do with such a quarrel, and merely observed that if the Prussians were troublesome to Austria, the English were equally so to France. Kray, who had, no doubt, his instructions from Prince Charles, whose friend and counsellor he was, said he cared as little about England as Hoche cared about Prussia. He did not therefore go out of his way to laud those islanders, but stuck to the object he had in view.

His mode of argumentation was powerful, intellectual, and full of point. He demanded with a species of ascendancy in his manner, that the armies should remain in *statu quo*, or at all events not resume the campaign until the harvest was over. He urged the state of exhaustion of the right bank, and insisted upon the necessity of awaiting the result of the negotiations begun in Italy. Hoche took care not to yield to such arguments. He knew that the Austrian government was making levies, and that recruits were reaching the Rhine from all parts; he therefore resolved not to give his adversary time to bring them into line.

The conference had lasted four hours, when Hoche put an end to it, and expressing to the Field Marshal the esteem he had for his noble character, took his leave.

Chapter 19

Ney Taken Prisoner

This long conversation revealed to Hoche the anxiety with which the Austrians contemplated their future prospects, and the little confidence they had in their own resources. He therefore hastened his preparations, which were nearly complete. Ney having laid in stores of forage, and Championnet collected some provisions, the army was put in motion, and the left wing crossed the Sieg on the 17th of April. The remainder of the forces assembled in the environs of Andernach, crossed the Rhine at Neuwied, and debouched, on the 18th, at daybreak, in front of the formidable positions occupied by the Austrians.

Kray, who for some days past had constantly talked of peace, and had even proposed an armistice, thought that Hoche would become more complying when he saw the obstacles he had to encounter. The two armies were within cannon shot of each other, and the field marshal made proposals to the French general to suspend the attack, and see if they could not come to an accommodation. Hoche consented; but insisted upon the surrender of Ehrenbreitstein and the evacuation of the Upper Lahn, as a preliminary measure. The bearer of the Austrian flag of truce rejected such conditions, and both parties prepared for battle.

The front of the imperialists was covered with redoubts friezed and palisaded, and their two wings occupied strongly fortified villages; the right Hellesdorf, the left Bendorf. The little river Seyn increased the strength of a position already covered with fortifications. Hoche determined to attack it, and pointing out the redoubts whence the enemy were pouring death upon their ranks, "A thousand *francs* for each piece of cannon," he exclaimed.

"Agreed," the soldiers replied. The infantry was formed, and the cavalry and artillery occupying their respective stations, advanced with the infantry, and soon came to close action. The attack was fearfully impetuous, and the bayonet was soon resorted to; it overcame all resistance, and in a very short time the right wing of the Austrians was overthrown. On the left, the action was longer and more obstinate. Lefebvre, Gratien, and Spital threw the ranks of the imperialists into disorder, without, however, being able to break them. Ney was more fortunate: he had taken up a position in front of Neuwied, and having despatched the 2nd Hussars to occupy the space between the redoubts at the bridgehead, threw himself with the 3rd and 4th into that between the redoubts at Hellesdorf, cut to pieces the infantry which guarded it, and took a great many prisoners, with several pieces of cannon; then falling with the same impetuosity upon the masses which covered Hellesdorf, drove them into the defiles of Braunsberg.

But the Austrians were scarcely dislodged from the village, ere they became aware how. critical their situation was. Having perceived the impossibility of maintaining themselves upon the line they had formed, they immediately took measures for occupying the woods and defiles leading to Neuwied. Heavy masses of their troops advanced for this purpose; and two columns with a numerous artillery were about to attain the position; but Ney, who perceived all the importance of the movement, and that if it succeeded, the fortune of the day would again become doubtful, did not hesitate with his comparatively small force to attempt counteracting it.

Notwithstanding the fatigue which the men had already undergone, he divided them into two bodies, and marched up to the enemy. Though the nature of the ground, and the exhaustion of his troops, gave him but slender hopes of success, both men and horses seemed on a sudden to arouse at his voice, charged the Austrians with irresistible spirit, and made great havoc in their ranks. They gave way, and those who escaped death, being stopped in their flight by the baggage-wagons with which the road to Neuwied was covered, were obliged to ask for quarter. The whole of the Austrian column was either taken or destroyed; Ney established himself in the plain, and took up his position on the road to Dierdorf at the entrance of the mountain gorges.

His attitude was threatening; and the Austrians, broken throughout their line, perceived that they were in danger of being shut up in the plain of Neuwied. They therefore resolved upon a fresh attempt to occupy the woods. Columns of infantry, much stronger than the former, advanced under the support of a numerous body of cavalry and artillery, but were unable to debouch. Ney's hussars kept them in check, and drove them back each time they attempted to force their way. The battle had now lasted many hours, and the manner in which the French troops behaved was fully appreciated by their general-in-chief, who did ample justice to the decision and ability which Ney had shown. Hoche, in his despatch, thus speaks of him:—

> Ney proceeded with rapidity to Dierdorf, where he found the reserve of the Austrians, six thousand strong, and still untouched. With less than five hundred hussars, he engaged this body during four consecutive hours, and by his skill and energy succeeded in gaining time until the arrival of our infantry and reserve of cavalry.

The French were now a match for their adversaries, whom they overthrew on every point. Ney pressed upon them, and allowed them no time to breathe. He had already driven them from Dierdorf and Steinberg, and was preparing to force them beyond the Lahn, when they again sounded the charge, and came towards him. Unable to account for this sudden change, he advanced and soon discovered its cause. The French hussars had forced an Austrian column to lay down its arms, but were still stopped by a line of sharp shooters. Anxious to disperse these, and drive them from the heights which they occupied, the

French had brought a field-piece into play. The Blankestein Hussars, perceiving this fault, hastened to take advantage of it, and, supported by the Cobourg Dragoons, made a desperate charge. The troops advanced on both sides, fought round the gun, and both parties struggled for it as the prize contended for.

The ground was bad, and the numbers of the Austrians very superior; but Ney succeeded in throwing their ranks into confusion, and they gave way. The French were now in hopes that they should be unable to return to the attack, and were congratulating themselves on their victory, when fresh squadrons came up to the assistance of the Austrians. The republicans were broken in their turn, and it was in vain for Ney to resist the torrent which swept his forces along. His horse fell, and rolled with him into a ravine.

He was covered with bruises and blood, and to complete his disaster, his sword snapped in twain. The enemy surrounded him, and he had no further hope of escape. He resisted, nevertheless; for perceiving the 4th about to make a fresh charge, he was anxious to give them time to come to his assistance. He therefore used the stump of his sword, struck, parried, and kept in check the crowd which pressed upon him. Such a contest could not last long;—the ground was slippery, Ney's foot slid, he fell to the ground, and the Austrians succeeded in seizing him. He was thus made prisoner, and conveyed to Giessen.

The fame of his capture preceded him thither, and everyone was eager to behold a man whose deeds seemed fabulous. The women more especially could not imagine how he had dared to resist a whole squadron, and, for a time, with some appearance of success. As they were taking him to head-quarters through a by-street, these fair admirers of courage begged that he might be led through the public square.

"Really," said an Austrian officer, annoyed at their importunity, "one would suppose that he was some extraordinary animal."

"Extraordinary indeed," replied one of the ladies, "since it required a whole squadron of dragoons to take him."

This sally put everyone in good humour, and each yielded to the admiration which Ney's heroism inspired;—some among the fair Germans calling to mind his valour on one occasion,—others the humanity and disinterestedness with which he always treated the people he conquered.

Ney was received at the Austrian head-quarters in a manner worthy of his high reputation. Each condoled with him on his mishap, and on the vicissitudes of war. But the conversation soon turned on battle and military manoeuvres; and the prisoner was discussing each general's share of merit, when he perceived his horse, with an Austrian upon its back. The animal seemed weak, lazy, and obstinate; in spite of the spur, it would not advance. Ney exclaimed against the awkwardness of the rider, and was answered by a joke about the worthlessness of the animal. An officer jestingly proposed to purchase it; and its points and capabilities seeming matter of doubt, Ney approached it.

"I will show you," said he, "the value of my horse."

An opening was immediately made, Ney sprang upon the saddle, and taking the direction of the French army, soon left in the rear those who accompanied or followed him. The horse which had appeared so worthless to the Austrians, carried him off like the wind, and he was near escaping; but the trumpets sounded, and the heavy and light cavalry rode off and soon stopped up every issue. Ney then turned back, and with equal celerity reached the spot where the Austrian generals stood aghast.

"Well, gentlemen," he said, "what think you of the animal now? Is he not worthy of his master?"

Their scattered squadrons sufficiently proved the affirmative. A little confused at their mistake, they guarded their prisoner more carefully, and took care not to jest again about his horse.

A French orderly having been sent to the Austrian head-quarters with intelligence of the preliminaries of peace, signed at Leoben—news of which had just reached the army of Sambre-et-Meuse—the attention of the generals of both armies was turned to the terms of an armistice, in order to stop the effusion of blood. But the communication of this important circumstance was not the sole object of the message. Hoche was attached to Ney, whose loss he regretted; and he wrote to the latter expressing deep regret at his captivity, and the steps he had taken to bring it to a close.

> "You know me sufficiently, my dear general," he wrote, "to give me credit for the affliction I feel at your misfortune. I depend sufficiently upon the reciprocity with which the Austrian generals will act, to trust that they will treat you as we have treated those of their colleagues whom we captured in Italy. I have requested M. Elsnitz to send you back on parole, and I am awaiting, in the most anxious impatience, the moment when I shall embrace you. Write to me, and inform me what pecuniary assistance you require. *Adieu*, my dear Ney; rely upon my sincere and constant friendship."[1]

Ney required no assistance. Meantime, Hoche expressed to the officers under Ney's command, how highly he was satisfied with their conduct. He gave a horse to one, a sword to another, a sash to a third; he also insisted upon Ney's receiving a memorial of his esteem and friendship, and accordingly forwarded to him a magnificent belt, with a letter still more flattering.

> "In sending you," he wrote from Friedberg, three days after, "the belt which the bearer will deliver to you, I do not pretend, my dear general, to reward either your success or your merit. Pray therefore accept it only as a feeble pledge of my personal esteem and unalterable friendship. Give me news of your health."

The Directory, who did not evince less kindness or less regret at the accident which had placed Ney in the power of the Austrians, sent him a strong and flattering letter. And indeed his talents, his impetuous valour, and the ability he had displayed before Giessen, made the Government the more sensible of the loss of his services; but it trusted that one of the most efficient

---

1. Head-quarters, Giessen, 2nd *Florial*, Year 5. (April 1st 1797.)

officers in the service would speedily be restored to the army, and that his future deeds would soon avenge the check which the French cavalry had received.[2]

Warneck, who commanded the Austrians, had no desire to set Ney at liberty. Several communications had taken place on this subject, and the captive, who was expected to return every hour, did not appear. Hoche at length got out of patience; he knew that the archduke had forbidden his officers, under the severest penalties, to disoblige the French generals, and he threatened to complain to that prince. The Austrian field-marshal was not proof against this, and pretending to perform an act of courtesy towards his prisoner, sent him back on parole.

Hoche received him with most lively satisfaction. The share which Ney had taken in the victory of Neuwied, and the talents he had displayed before Giessen, were subjects of high eulogy on the part of the commander-in-chief, who, as if these praises were insufficient, determined that his impatience to see such an officer again in activity of service, should be stated in a public document. It was so, and in the following terms:—

> Head-quarters, Friedberg, 17th *Florial*, Year 5.
> (May 6th, 1797.)
> Brigadier-General Ney may retire to Giessen, whenever he pleases, until his exchange, so anxiously desired by the general-in-chief, can be effected. And in the event of his private affairs requiring his presence in another part of the territory occupied by the army of Sambre-et-Meuse, he is at liberty to proceed thither and remain as long as he may find it necessary. Hoche.

---

2. The Directory to Brigadier-General Ney, Employed in the Army of Sambre-et-Meuse.
The Executive Directory is truly afflicted, Citizen General, at the accident which made you fall into the hands of the enemy. The impetuosity of your courage before Giessen, and the brilliant manoeuvres which you executed at the head of the squadrons under your command, make this event still more to be regretted.
The Directory trusts that the army will soon again behold one of its bravest general officers, whose absence is particularly regretted by the general-in-chief.
Letourneur, President
.Paris, 12th *Florial*, Year 5. (May 1st, 1797.)

The wished-for exchange at last took place. The Directory set General Orelly at liberty, and the Aulic Council liberated Ney from his parole. This negotiation lasted three weeks, and no sooner did Hoche learn its termination than he forwarded the news of it to Ney.

"I send you, brave Ney," he wrote, "the certificate of your exchange, which has reached me through the Government. Come and resume your station in the army; and be assured that when we begin again, I will place you in a situation to win the praises of both our friends and enemies."

This promise was flattering, and Ney determined to justify its performance. Though the campaign had been short, it had been attended with great loss of life; and Ney applied himself to repairing the losses among his hussars, by filling up the gaps which the different battles had made in their ranks. He collected horses, mounted and drilled recruits, and in a few weeks his division was more numerous and stronger than at the outset of the campaign.

This circumstance, which would have rendered him more formidable in the field, was rather an impediment to him in cantonments. The general-in-chief had imposed upon the country contributions in kind, but the bailiwicks were slow in their supplies, and had become much more so since peace had been talked of. The evacuation of the territory by the French seemed at hand; and they flattered themselves that, by delay, they might possibly elude the burthens which weighed upon them. The French, moreover, had neither warehouses nor the means of making bread; and Hoche had just given up to Moreau the million of *francs* which the army of Italy had presented to that of the Rhine.

Thus the situation of the troops was not very brilliant. But Ney, anxious to avoid extreme measures, had recourse to an expedient which succeeded. He knew that the inhabitants, so averse to the delivery of their produce, were easy enough on the score of domestic consumption. He therefore humoured this feeling, and in lieu of contributions, quartered his men upon the villagers.

The peasantry of these countries are naturally hospitable; the soldiers did little jobs for them, and everything went on amicably. The peasants consumed only a little more bacon and vegetables, and an additional quantity of milk and cheese; whilst the soldiers had abundance of food, and soon regained that strength which lightens the burthen of life, and disposes the mind to acts of daring.

The negotiations, meantime, dragged heavily on Royalism had once more reared its head; it agitated the French nation and reigned in its councils. The revolution seemed again in danger, and Austria, emboldened by the royalist conspiracies, became daily less complying and more haughty. But the armies destined to defend the liberties of France against kings, defended them also against treacherous legislators; the emigrants were punished, and the empire, deprived of its auxiliaries, at length signed a treaty of peace.

The Continent was now undisturbed. Great Britain alone remained hostile, and it was determined to assault her upon her own shores. An army was formed for this purpose, and called the army of England. The pacificator of Campo-Formio was to command it; but being obliged to pursue, in Germany, the negotiations, which he had commenced in Italy, he left to Dessaix the care of assembling and distributing its force along the sea-coast.

This general, an able statesman and warrior, was anxious to put an end to the wars which desolated Europe, by destroying the source whence they sprang. He considered this a great national undertaking, and was therefore anxious that all the armies of the republic should share in it. This induced him to select troops from those armies which had fought in the North, as well as from those which had rendered themselves illustrious in the South.

Ney was put at the head of part of the forces supplied by

the army of Sambre-et-Meuse, and accordingly set out with his division of hussars for Amiens, where he arrived on the 14th of March 1798. It soon, however, became evident that the means of execution were not adequate to the greatness of the project. The warehouses were empty, the arsenals without arms or ammunition, and the pay of the troops, which their victories did not afford the means of discharging, was ten millions of *francs* in arrear for the armies of the Rhine alone.

General Bonaparte was not discouraged: he considered that an invasion of England would secure for many years the peace of the Continent, and he resolved not to forego his intention of trying it, until he had a firm conviction that it was impracticable. He therefore directed General Dessaix to survey the coast from Havre-de-Grace to the mouth of the Loire; and he sent Berthier to survey the coast along the British Channel.

Both were directed likewise, to ascertain the number of ships, together with the nature of the stores in each sea-port, and to examine the state of the arsenals. They found distress, neglect, and want everywhere, and both returned with the conviction that an attempt upon England could not be made with any prospect of success.

Unable to reach England in a direct manner, General Bonaparte resolved to attack it indirectly. The peace had brought back an expensive army to France, the treasury was empty, and a host of necessitous and enterprising men whom the war had trained to arms, already tired of peace, displayed the uneasiness attendant upon forced inaction.

The Directory, fully aware of the critical state of things, saw that it was as impossible to meet the public expenditure, as to keep down the effervescence of these men. General Bonaparte therefore offered to diminish the former and give employment to the latter. He proposed, that after the example of Spain, Portugal, and Holland, these individuals without employment should be sent beyond seas in search of adventures, and their activity of mind, which at home might become dangerous to the state, thus turned to its advantage. The Directory accepted the proposal, and the expedition to Egypt was resolved upon.

The plan was not, however, suffered to transpire; on the contrary, every exertion seemed to be directed towards hastening the expedition to England; but the forces which were to have formed it, were distributed for the undertaking they were really to pursue. Some recrossed the Alps, others marched westward and reached the frontier. The hussars were included in this last measure, and Ney was despatched to Lille to take the command of the 6th and 10th Dragoons, and 10th Chasseurs, forming the cavalry of General Grenier's division.

Everything was again prepared for a renewal of war. Italy was in violent commotion. The new republics, though disagreeing among themselves, had united to attack and revolutionize Piedmont. This state, supported by all that was still monarchical in the Peninsula, prepared to make a stout resistance; whilst Austria, on the other hand, daily assumed a more hostile attitude. It had already agitated the Grisons, made military movements upon the Adige, and seemed now prepared to come to extremities, when an incident occurred which placed its intentions beyond a doubt. Bernadotte, who represented the French Republic at Vienna, had received instructions to endeavour to overthrow Thugot, then directing minister.

The French general accordingly applied to the Empress, revealed to her certain double dealings on the part of the minister, and the rich reward he was to obtain for certain acts of perfidy, The Empress was indignant; but Thugot obtained intelligence of the scheme of the French ambassador, and perceiving his danger, hastened to put a stop to such dangerous conferences.

The French embassy being about to be adorned with a tricolour flag, he seized this opportunity, raised the populace, and directed their fury towards the French ambassador's house. Bernadotte, indignant, demanded satisfaction, but finding it. neither prompt nor sufficient, quitted Vienna. This insult, the object and particulars of which were unknown, seemed a declaration of war. Ney left his dragoons to proceed to the army at Mayence, and arrived on the 1st of September 1798, at Friedberg.

Bernadotte to General M——.
26th *Florial*, Year 5. (March 15th, 1797.)

Thugot, the soul of the coalition, who seeks to renew it, and is a sworn enemy to the republic, was near falling into the snare which I had laid for him. But as a clever and experienced courtier, he felt that my third audience of the Empress would have either totally ruined him, or at least have placed him in inaction. To avert the storm, he conceived the project of getting me either assassinated or ill-treated. The affair of the flag was adroitly taken advantage of by him for this purpose. This flag had been ordered at the tailor's three days before, and there was plenty of time to get up the riot.

The planting of the flag, however, which was done without thought, frustrated my measures. Nevertheless, Thugot's perfidy has furnished me with fresh weapons against him. The information given to me after the danger was over, has fully convinced me that he was one of the principal promoters of the disturbance. His silence during five hours, and the tardy arrival of a military force; the inertness of the latter, and of the police;— all these circumstances authorise me to cease communication with him, and to accuse him before the tribunal of public opinion, as well as before the supreme chief of his nation. The sovereign has replied to my complaint through the medium of another minister;—thus Thugot's credit and respectability are on the wane. The Government has only to pursue the plan laid down by its ambassador &c.

Nevertheless, the political horizon seemed to clear up a little; negotiations were opened at Seltz, after the turbulence of the Italian republics had been suppressed. For a moment there were hopes that no fresh conflagration would burst forth; but principles, such as gave rise to these commotions, must receive their full development, and it is impossible to avoid their consequences.

CHAPTER 20

Invasion of Helvetia

The French were announced as the avengers of nations, and the award which, as umpires, they had rendered in the affair of the Valteline, sanctioned this title. It is known that the Valtelinians, having submitted to the Grisons, were soon after abandoned to the latter by the house of Sforza; but only on certain conditions, and with franchises for which this princely house became guarantee, but which the Grisons had never yet allowed them to enjoy.

The yoke of the latter had therefore become intolerable, and the Valtelinians attempted at different times to shake it off; but each time that the Sovereign people[1] had the disadvantage, the federal aristocracy came to their assistance, and riveted still more firmly the chains of the poor oppressed mountaineers.

The popular cause at length triumphed, and General Bonaparte having subjected Italy to his laws, the oppressed Valtelinians submitted their grievances to him. As this affair was closely connected with the interests of Switzerland, it might from that very cause endanger the peace of Europe. Bonaparte, therefore, felt repugnance to interfere in these differences; but having conquered the Milanese territory, he had thereby become invested with the rights of the Dukes of Milan, and could not consistently decline their duties.

He accordingly accepted the office of umpire, and having admitted that the stipulations had been violated, decided that a people could not be the subjects of another people, and that the

Valtelinians were free from the yoke of the Grisons. This decision soon spread through the valleys of Helvetia; the sovereign population perceived what they had to fear, and the enslaved mountaineers saw their franchises acknowledged and supported by a powerful nation. All was in agitation in Switzerland; some cantons claimed their rights, others defended their privileges, and, as it always happens when states have no confidence in their own strength, and have powerful neighbours, each appealed to the particular government whose political doctrines favoured its own peculiar views.

The people of Argau, St. Gall, and the Pays de Vaud, appealed to France; the aristocracies of Basle, Soleure, Berne, and Zurich, to Austria. Thus the balance was far from even; the people were in favour of the French, but their rivals were all powerful in the council. The former only elicited a useless sympathy, the latter wielded the power.

Such a state of things was not to be endured. France could not allow Austria to obtain such ascendancy in Switzerland, and thus dispose of all the resources of the confederation. The internal struggle in the cantons became daily more intense; the Pays de Vaud claimed its rights and privileges, and Berne overran it with troops. This territory was contending against evils of the same nature as those which had afflicted the Valteline. Like the latter, it had been alienated, but on condition that its franchises should be respected. It now only demanded the execution of the solemn treaty made at that period;—it required nothing more than the franchises specified in the declaration of rights guaranteed by France, The Directory unable, under such circumstances, to do less than one of its generals had done, interfered; but in a manner worthy of the government of a great people,—with a view only to conciliation.

The effect of such interference did not answer the expectations of the French government. Battles were fought, much blood was shed, and whole tribes were swept from the face of the earth. But these troubles had their origin in the noblest feel-

---

1. The Grisons assumed this title;

ings; and if they led to fearful results, it was because foreign ideas, combined with local influence, had obtained too much weight in the Swiss councils. This is proved by the following despatches, which, though they have no direct connexion with Ney's life, point out the causes of a struggle in which he afterwards became an actor. They also show the feelings existing in a country which at a subsequent period he was sent to pacify; and they clear one of his brethren in arms, afterwards proscribed and sacrificed, from the base imputations with which it has been lately attempted to stigmatize his memory.

1

General Brune, Commander-in-Chief of the French Army in Helvetia, to the Executive Directory,
Head-Quarters, Berne, March 17th, 1798.
Citizens Directors,
I yesterday saw the deputies of the democratic cantons of Ury, Underwalden, Schweitz, Glaris, and Lower Zug. In their address to me, you will find the profession of friendship made by their constituents, to the French republic. Twenty deputies from Argau came, at the same time, to ask me for authority to form a separate canton. It was granted to them immediately; and they promised me to proceed with activity in constituting new authorities, enlightening the people, urging the neighbouring countries to adopt the same resolution that they had done, and carrying into execution the constitution drawn up by M. Ochs. In these deputies I perceived great ardour, zeal, and openness. I send you the address; it contains thanks on the subject of the instructions I sent them.

The canton of Zurich, torn by hostile parties, has yet come to no decision; nevertheless the friends of the new constitution are very numerous there, and will carry it into effect without being obliged to secure their triumph by an appeal to arms. At first, Citizens Directors, you desired that Switzerland should form a single republic, one and indivisible; but on taking into consideration some difficulties in the constitution which was to have served as its basis,—and perhaps on reflecting upon the consequences which might result from the neighbourhood of a great political machine, whose motions would be prompt and uniform, and from the effects of which we should have greater occasion to preserve ourselves than to make any use of it, you have come to the conclusion that the whole of Helvetia ought to form three independent republics.

This plan is now being carried into effect. One of the three republics, consisting of all those parts of Switzerland in which French is spoken, is almost wholly formed. You will find its composition in the document of which I enclose a copy.

The canton of Berne, already deprived of the Pays de Vaud and Argau, will further lose the whole of Oberland, which begins at the lake of Thun and terminates on the other side of Mount Grimsel. It will also lose the country between the lake of Brienz, the Sanen, and the Aar, as far as Buren. The territory of the new republic requiring width, and it being necessary to secure to France good communications with Italy—such communications being more difficult in the south of Switzerland, the inhabitants of which are refractory and ill-disposed—it is expedient to form, at the two extremities of the lake of Neufchâtel, points of contact which may facilitate our influence. As the Rhone runs through a considerable portion of this republic, and supplies with water, if it does not pass through, the beautiful lake Leman, I have called this country Rhodania. Thus we may say the Rhodanians, and the Rhodanian republic.

As it is not your intention to trouble the small democratic cantons of Ury, Schweitz, Underwalden, Zug, and Glaris, their federative form shall not be meddled with. They will compose a confederation, with a central and representative body to watch over its general safety and manage its foreign relations. In this confederation the Grisons may join. There is nothing to prevent this country from being called Tellgau, or Tellgovia, which signifies country of William Tell; and we may denominate its inhabitants Tellgovites. The capital might be Schweitz, or Altorf in the canton of Ury.

The third republic, the most important in extent, commerce, and population, will consist of twelve cantons or departments. Its metropolis may be either Lucerne or Zurich. This country may be called Helvetia. It will be easy, after what I have done to prepare the public feelings on the subject, to establish in it the constitution drawn up by M. Ochs; but with some modifications,—perhaps the same which I have thought necessary for Rhodania.

I must now explain why I have not placed Appenzel among the number of cantons which remain pure democracies. Appenzel touches the hereditary states of Austria on several points; and by placing it in Tellgovia, Austria would be enabled to exercise a greater influence over that republic, and consequently over Helvetia, than it does at present. We ought not to neglect warding off danger, however distant and insignificant it may seem. If the Helvetian republic, which joins our territory in several places, contained Appenzel, we should be able to perceive the action of Austria upon this most important part of the country; for we may reckon as nothing any attempts of the enemy upon the country of the Grisons, which forms at the back of Tellgovia a rampart of inaccessible mountains.

Health and Fraternity.
Brune.

2

Brune, Commander-in-Chief of the French Army in Helvetia, to the Executive Directory.
Berne, 1st *Germinal*, in the evening,
(March 21st.)
Citizens Directors,
The resolution I had formed, and which I communicated

to you in my despatch of this morning, is no longer practicable. Your last plan was no doubt known to M. Ochs, for he invokes your will, and almost your name, to hasten the return to unity. In yielding to his sarcasms, the people think they are obeying the executive Directory of the French republic, and by this line of conduct he has obtained an almost unanimity of suffrages.

M. Ochs has evinced towards me a degree of cunning which approaches duplicity. After applauding the motives which induced me to delay for some days the execution of your plan, he had no sooner left me than he used the most impetuous haste in precipitating the union; thus depriving me of the merit of bringing it about myself. He travels as president of Switzerland rather than of the canton of Basle. He has two flags suspended to his carriage: one green, and the other red, white, and black. He is likewise attended by a numerous escort. I must end what I have to say concerning him by stating, that he gave me an almost scandalous account of the formation of his constitutional project.

Health and Fraternity.

Brune.

3

To the Executive Directory.

Head-quarters, Berne, 5th *Germinal*, Year 6.

(March 25th.)

Citizens Directors,

The work of Swiss liberty is in progress, and I shall have the satisfaction, before I leave, of seeing it sufficiently advanced to make the enemies of the federative system lose all hopes of success. Berne has appointed its electors and municipal officers; and the primary assemblies have met without any disturbance. In your last despatch you directed me to complete the overthrow of the Bernese oligarchy, and prevent the provisional government from publishing the project of a constitution, in preparing which several of its members were occupied. I informed you in my last that all this had been done. The exclusion is pronounced. In my last, I also sent you copies of the several decrees which I have felt it my duty to promulgate; I now transmit you a copy of an explanatory letter I wrote to the commune of Berne, and in which I extend the exclusion even to the families of the oligarchs in office.

There is a difficulty on this head with regard to Zurich. It is well known, that, in the council of that city, ten or twelve members formed, in spite of the aristocracy, an opposition which has resisted the greatest political storms. The courage of these citizens deserves to be rewarded, and the inhabitants of Zurich are desirous that it should be. The national assembly of Zurich have sent deputies to me to express a wish that the people should have the power of placing among those whom they intend to honour with their confidence, the men who have earned their share of it by such generous sacrifices.

You will perceive the precautions taken by the assembly of Zurich to prevent this exception from being made an improper use of; and I scarcely know how a general measure, whatever be its rigour, could resist such considerations as these. Besides, the men in whose favour Zurich makes such a demand, have protested against the petition, and declared that, for the term prescribed, they renounce all public employment. This new species of courage renders the members of the Zurich opposition still more deserving of the confidence of their fellow citizens, and I have deemed it right to yield to the wishes of the national assembly.

Although the aristocracy of Friburg are not worthy of so extensive an exemption, nevertheless, the citizens Montenach and Wonderveïdt ought to be included in it. Both enjoy the esteem of the friends of liberty; and I am indebted to the latter for much useful information, given prior to the capture of Friburg.

Claims have also been made in favour of certain members of the council of Soleure; but as General Schauwenburg is exclusively acquainted with everything which takes place in that canton, whether political, military, or financial, he will act in this matter to the best of his judgement.

As for Berne, there may be some patriots among the members of the ex-council, but I regret that I do not know them; and I am of opinion that, in this part of Switzerland, the exclusion should remain entire.

I leave on the 8th instant for Italy, in conformity to your orders; and I therefore do not think it necessary to trouble myself about the aristocracies of Lucerne and Schaffhausen, which can inspire but little interest, as not a single voice is raised in their favour.

The lesser cantons may become alarmed at the reports circulated, in spite of my protestations, regarding the necessity which would be imposed upon them of joining the rest of Helvetia, and changing their democracy into the representation system; but I know your intentions sufficiently, Citizens Directors, to be persuaded that the inhabitants of these little states will not be troubled. The openness, and even freedom of their declarations, prove that you may depend upon their attachment to, and their faithful observance of the treaties.

The resident Mangourit, who arrived here the day before yesterday, informs me that the Valais is extremely averse to form part of Helvetia, and that it would object to belong to any republic of which it did not form the total. This feeling, in the event of its not being overcome by persuasion, would not be in any wise disadvantageous to us, because, by way of the department of Mont Blanc, we have only the Valais to cross in order to establish our passage into Italy. Thus the formation of this country into an isolated state, could not, at all events, prove a very great political error.

Generally speaking, the political state of the whole of Helvetia is satisfactory. The different ranks of constitutional authorities are in progress of being established there, and an ordinary degree of watchfulness is alone necessary to prevent an injury to the interests of France.

I must inform you, Citizens Directors, that copies of the letters and instructions which you send me, are in circulation through the country, and more particularly at Basle and Lausanne.

I am certain that Citizen Laharpe has written from Paris—from the Directorial palace, nay, from the very Salle des Drapeaux—that you are about to determine upon the unity of Helvetia, and that no attention is to be paid to any measures that may be pursued by the French ministers and generals in opposition to this determination. You may easily imagine, Citizens Directors, the difficulties which may be raised by these communications, and their effect in delaying the execution of your orders.

I send you all the securities of monies due, which I have been able to procure. They are very considerable, and bear not only upon England, but upon Austria, Denmark, and several states of Germany. All these bonds form a deposit which I send to Paris, and which my *aide-de-camp*, Captain Guillemot, is instructed to take care of, and deliver into the hands of any person you may appoint to receive them. I dispatch at the same time the ex-treasurer and ex-director of the mint at Berne, now military commissary-general of the same canton. His name is Jenner. He is able to give you every information concerning both the bonds and the mode of converting them into cash; likewise the amount of the specie at the mint and in the treasury. You will see, by the accompanying copy of an abstract, of which he will deliver to you both the original and the several *procès-verbaux* connected with it, that the sums found in the treasury pretty well correspond with the entries in the books.

The sums which I have applied to the use of the troops,

amount to nine hundred thousand *francs*, taken at two different periods: namely, five hundred thousand *francs* the first time, and four hundred thousand the second. I send you the account of the paymaster to the division of Italy,—a document proving the taking and application of this money, and showing that the troops have been paid up to the 15th instant, as you desired.

Sufficient still remains in the treasury to meet the wants of the troops under the command of General Schauwenburg, until contributions, which may certainly be abundant, and the amount of which you will fix, are raised to supply any other exigences that may occur. The surplus of the treasure shall be sent to Mayence; I will leave instructions for my successor to this effect.

I likewise send you a list of the bonds belonging to the canton of Friburg, for sums due by the inhabitants of the country, as well as by France and foreign nations.

You will, at the same time, receive an account of the ordnance taken from the enemy. It amounts to two hundred and ninety-three pieces of cannon of different calibres, thirty-eight howitzers, and thirty-two mortars. General Schauwenburg is directed to evacuate these pieces upon Huninguen and Carouge. One hundred and sixty-three are already evacuated.

Health and respect.

Brune.

This correspondence shows the injustice of the imputations lately raised against Marshal Brune; it shows how little this General deserved the reproaches of perfidy and cupidity applied to him. It also shows that, far from taking an undue advantage of his victories, he constantly pleaded the cause of the conquered inhabitants; that he felt in them the same confidence which he sought to inspire; and that no one could be more careful, or take greater precautions in verifying and proving the amount of the treasure that fell into his hands.

CHAPTER 21

Second Coalition

The French having made an irruption into Switzerland, the Austrians penetrated into the country of the Grisons; and besides increasing their force upon the Lech and in the Tyrol, sent troops into Brisgau. The attitude thus assumed by them was formidable: they could, on the one hand, cross the Spulgen, reach Chiavenna and Lago Maggiore; on the other, they had it in their power, by penetrating through the valley of Urseren, to occupy Mount Tavesch, force the St. Gothard, and reach Airolo and Bellinzona. They might further direct a movement upon Schaffhausen, spread their forces through the Frickthal, force the valley of Scion, debouch upon Aost, rally the Piedmontese troops, involve the French army in a system of irremediable manoeuvres, and divide the army of Italy into two parts, cutting them off from each other.

The Directory, anxious to provide against the power of producing such serious consequences, seized the strongholds of the King of Sardinia, reinforced the French armies in Italy, in the Roman states, and in the cantons of Helvetia, and organized two fresh armies upon the Rhine. The one intended to operate in Suabia and Bavaria, under the command of Jourdan, was called the army of Mayence; the other, commanded by Bernadotte, was denominated the army of observation. The latter was intended to protect the forts on the river Huninguen at Dusseldorf, prevent an invasion of the left bank, spread through Hesse-Darmstadt, and take Manheim and Philipsburg. Ney, who had been for several months on the banks of the Lahn, naturally belonged to the latter army, which was to have contained forty thousand men, but was reduced much below its complement.

Nor were the men in a fit condition to enter upon a campaign;—one had no musket, another no bayonet—and what was still worse, the whole of them, worn down by a long agony of want, displayed no appearance of regularity, order, or even primitive organization. Coats in rags, waistcoats of different materials, rent breeches, and gaiters of all colours;—such was the condition and appearance of these patriotic soldiers, cruelly pinched by hunger, and yet most ardently devoted to their colours.

In vain did the superior officers interfere to alleviate the sufferings of their men; if their exertions were sometimes successful, and they obtained a little forage from the administration, the quality of the article was so bad that it was really not worth the trouble taken to procure it. If ready-made articles of clothing were given out, the shoes were not sewn, or the cloth had never been wetted: thus, the former fell to pieces at the commencement of a march, and the coats burst on the first shower of rain. If the materials were demanded instead, it was still worse; the applicants were made to come and go, and wait, and the most tedious and painful solicitations often remained unanswered.

The stores were distributed throughout the territory of the republic; each town had its well-filled warehouses, and yet none contained all the different items of a soldier's dress and accoutrements. At Cologne there were plenty of coats, but neither waistcoats nor breeches; there was at Mayence a large store of stout leather for soles, but no upper leathers. There were shirts at one place, stockings at another, gaiters at a third.

The same confusion reigned in the ordnance department. At one place there were swords, but no belts; at another plenty of *cartouches*, but nothing to hang them upon. If an officer overcame the disgust he felt at such a system, and made an application in behalf of his men, he would generally receive an order on the stores of Liege, or Brussels, or any other place than the one he was at. If he required, for instance, fifteen hundred coats, he was obliged to send for them at a great expense; and then, perhaps, instead of obtaining what he wanted, he received only a few yards of cloth to clothe a whole brigade; or blue cloth was perhaps given him for the coats, but no red to make the facings; or if there was red cloth, there was no white, and nothing for linings;—in fine, the delivery was never complete. All this was monstrous, but it must in justice be stated that the government was not alone the cause of it.

The conscription had just been adopted; it was the only mode of recruiting the army which the local councils had left to the government, and the formation of the list of conscripts, as well as the examination of all claims to exemption, was entrusted to the communal administrations.

Now, it is well known that lukewarm zeal is always shown by the municipal magistrates in such cases; and to this cause of delay was added another equally powerful. The treasury was empty, and the minister, obliged to meet an immense consumption, had only national property and delegations at his disposal. If horses were wanted, a delegation was offered upon the door and window tax; if new clothes were required, a domain was offered in payment. For arms and stores, the same means of purchase were proposed. But be the cause what it might, the state of absolute wretchedness to which the troops were reduced, rendered their situation deplorable.

Before appearing on the field of battle, it was necessary that the French army should have the means of doing so with effect. General Ney, who had fought and sojourned in the country, well knew its localities and resources. He commanded men in want of everything, even the greatest necessaries of life; but at a little distance from their cantonments, commanderies were to be seen which contained everything in abundance, and whose superfluities he thought might be applied to the craving wants of his soldiers. His means were, however, greatly out of proportion to the obstacles he had to contend against; but celerity and boldness are likewise powerful means, and he resolved to try his fortune.

When on the point of setting out with his little force, some unexpected occurrences increased his danger, though they gave great additional importance to his undertaking. Manheim and Philipsburg were garrisoned by troops who seemed but little disposed to defend them. The French revolutionary principles had penetrated among the soldiers: they had become agitated and uneasy; they were weary of shedding their blood only to rivet their own chains; whilst their officers, disgusted with a war in which no personal renown was to be gained for themselves, felt only a more ardent longing for those generous and liberal institutions, which could alone permanently fasten their colours upon the car of victory.

There is always a great advantage in cultivating the favourable dispositions of an enemy; but in the present instance they derived a most powerful importance from their local power. If these two places were carried, Lower Alsace would be covered, and a portion of the Palatinate sheltered from irruptions. The petty princes of the empire would then be forced to subscribe to a treaty of peace, and the French would take the lead in the campaign. This changed altogether the object of Ney's operations.

His plan was therefore altered, and he resolved to attempt to surprise Manheim, and if successful, to force Philipsburg. But the troops he had at his disposal were scarcely sufficient for this double undertaking; and yet an attack upon the one would give the alarm to the other. He resolved, however, to ascertain in person the extent of the difficulties he had to encounter, and accordingly crossed the Rhine under the disguise of a peasant. Having entered Manheim, with a basket on his arm, he proceeded through the streets, made his observations, and obtained precise information concerning the force which defended it, and the provisions it contained.

The garrison were ill disposed to defend the place, and the duty was carried on in a slovenly and unequal manner. He was about to leave the fortress full of hope, when he perceived a soldier of the garrison supporting a female in the last stage of pregnancy. Having accosted the woman, he expressed an interest in her situation, and his fear that her illness might begin before the night was over.

"No matter if it does," the soldier replied; "should this be the case, the commandant will allow the drawbridge to be let down at any hour of the night, so that the instant she is taken ill she can have assistance."

This was all Ney wanted to know; and he soon recrossed the Rhine to make his preparations.

Having selected a hundred and fifty of his bravest soldiers, he crossed the river with them in skiffs, marched rapidly forward, and concealed them under the walls of Manheim, in the hope that the woman's labour-pains would soon come on. She did not disappoint him: her sufferings began, the bridge was lowered, and an instant after Ney and his men took possession of it. They then pushed forward with their general at their head, and the weakness of their force was masked by the darkness of the night. Ney threatened and alarmed the garrison, and succeeded in obtaining a surrender of the place.

Being master of Manheim, Ney advanced towards Philipsburg. But the garrison of that town having taken the alarm, he was obliged to halt and wait till fortune should come to his assistance. He established his force in the neighbouring villages, and the garrison having pleaded negotiations that' were open, hostilities were suspended. The: hostile forces lived at first in the most perfect understanding; but the French dragoons at length got tired of seeing the enemy's patrols going through their quarters. Disputes arose, and the hussars of Bamberg were very roughly handled. The governor immediately took the alarm, and cried out against the aggression. Ney sent to quiet his fears, and mounting his horse, proceeded to ascertain how things were.

He pushed on towards Waghausel; and the enemy's troops stationed in the villages, retiring on his approach, he followed them and came in sight of Philipsburg. Being so near the place, he resolved to demand an interview with the governor, the Rheingrave of Salm, a haughty, reserved, morose, and bigoted aristocrat. This proud chieftain did not condescend to see the French general, but despatched as his representative the chief of the advanced posts, with authority to accept any proposals which Ney might make. This was of good augury. The French general feigned to be desirous of sparing the garrison, and offered a suspension of, arms. The chief of the advanced posts at first eluded the proposal; but being a man of weak judgement, and devoid of energy, he soon suffered himself to be led by Ney, and the suspension was accepted.

Thus was Philipsburg blockaded upon parole, and Ney became free in his movements. During this interview he had found an opportunity of ascertaining that everyone in the place was not averse to being treated with, and that a little gold was alone requisite to obtain all he desired Now, his troops had nothing immediately on their hands, and the rich convents of the Necker were not far off. He therefore boldly offered the wealth of these convents to those of the inhabitants or garrison who would deliver up the place. The proposal was eagerly accepted; but each estimated himself at a very high price. To save appearances, bridges were to be constructed, a pretended attack was to be made, and a place of retreat provided for the traitors in the event of failure.

A first excursion supplied the means of meeting these expenses. Generals Gudin, Sorbier, and Darnaudat, had assembled the men they wanted to secure the passage of the river, and begin their march. Ney, full of confidence, pressed Bernadotte to come and assume in person the direction of the siege, which he required only four hundred horse, four companies of infantry, and two pieces of cannon, to cover. But the Austrians were advancing, and Bernadotte knew not where Jourdan and Masséna were. He feared the coming of the archduke still more than he coveted the possession of Philipsburg; and he adjourned the capture of this place until he had ascertained the motions of the Austrian prince.

This delay led to other difficulties. Great Britain had her emissaries everywhere;—burgomasters, editors of newspapers, and postmasters, richly remunerated by that power, embarrassed and watched the movements of the French army, giving publicity to every attempt made by its generals to open secret negotiations. Nevertheless, Ney contrived to keep open a channel of communication with the inhabitants. He had moreover established a sort of agency whose members had explored the country-extending from Ulm to Wurtzburg; being thereby able to allay the apprehensions of the general-in-chief, he repeated his former demand of troops.

"You fear," he wrote, "that the Austrians will come upon us. They may doubtless do so, and it is a miracle that we have not before now been confined to the walls of Manheim. But you know their tendency to procrastination; and so slow are they in their operations, that we should have time to take Philipsburg, and afterwards go to meet them. Send me, then, some troops and a few pieces of cannon. As for the money demanded, I will undertake to raise it upon the convents and the seats of the nobles. I will not touch the cottages."

This was all well; but easy as Bernadotte was on the score of funds that came not from his own military chest, he was nevertheless not so when troops were to be displaced. He did not consider himself in a state to attempt to carry the place by storm, and he therefore confined his efforts to seduction.

"It is very unfortunate, my dear Ney," he wrote to the latter, "that I cannot spare a body of troops sufficiently numerous to invest Philipsburg. You know how feeble my means are, and they have not increased since our last interview. I am waiting until the orders which the Government must have given, are executed.

"Promise five hundred thousand *francs*—promise six hundred thousand, or more if necessary: I pledge my word of honour that the money shall be paid on the very day the fortress is delivered up to us, or at latest within twenty-four hours after, by means of contributions. We will raise funds to meet everything. Satiate your emissaries with gold. Endeavour to correspond with the most influential among the officers; for he who is not brave, my dear Ney, will always allow himself to be corrupted with gold. To profit by his weakness, is an art which must be used; and when once an opportunity has been let slip, another is not easily found. Busy yourself in sowing dissensions among the troops composing the garrison; this might induce the commandant to put us in possession of at least one of the city gates.

"Manage this business, my dear Ney, with discretion and foresight. It would be striking a great political blow to obtain Philipsburg by our secret negotiations alone; for besides the advantage which our armies on the Rhine would derive from the occupation of that fortress, it would raise suspicion and uneasiness among the leaders of our enemies, and we might thus lay the foundation of a brilliant campaign.

"It is lawful, my dear Ney, to employ all kinds of means in the service of our country, and in contributing to the glory of its arms. Let me hear from you every day by express.

"Yours ever,

"Bernadotte."

"Mayence, 19th *Ventose*, Year 7 (March 19th, 1797.)"

This theory may be true enough; but the governor was also putting it in practice, and was very near obtaining all the advantages of it. He had called the Austrians to his aid, and set the peasantry in commotion. The arms and ammunition were ready, and the insurrection was about to burst forth, when Ney discovered the plot, and prevented its execution. He was unable, however, to seize the noble emigrant who was to have headed it. The officer to whom he had entrusted that mission failed in address. The Baron escaped in his shirt, and went further off to plot the assassination of his countrymen.

The governor was unable to deny having participated in the conspiracy; he was therefore confined to his walls, and the place rigidly invested. He had the assurance, nevertheless, to complain, and inveigh against what he termed an act of hostility. Ney took no notice of his complaints, but so disposed his forces as to intercept all communication with or egress from the town. Certain that he had succeeded in this, he wished Bernadotte to come and judge of the fact.

"Come hither," he wrote, "and you will much oblige me. Come and tell me whether my position is well chosen."

He was less courteous towards the Rheingrave. The latter complained bitterly both of his aggression and of his silence.

"The aggression," replied Ney, "was of your own seeking; it was a mere act of reprisal; and my silence is the effect of pure provocation. You wanted to introduce the Austrians into Philipsburg, and thus commit me with the inhabitants. I have taken measures for my own security. Hostilities are opened with you personally, but the armistice continues with regard to your soldiers. You shall have a proof of this: the prisoners I made this morning shall be set at liberty."

Though Ney thus harshly treated the Rheingrave, he did not the less follow up his communications within the fortress. As appearances could no longer be saved, it was necessary to increase the bribe. Ney again undertook to supply the surplus funds. He resumed his excursions, levied an impost upon Heidelberg, and contributions upon the feudal castles and commanderies throughout the country. But whilst he was collecting this money, and purchasing or making requisitions for horses, an act of imprudence divulged the plot which had so far been successfully carried on. The governor was himself applied to, and an attempt made to seduce him, whereby everything that he should have remained ignorant of, was revealed to him. The conspirators were seized and shot, and the whole plan frustrated.

Its execution, so far as it went, was not however without advantage. With the proceeds of the contributions levied upon the convents and feudal estates, Ney purchased a considerable number of horses from the peasants. Upon these he mounted recruits, which he had sent for on purpose. Thus his three cavalry regiments, which contained only six hundred men when he first approached the Necker, now amounted to more than double that number. His soldiers were armed, clothed, and full of ardour. He could now take the field with good effect, and he hoped the time would soon come when he should be again called upon to appear in line.

CHAPTER 22

Ney Accepts the Rank of General of Division

This period arrived. Austria had invaded the country of the Grisons; its forces were assembling near the Lake of Constance, and upon the Lech in Franconia;—the imperial government, in short, had assumed a hostile attitude. Nevertheless the Directory still evinced the same want of energy. The army of Mayence had reached the sources of the Danube; and the sapient Directors were content to order that of Helvetia to make the Austrians evacuate the country of the Grisons. Masséna forthwith commenced operations, and had overthrown the imperialists, before Jourdan knew whether he was to support him or not.

The odds were however too great against the former general, and Jourdan determined not to allow the forces of his colleague to be overpowered, for want of receiving instructions to co-operate with him. He therefore resolved to attempt a diversion, and accordingly advanced towards the archduke's army. A warm and obstinate encounter took place at Stockbach; and the French, after a long struggle against very superior numbers, were forced to give way. They were defeated and driven into the mountains.

Had they proved successful, each among them would have been ambitious of sharing in the glory of their arms; but as they were unfortunate, they could scarcely find anyone to lead them. One quitted his post whilst the battle still raged; another, before he knew that it was lost, was attacked with sudden indisposition and withdrew from the field. Of those who did not desert their colours, one could not execute a mission because he had an open wound; another, because he considered it above his capacity;—each found an excuse for not fighting, and the army seemed on the eve of dissolution.

If some men are discouraged by danger, there are fortunately others whom it excites and renders capable of the boldest deeds. Masséna had great reason to complain of the Directory. Appointed to the command of the French army at Rome, he had joined his troops only after they had taken possession of the capital of the Christian world. He was as much a stranger to the disorders of their march, if there were any, as to the excesses committed on their entrance into Rome. The different corps, however, broke out into open revolt; and the insurgents, at first obsequious towards the general, soon included him in the general reprobation. He summoned them to return to obedience; and they decreed that they no longer acknowledged his authority. He took no notice of this decision; but the moment he attempted to enforce an act of command, the tumult exploded with fresh fury.

The Directory gave way, and Masséna, abandoned by the arm of power, which ought to have upheld him and punished the leaders of the mutiny, was obliged to withdraw. He afterwards assumed the command of the army in Helvetia; but in spite of his commission and the personal talents of which he had given so many proofs, he was never master of his own movements and operations.

Left to his own resources, when he had to effect all that the administration should have done, he was under severe control in those matters which ought to have been left solely to his own judgement. His manoeuvres were always subordinate to those of the army of the Danube. Invested in appearance with a chief command, he was in fact only the commander of a wing. He was justly hurt at this conduct of the Directory towards him, and had already sent in his resignation; but the defeat at Stockbach took place, and all other considerations yielded to that of the peril which threatened his country. Far from deserting the post confided to him, he met the danger in its fullest extent, and generously assumed the command of the wreck of an army which the other generals had abandoned.

Tharrau, Legrand, Ney, Gozan, and some others remained unshaken. They did not withdraw under pretence of ill health, nor decline responsibility under that of incapacity; and Masséna, desirous of honouring in them the disinterested bravery of which he had set the example, reported their noble conduct to the Directory. Having had occasion to appreciate the ability and precision of Ney's manoeuvres, he appointed this officer to the command of the cavalry attached to his right wing.

The theatre of the military operations of the French being now transferred to Helvetia, Ney proceeded thither, and assumed the command to which he had been appointed. His corps consisted of ten regiments of light cavalry and three of dragoons. As they had been neglected daring the peace, he first applied himself to break them into manoeuvring, and familiarize them with movements in line, to which their dispersion and want of horses had made them almost strangers.

Their progress was so rapid, that he flattered himself he should in a short time lead a formidable body of cavalry to victory, when an incident, which ought to have flattered his ambition, threw him into a strange perplexity. He was appointed on the 28th of March, general of division; but his modesty taking the alarm, he considered the charge too much for him, and received his commission only to send it back. He deemed himself qualified to command a brigade, but not a division. He examined and measured his own powers, and determined that, for his personal advantage, the honour of the French arms should not be placed in jeopardy.

> "I have received," said he in his despatch to the minister, "your letter of the 8th of *Germinal* (28th March), in which was enclosed the decree appointing me general of division. The Directory, in conferring this promotion upon me, probably yielded to advantageous reports of my

conduct; but it is my duty to be more severe on my own merits. If my talents were truly such as the Directory has conceived, I should not hesitate to accept the promotion; unfortunately such is not the case, and I am forced to decline the honour the Government would confer upon me. I trust that this refusal will be considered nothing more than a proof of the sincere patriotism by which I am actuated, and of the disinterestedness with which I perform my professional duties. May I beg you will assure the Directory that I shall never have any other aim than that of deserving its esteem."
"Waghausel, 15th *Germinal*, (April 4th, 1799.)"

Nothing could be more modest or disinterested than this; but a government cannot always overlook the talents of which the possessor is ignorant. The Directory therefore maintained its decree, and the minister who forwarded Ney's refusal was directed to make known to him that the Government persisted in its decision. The following was the despatch:

Citizen General,
The executive Directory, before whom I laid your letter requesting me to tender your refusal of the rank of general of division to which you had been appointed, has directed me to inform you, that it persists in the decree which promotes you to that grade. It sees in your modesty only a stronger claim to reward for the services you have already rendered, and a valuable earnest for those you will hereafter render to the republic. In consequence of which, I herewith again forward the decree of your appointment.
Health and Fraternity.
Millet Moreau."
Paris, 15th *Florial* (May 4th, 1799).

This despatch was flattering; nevertheless the new rank to which Ney was raised seemed to him so great and imposing, although he had already performed its duties, that he dared not accept the title. Fortunately he had continued to correspond with Bernadotte, to whom he stated his fears, his conjectures, and the chances offered by the field of warfare to which he was called. His forebodings were by no means consolatory. Victory had inspired the Austrians with confidence; and, as it always happens, defeat had spread discord through the French ranks. The troops were irritated, discouraged, and deprived of necessaries. Ney made no secret either of the uneasiness to which this general want of confidence throughout the army had given rise, or of the perplexity into which he was thrown by his own promotion.

But Bernadotte did not encourage his scruples with regard to this latter point. He well knew Ney—he well knew his vigilance and talents; and he blamed his misgivings still more strongly than Masséna had done.

"I have received, my dear Ney," he wrote to the latter, "your letter of the 16th. The particulars you gave me are not of a nature to make my mind easy with regard to future operations. But the spirit of freedom is indefatigable, and will, I trust, still perform miracles. You have doubtless read Garat's speech upon the assassination of our plenipotentiaries. It reminds me of the most prosperous days of Lacedæmonia and ancient Rome. Every man who is a Frenchman, and above all a republican, must think as he does. It is no doubt more than necessary to destroy parties if they exist, and not to create any if their existence is only ideal. Parties raise factions, and the latter overthrow states, however powerful.

"I expect shortly to set out for Paris. After I have nursed my body, and tranquillized my mind for a few days, I shall return and share the toils of our comrades. I shall enjoy a delicious satisfaction if I am able to share in their successes, and if chance is sufficiently favourable to me to enable me to include you among the number of those with whom I shall fight my country's battles.

"I recommend your not displeasing the Directory by your refusal of the promotion which it persists in conferring upon you. Look around you, my dear Ney, and say candidly whether your conscience does not call upon you to lay aside a modesty which becomes out of place and even dangerous when carried to excess. We must have ardent souls, and hearts as inaccessible to fear as to seduction, to be able to lead the armies of France. Who, more than yourself, is gifted with these qualities? It would be an act of weakness, then, to shrink from the career that is open to you.

"*Adieu*, my dear Ney. You perceive that, yielding in my retirement to the reflections excited by the quietude I enjoy, and the peaceful banks on which I dwell, I assume somewhat the tone of a mentor; but you will, I know, listen to everything from one who is attached to you by the ties of the warmest friendship, and the most perfect esteem.
"Bernadotte."
"Simmern, *25th Florial*, Year 8. (May 14th, 1799.)"

The following details concerning that horrible event, are not without interest, and are little known.

The Baron de ———, minister plenipotentiary of the Elector of Bavaria, came to spend the evening with me. Our conversation naturally turned upon the subject of those men who had exercised more or less influence in the affairs of Germany.

The Archduke Charles and M. de Thugot were in the foremost rank. An examination of the political principles of the latter led us to speak of the murder of the French plenipotentiaries at Rastadt, of which I affirmed that public opinion accused M. de Thugot, and acquitted Prince Charles.

M. de ——— manifested the same opinion. I had nothing but conjecture to support my belief; but he offered to give me the most convincing proofs, arising from what he knew and heard from the very mouth of M. de Lerbach. He then related what follows.

A few days prior to the murder, M. de Lerbach, imperial-commissary in Prince Charles's army, came to Munich, to make arrangements relative to the passage of the Austrian troops through the states of Bavaria. He lodged at an inn which was also inhabited by M. de ———. The two apartments were separated only by a large but very thin door. M. de Lerbach was out all day upon business, but regularly spent his evenings in his room with M. Hoppé, whom we had seen at Paris, as secretary to M. de Cobentzel.

M. de ———, who was attached to the mission of Commander Jalabert, minister of the Elector at Frankfort, had been sent to Munich with despatches relative to the matters in negotiation at Rastadt. He was accompanied by M. ———, who at present holds an appointment under M. de Mongelas, but was then employed in the chancellerie of foreign affairs at Munich.

One evening, M. de ——— having perceived that the conversation between M. de Lerbach and M. Hoppé related to the different interests of the German princes, had his candles taken into the next room, whence they could feebly light that in which he sat, without being visible through the door of communication,—thus indicating that the room was not occupied.

He then listened in profound silence, and took notes, as did also M. ———, of all that they heard. After each conversation they compared their notes, and formed them into a single narrative, which both of them signed, and took each day to the office for foreign affairs.

The first conversation gave them the following information:—M. de Lerbach had gone to Prince Charles, and represented to him that it might prove of the greatest advantage, if the Austrian monarchy became acquainted with the connexion suspected to exist between the princes of the Empire and France; that numerous communications had been made on this subject to the plenipotentiaries, and there was no doubt of the positive existence of such a connexion; but that a moral certainty alone was insufficient; that the house of Austria, to justify its conduct towards the faithless princes of the German empire, must possess tangible evidence, and that such evidence existed abundantly in the papers of the French ministers; that under the circumstances in which Europe was placed, and in consequence of the personal conduct of these ministers, no measures ought to be kept with them; that the end was moreover of such magnitude as to justify the means, whatever they might be.

From these motives M. de Lerbach requested that Prince Charles would give him an armed force, in order to arrest these plenipotentiaries on their way to Seltz, whither they would proceed after the rupture of the negotiations, which was certain of taking place. Prince Charles opposed his repugnance to such a measure, which was only overcome on reading M. de Thugot's instructions. He yielded to a formal requisition, and placed at the orders of M. de Lerbach, Colonel Barbaczi of the Szecler Hussars, and one Bourchart, who were to receive and implicitly follow the instructions of the imperial commissary.

M. de Lerbach directed these men not only to seize the papers, but at the same time to drub well *(bien houspiller)* Jean de Bry and Bonnier, upon whom he had a vengeance to exercise, for the rudeness of the one, and the insolence of the other. He also recommended to their attention, provided he fell into their hands, the Baron d'Albini, whom in this conversation he talked of in the same manner as of the French ministers.

On the following evening, the conversation ran upon the same topics. It was interrupted by a messenger, who brought M. de Lerbach the news of the tragic result of the expedition he had ordered. His delight at the double success obtained by his vengeance and his policy was poisoned by the horrible murder which he must have anticipated, and was therefore guilty of having perpetrated.

Remorse and hatred drew from him the most contradictory exclamations.

'The unhappy men,' he exclaimed, 'they have been murdered! That scoundrel, Bonnier, well deserved his fate! But poor Roberjol! If, however, they had not let Jean de Bry escape!'

This evidence of M. de Lerbach against himself, put in haste upon paper, and as he uttered it, must now be among the state papers of Bavaria.

Ney yielded to this advice, assumed the rank to which the Directory had raised him, and was preparing to lead his cavalry towards the Thur, when an unexpected event called him to another place and to the command of a different kind of force. The following is the report of the circumstance made by the *aide-de-camp* of the general-in-chief.

> I arrived at Coire on the 13th of *Florial* at ten in the evening, and found everybody in the greatest consternation. The peasants of the vale of Disentis, those of the valleys of Medels, and Maderanerthal, and those of the Italian bailiwicks, had risen in open rebellion. They had assembled in great numbers, and were forcing the peaceable inhabitants of the other villages to join them, on pain of seeing their houses burned and their families massacred. That which was at first only a spark, soon became a dreadful conflagration. The fanatic people followed the torrent, became partners in the excesses of the peasantry, and cooperated in an unheard-of refinement of barbarity.
>
> The vigilance of General Menard, commanding the Grisons at that period, had, so early as the 10th, led to the discovery of the intended insurrection. He accordingly wrote to Citizen Salomon, commanding the detachment at Disentis, calling upon him for particulars concerning the situation of the country, and the agitation which was becoming manifest. This officer, too credulous and too confident, replied, on the 11th, to the General, that

it was true a certain agitation had lately prevailed during a few days, but the peasantry had since become tranquil and gave no further cause for uneasiness; that he answered for everything, and his care and vigilance would suffice to make the remainder of the storm blow over.

The rapidity with which events succeeded each order,— the attack of Lucistig, that of Davos, and the demonstrations of the enemy upon other points, prevented this affair from being treated with all the importance it deserved. The insurrection was organized without opposition, and on the 13th the insurgents marched toward Disentis. The peasants were armed with muskets, and hatchets, and with long sticks, through the ends of which two or three sharp-pointed iron pegs were driven, thus forming a very dangerous weapon. In this state they proceeded to the church, where they heard mass with profound respect.

The officer, Salomon, in spite of his confidence, became alarmed, and assembled the municipality, to whom he expressed his surprise and uneasiness at this rising. But he again suffered himself to be deceived by the treacherous mountaineers, and was satisfied with the assurance given to him that this vast assemblage had no political object, and that the shepherds who swarmed around him, had met for no other purpose than to repair the bridges on the Rhine. As the confusion, nevertheless, went on increasing, he once more became alarmed, and again convoked the municipality. It was now only five o'clock in the afternoon, and night was not yet nigh. The protestations made in the morning were therefore renewed; Salomon again gave faith to them, and contented himself with throwing the responsibility of passing events upon those who brought them about.

The soldiers, having been invited to share in the festivities, spent the remainder of the day in imprudent libations; but when night came, some of the insurgents entered the dwelling of the commandant and ordered him to surrender his sword. He then felt how fatal his foolish confidence was likely to prove, and asked a thousand questions, to which no reply was made. As he delayed delivering up his arms, they were taken from him, and he was escorted to the convent. The officer was now in safe custody, and the troops dispersed; the insurgents therefore no longer fearing a combined action, or an organized resistance, threw themselves upon the French soldiers whilst they were carousing, and beat and otherwise ill-treated them. Some of them were killed in defending their arms; the remainder were placed in the corridors of the convent.

A sub-lieutenant had assembled a dozen men who lodged in this building. They fired from the windows, and for a long time resisted the insurgents who were trying to force it; but a menial having admitted the multitude through a side-door, the whole of our unfortunate men within its walls were instantly put to death.

Five thousand of the insurgents then marched upon Trons, where half a company was cantoned. These brave men were prepared for the attack, which they met with the greatest resolution, and succeeded in effecting their retreat to Ilantz. They were however forced to evacuate this place, leaving some of their wounded companions behind them, who were immediately butchered. The insurgents continued their movement, and reached Reichenau, the same evening, where they carried the bridge by storm.

Those who had remained behind, arrived successively at Disentis. All of them were eager to vent their rage upon the bodies of the slaughtered French, and wallow in their blood; and the atrocious municipality who presided at these cannibal scenes, distributed, according to the numbers of the claimants, one or two of the unhappy soldiers who had not yet expired, and whose lengthened death-throes intoxicated this ferocious rabble with delight.

Such was the state of affairs when General Menard received intimation of what had occurred. He instantly took measures to put a stop to such horrible scenes. Having assembled six companies, he placed them under the command of Citizen Baulard, commanding the 109th Demi-Brigade; and he begged I would join his *aide-de-camp* in directing the attack, leading the column to Disentis, setting fire to that den of brigands, and sacrificing to the manes of our deceased comrades, a hecatomb of their murderers. Meanwhile, the general undertook to make the report to you of my mission to Engadine. Convinced that my duty called me wherever there was danger, I set out to execute these orders.

The number of insurgents had increased very considerably. They crossed the bridge, forced the five companies back, and drove them to the gates of Coire, after wounding a hundred and fifty men. Six companies from Sargans and its neighbourhood had just arrived at Coire. The rebels, to the number of eight thousand, had retired to Reichenau, and taken up a position there. We marched thither. Citizen Baulard had scarcely eight hundred men; but he took his measures with prudence. He formed his troops in line of battle, and placed his two pieces of artillery, which he supported by two companies of grenadiers, between the *corps-d'attaque*, and the *corps d'éclaireurs*.

In this order we reached the platform commanding the bridge, which we cannonaded with all our might. Two companies of grenadiers, who had passed the Rhine to turn the enemy, having reached our parallel, we beat the charge, and rushed upon the bridge with fixed bayonets. The peasants defended it with vigour; but we had cut off their retreat. Some died at their posts, others threw themselves into the castle, whence they opened a destructive fire; unable, however, to resist our attack, they were forced and put to the sword.

A thousand of these wretches were slain. The night was approaching, and the survivors effected their escape under cover of the woods and of the darkness. As our men were sinking with fatigue, we made no attempt to pursue the insurgents. On the 15th, at daybreak, we resumed our movement, and occupied Ilantz and Trons. But we only followed the insurgents, without overtaking them;— fear seemed to have given them wings, and they were on the point of escaping from us, when the idea struck us that we had better quiet the alarms of the innocent; by separating them from the guilty; and thus we might succeed in putting an end to a contest which had already lasted too long. We accordingly issued the following proclamation:

'Your credulity is imposed upon; and you have proved culpable towards a people who were your friends and allies; but there are still means open to you of deserving pardon and obtaining the clemency of your conquerors. Repentance is all you have left. Deliver up those who seduced you to this criminal action, and you will find that the French are generous after victory: that they know how to distinguish error from crime, and are only to be feared by those who are still in arms.

'Such among you as do not immediately return to their homes, shall from that single circumstance, be considered leaders of the revolt, and treated accordingly. Their property shall be destroyed.

'Woe to him whom the feelings of humanity and the interests of his fellow citizens shall not induce to return to his duty! He must expect no mercy—he will become the victim of his own obstinacy.

'The inhabitants, in whose houses arms or ammunition are found, shall be immediately shot, and their premises burnt to the ground.

'The present proclamation shall, in each commune, be translated into the language of the country.

'Baulard, *Chef-de-brigade, Commandant.*
'Burthe, *Aide-de-camp* to General-in-chief.
'Masclary, *Aide-de-camp* to General Menard.
'Ilantz, 15th *Floreal*, Year 7. (May 5th, 1797)'

This proclamation produced the best possible effect upon the peasants, and before we reached Trons several communes had submitted. The same thing occurred at Disentis, the municipalities throwing themselves upon our generosity. They expressed regret and repentance for the foul crimes which had been committed. We were here upon the exact spot where humanity had been so cruelly outraged—we were here opposite to that hateful building in which a hundred and eighteen Frenchmen had been slaughtered; and we could still behold traces of that blood which ought to have been shed only in defence of the commonwealth. I know not what may have been the feelings of our soldiers, but it required all our ascendancy over them, and all the vigilance of their officers, to prevent them from committing the most violent excesses.

This was not, however, the most affecting part of these bloody recollections. The inhabitants, alarmed at our approach, had carefully put out of sight all that could serve as evidence of their guilt, or even of their participation in the crime which we came to punish. They had taken from their dwellings everything that denoted an act of violence. The arms and clothes of their victims were shut up in a cellar of the convent. The door of the building was broken open, and our men rushed with precipitation into the dark passages leading to these relics. Good God! What a sight! Muskets, clothes, and belts, pell-mell, formed a pile six feet high.

Whilst the soldiers, in a stupor of grief, were contemplating these trophies of the bad faith of the mountaineers, six light infantry soldiers appeared, who had escaped, as by a miracle, from the fury of these barbarians. They had succeeded in reaching the wood, and had eluded every search made to discover them. Having at length perceived us driving before us the ferocious shepherds, they had come from their place of concealment to resume their arms and baggage.

One perceived the coat of a friend slaughtered before his face; another raised the cap of a grenadier whom he had been unable to defend; a third recognized a knapsack; a fourth a *cartouche*. The silence was profound, the emotion general; at length an old soldier sprang forward and seizing a belt with a sort of nervous convulsion, fell down in a swoon.

At this instance of grief, no one placed any further restraint upon his feelings, and groans, and sobs, and tears served to express the most painful emotions. The scene was dangerously affecting, and might have rekindled the rage of the men, had I not put an end to it by making them withdraw and ordering the doors of this horrible place to be closed.

On inquiring into the cause of this insurrection, we were informed that it was solely the work of the priests: those fanatics having published a statement that the Austrians had taken possession of Lucisteig and Davos, that General Lecourbe had no farther place of refuge, and that the last hour of the French in Helvetia was arrived. Among the atrocities committed, we learnt that the French officer in command had expired after several hours of torture; that his sub-lieutenant had one of his legs broken, and was afterwards thrown upon a sledge, where he was exposed to the blows and abuse of this savage people, and died after a long and painful agony.

A storekeeper had escaped from the fury of the multitude, but his wife still in the confinement of child-bed, together with her infant babe, remained in their hands. He returned to deliver them; but was recognised, seized, and brutally mutilated. In this state he asked for a priest: one came, who declared to him that his death was inevitable, that the people insisted upon it, and that he could not possibly escape. The unhappy man, still not discouraged, begged that a second priest might be sent to him, and then a third. But neither of these ministers of the Gospel would exert any influence to save his life. They all told him, that no kind of subterfuge could avail him, and he must submit to his fate. At length after thirty-six hours of suffering he was shot, notwithstanding the supplications of his wife on her knees, who held up to the view of the murderers the innocent babe in her arms. Being repulsed with, violence, she was herself dreadfully outraged, and escaped with her life, in consequence only of the approach of our forces. We gave this unfortunate woman a thousand *francs*, as a first aid in her deplorable situation.

The moment of retribution had now come. An example was necessary, and it was considered that the destruction of the very place where the revolt first broke out would best serve as one. We accordingly assembled such of the inhabitants as had taken but a slight share in the revolt, and. these, together with the women, children, and old men, we ordered to withdraw; we then set fire to the village and convent.

We however attempted to save the house of a member of the provisional government of Rhetia, and also that of a widow, who had shown kindness to the French. The wind was too high, and we did not succeed; but we saved the goods of these houses, and put a guard over them. Nothing was missing.

Several leaders of the insurgents, among whom were two monks, were concealed in the village. The fire forced them to leave their place of concealment, and they were taken and shot. The communes were not very severely treated. They had plundered the military chest, and carried off three months' pay of the soldiers; they had likewise damaged the corn deposited in the convent. We therefore laid a contribution upon the most culpable and thus forced them to repair the damage they had caused.

Such was the issue of this deplorable insurrection. One hundred and eighteen Frenchmen lost their lives through the confidence they had placed in the hospitality of the inhabitants. Twenty-two perished in avenging this dreadful butchery, and one hundred and fifty were put *hors-de-combat* in the different actions that took place for this purpose. Of the inhabitants, twelve hundred peasants were killed, and a much greater number bearing musket-shot and bayonet wounds, have since been found dead in the woods. Never was such an attempt more severely punished.

This revolt, combined with the attacks of the Austrians, might have been attended with serious consequences, had it not been immediately suppressed. It was necessary to strike at the root of the evil, and thereby prevent a recurrence of such scenes.

The insurrection of these peasants has been stamped with a character of cruelty never remarked in any other. The cause of this seems to lie in the great influence exercised by the priests and monks, who in the other cantons have had a less share in such risings.

Burthe, Captain and *Aide-de-Camp*."

Thus was the insurrection put down at Disentis; but it had unfortunately spread beyond the narrow limits of that valley. Schweitz and Altorf had taken up arms, and there was also a rising at Engadine. General Loison, unable to make head against the swarms of insurgents that assailed him, evacuated Chiavenna; whilst Lecourbe, who directed the defence of these valleys, had been obliged to give up Zernest, and was with difficulty retreating towards Lientz. Menard was uncovered; the road which leads to Coire by Davos offered no defence, and the right wing of the French army was placed in a very critical situation.

But the measures taken were as prompt as the necessity was urgent. Soult went against the insurgents of Schweitz, Loison pressed hard upon those of the Valteline, and Ney, leaving his cavalry, which could not venture into the deep glens, placed himself at the head of a few companies of light infantry, with which he reached Alberta. Lecourbe, who had pushed towards Bellinzona, descended into the valley of Roveredo, and beat and dispersed the insurgents.

The remnant of their forces took refuge in the valley of Missox; Ney pursued and again routed them; but, this wild country offering great natural means of defence, he soon perceived that he had something else to do besides fighting, and must be content to depend upon the measures which his own skill might induce him to adopt. He accordingly went to Claro, studied the ground, and possessed himself of the passes which opened in front of the right wing. He extended his posts from the foot of Mount Bernardin to the valley of Roveredo.

All that part of the line was thus sheltered from the incursions of the Austrians, who, unable to penetrate through the passes, in which, from their being more strongly defended, the obstacles daily increased, threw themselves into the still open glens, and poured a large force into that of Furcula. It was rugged and difficult, and Ney did not resist their entrance into it; but having seized the defiles and destroyed the bridges, the moment he saw the Austrians engaged in its intricacies, he fell upon them, broke their ranks, and put them to the rout. But it was impossible to pursue them far, and he was therefore soon obliged to remain inactive.

At length he caught a distant view of the whole Austrian army in full motion;—he saw it form, extend its line, and ultimately disappear in the woods. Where was it going?—what could be the object of its present movement?—were questions which naturally arose in his mind. There seemed but little probability of its intending to enter the valley of the Rhine; and for him to penetrate into the country of the Grisons seemed still more hazardous than to remain where he was. He knew not what to conjecture, or what steps to take. His scouts, having reached the summit of Mount Bernardin, discovered the remains of fires which had been kindled there the night before. They reported that the Austrian forces had passed, and that was all;—they could give no intelligence as to the road which the imperialists had taken. He therefore sent out reconnoitring parties, with directions to advance further on; but the rain fell in torrents, the warmth of the season began to penetrate among the mountains, and bad weather, hunger and fatigue, compelled them to return without information. But intelligence of some sort being indispensable, the general took measures for sending out a party with better success. Bread was scarce, and a small addition to the soldier's ration was an object of great desire among the troops: he therefore collected all the bread he could dispose of, and adding a few pints of wine to this meagre store, sent forth a third detachment among the eternal snow on the mountains.

This body of men being better provided with provisions than the former parties, penetrated much farther. They reached Splugen, and explored the woods and villages on their road; but not a trace of the Austrians could they discover. Nevertheless, the successes of the latter were loudly trumpeted wherever the detachment passed. The party returned, and acquainted Ney with what they had heard. They reported that an Austrian column had taken possession of Lucisteig, another invaded the valley of the Rhine, and that the French ran the risk of being destroyed. This news seemed so improbable that Ney at first would not believe it; but a despatch from Lecourbe gave him still further particulars. The French had lost not only Lucisteig, but Coire, and the whole country of the Grisons; and a speedy retreat had become necessary.

Ney called in his detachments, and reached Urseren. His operations were again becoming more extensive, and his cavalry was about to resume its former importance, when he received orders to join the army which he had before left. Lecourbe, who forwarded the despatch to him, would not allow him to depart without expressing satisfaction at his co-operation. He wrote as follows:—

> I enclose you, my dear General, a letter from General Masséna. I regret not having the benefit of your services for a longer period. Receive the assurance of the esteem and friendship which I fed towards you. Ever yours, Lecourbe.
> Giornico, 3rd *Prairial*, Year 7 (May 22nd, 1797)

CHAPTER 9

Action at Winterhur

Ney, having joined his cavalry, took up his position upon the banks of the Thur, in pursuance of his instructions. The Austrians having debouched in strong force, occupied Andelfingen and Frauenfeld; and fresh columns continuing to advance, everything denoted their intention of speedily giving battle.

Masséna would not, however, allow them to complete their preparations, but boldly bearing down upon their line, resolved to anticipate them. Paillard led the left, Ney the centre, Oudinot the right, and Soult, with the reserve, was ready to carry his forces to the assistance of such of his colleagues as might require it. The French troops, highly excited, and impatient to avenge their late defeats, made their attack with dreadful impetuosity. The Austrians gave way under the shock, but soon rallied, and having taken possession of the heights of Andelfingen, formed on the other side of Altikon, and opposed a resistance which Paillard and Ney were a long time in overcoming.

The danger served but to animate the latter of these generals: he formed his cavalry into a close mass, and threw its full weight upon the columns opposed to him; still he could not succeed in breaking them. He then rallied his men, brought them up again, and charged with such impetuosity that he broke through the Austrian battalions, and his horsemen penetrated into their ranks, now thrown into confusion. He drove the infantry to the bridges, the cavalry into the Thur, and rapidly pursuing those who had escaped scathless from the battle and from the river, forced them upon the columns of Paillard, who had just carried Andelfingen. The carnage then recommenced. The adverse troops mingled and fought hand to hand in the narrow streets of that town, until in the course of the action the Austrians found an opening, when they fled tumultuously, leaving twelve hundred prisoners in the hands of the French. Oudinot was less successful at Frauenfeld.

After making himself master of the place, he was unable to debouch. In vain did he several times renew his attempt; the difficulties of the ground, and the columns which constantly came up from the field of battle, always prevented him from effecting his purpose: at length Soult came to his assistance, and these generals in conjunction overcame the obstacles against which Oudinot had been unable to contend single-handed.

Masséna's object was thus gained: the Austrians were beaten and driven to the right bank, nor could they for a long time to come hope to be able to recross the Thur. But whilst Masséna was beating Hotze at Frauenfeld, the archduke reached Schaffhausen. The disproportion of the two armies now again became too great, and the adoption of other measures by the French generals was urgent: they were soon taken.

The Glatt was not far off; the banks of this stream were more rugged, and easier to be defended, than those of the Thur, and the republicans determined to retire behind it. This was, however, no easy matter: for Nauendorf was advancing with his forces, and the archduke was ready to debouch. But Ney had assumed the command of the vanguard; great confidence was placed in his firmness of purpose, and the army having begun the movement, soon reached the positions it was to occupy.

But this was not effected without trouble:—for an instant the troops lost their usual firmness, and the staff-officers forgot part of the orders they were to have transmitted. A demi-brigade upon the Thur was forgotten, and the army was already in its positions on the Glatt before it was discovered that this demi-brigade had been left behind. Ney, in anticipation of the accidents of the movement, had assembled his commanders of corps at the advanced posts, and concerted with them upon the measures to be taken. As soon as his preparations were made, he continued his route, and pushed on to Altikon. Great was his surprise when he perceived a demi-brigade in such a situation. The enemy had already thrown bridges across the river, and the firing was beginning to be heard. Ney hastily rallied his men, and ran to make head against the columns which were advancing. He has himself given an account of this fearful action, which we think will be acceptable to the reader.

To General Masséna
Zurich, 8th *Prairial* (May 24, 1799).

My dear General,

In consequence of the orders which I had given to the commanders of brigades in the division under my command, we proceeded, at four in the morning, to the front of the positions it had previously occupied. Shortly after the arrival of General Tharrau at Winterthur, the enemy attacked a reconnoitring party which I had sent towards Oberwyl, and pursued it almost as far as Wesindangen.

A column of Austrian infantry extended to the right of the high road to Frauenfeld as far as Hegt, and at the same time a second column advanced against my right wing. I immediately directed General Gazan to resume the offensive; but the weak state of his force did not allow him to do so. *Chef-de-Brigade* Roger, commanding the centre brigade, whom I had ordered to make a movement to the right, to attack the enemy's column marching upon Winterthur, probably manoeuvred according to circumstances.

I received no intelligence of him during the obstinate action I had to sustain, although he perfectly fulfilled the instructions I gave him. General Walther, who commanded the reserve, retired behind the Tosz at the moment when the enemy had forced me to retreat. General Tharrau had ordered me in your name to assume the offensive, promising to support me with General Soult's division; but whilst

I was fighting in front of Winterthur, I saw neither generals nor reinforcements.

The gunshot wound I received in my knee at the gates of that town, forced me for a short time to give up the command to General Gazan, who nobly acquitted himself of the trust. After having my wound dressed, I ordered a retreat upon the Tosz, which I defended during an hour and a half. The Austrian forces had crossed this river upon different points, and I was obliged to have the heights crowned. Soon after, I received a second gunshot wound in one of my hands, and again lost my horse.

Being thus personally *hors-de-combat*, I definitively gave up the command to General Gazan, who will render you an account of the end of the action. I shall only add, my dear General, that the enemy attacked me with at least fifteen or sixteen thousand men, and that I could only oppose to them, before Winterthur, three or four thousand. They have experienced a very heavy loss of men, arising from their obstinacy in making their cavalry and infantry constantly charge. I have from six to eight hundred killed and wounded; the prisoners made by the enemy do not amount to a hundred men.

The minds of the soldiers are singularly affected by our retreat from the Thur; and the more so, because the column of attack of *Chef-de-brigade* Roger was forgotten and left upon the banks of that river, whilst the columns of Generals Oudinot and Paillard retired at an early hour. General Tharrau, on the very day of the retrograde movement, wrote to me to proceed to Winterthur, and assume the command of the van-guard. It was fortunate I did not think proper to comply with this request; for when at nine o'clock in the morning I arrived at Altikon, the corps of Citizen Roger had not the least knowledge of the retreat of the army.

By this time, from twelve to fifteen hundred of the enemy, consisting of infantry and cavalry, had crossed the Thur. I nevertheless reached my former position without any loss, and it was not till my arrival at Sulzbach that I was made acquainted with the panic which had seized some of our troops at Winterthur, and of which I had the honour to acquaint you last night.

Adjutant-General Lorcet, who was by my side during the whole action, conducted himself with the most distinguished bravery. He had the misfortune to have a rib broken by a musket shot, and he begs you will allow him to remain with me until his recovery. As my wounds force me to retire for a while from the command you have conferred upon me, may I request you will permit me to go either to Colmar or somewhere else, for the benefit of my health?

Ney.

Masséna granted Ney's request without difficulty. He knew that this general had, at the very commencement of the action, been struck with a musket ball, which, after passing through his thigh, had spent itself in the shoulder of his horse, and that he had remained on the field after allowing some of the men to bind up his wound, and staunch the blood with their pocket-handkerchiefs. Masséna also knew that at the head of a small body of cavalry, Ney had charged a whole squadron of Hungarians; that being attacked by a foot soldier just as he had struck down a hussar, he had not time to turn aside the bayonet, which pierced through the sole of his foot; that he cut down his rash assailant, who however, in falling, fired his piece, and shattered Ney's wrist.

Ney's services, and the severity of his wounds, rendered it impossible for the general-in-chief to refuse him a short leave of absence; but he did not deem Lorcet entitled to the same indulgence. Aware, however, of Ney's friendship for that officer, he allowed Lorcet to accompany him.

"I would not have granted this to any other person," he wrote, "but I can refuse you nothing. He may go, since you wish it."

Both set out together, and on the road both ran a narrow risk of their lives. On their arrival at Sissach, they demanded an express to send to Basle for horses. This demand was sufficient to rouse a population already exasperated by the pressure of war. A mob assembled, and were about to offer violence to the French officers. The municipal authorities, far from repressing, rather encouraged this riot.

Ney succeeded, however, in keeping the rabble in check; and determined that the danger he had run should prove an advantage to the wounded soldiers of the French array, who each day expired under the poniards of this lawless mob. He accordingly, in the following letter, invoked the vigilance of the French authorities, and thus secured a safe retreat for the brave men who were wounded in battle.

> To General Souham.
> Sissach, 10th *Prairial* (May 29th, 1799).
> My dear General,
> In consequence of the wounds I have received, I am going to Plombières, accompanied by Adjutant-general Lorcet, also wounded on the 8th instant. Anxious to reach Colmar this evening, I wished, as I passed through the town from which I now write to despatch an express to Basle, in order to obtain horses from the commandant of that place. I must now inform you that, after diverse insults from Nicholas Ars, municipal officer at Sissach, during the conversation necessary to give this order, he threatened to have the alarm-bell sounded, and thus assemble all the inhabitants of the commune. This threat was followed by the commencement of a revolt, in the course of which the Commissioner of the Directory dared to add, that they were a hundred armed men.
> The revolt will doubtless soon be over, by the prudence which I oppose to the mob; but the fate of our unfortunate brethren in arms, treacherously butchered in other cantons of Helvetia by men calling themselves the children of William Tell, renders it incumbent upon us, for

the safety of the wounded, who pass here every day, not to leave such threats unpunished. Our cruel experience, purchased over the bleeding bodies of our slaughtered countrymen, particularly in the cantons I have just left, makes it our duty to take such precautions as prudence combined with resolution may dictate. I suggest to you no particular measures of repression, but you will adopt those which you may deem necessary to put a stop to the evil. Be they what they may, I beg that you will not notice me as connected with circumstances of which, for the safety of all, I have thought it right to give you information.
Health and Friendship.
Ney.

CHAPTER 24

March upon Stuttgard

Having spent two months at a distance from the field of battle, and his wounds being healed, Ney again joined Masséna. The latter was then in a most trying situation. The defeat on the Trebia had taken place; the allies were masters of all the valleys and mountain passes, and might every moment effect a junction between the columns which had been routed in Italy and those which had been forced upon the Limath.

Masséna, occupied in preventing this manoeuvre, which might prove fatal to him, hailed the return of Ney with considerable satisfaction. He immediately gave him the command of a division; and as he had no less to defend the army against the ravages of hunger than against the enterprises of the enemy, he directed Ney to provide against the one, at the same time that he counteracted the other. But this was a difficult undertaking; for the Austrian forces swarmed upon the banks of the Aar, and the Frickthal, long ravaged by war, was drained of both corn and cattle. Provisions must however be obtained; for the soldiers, who had received no rations for several days, were starving.

Ney, having ascertained the resources which the country still possessed, exacted supplies proportionate to those resources; he lowered the contributions of some, raised those of others, and thus relieved the troops without ruining the inhabitants. Under pretence of services and public works, the forests had been devastated and the woods nearly destroyed by the agents of the French army. Ney put an end to this odious abuse, and severely censured those who had participated in it. As cupidity does not readily quit its prey, these agents boldly declared their intention of following up the cuttings which they had begun.

"You state that you require wood," said Ney; "but have you a warrant from the commander of a wing for cutting it? Besides, is it in the forests of a country laid waste by war, or in those of the Emperor, that you ought to procure it? Go to the latter," he added, "and let monarchs pay for their own follies."

Whilst Ney was wasting his energies in such obscure duties—whilst he was employed in providing food for the troops, and at the same time protecting the interests of the inhabitants, Lecourbe, entrusted with a more brilliant mission, had again penetrated into the Upper Alps. His columns, after scaling the most frightful precipices, had simultaneously debouched upon the Mutten, upon Altorf, and upon Urseren. The Austrians, attacked from Zurich to the Upper Valais, had been driven beyond the mountains which separate the Reuss from the Lentz. The St. Gothard, together with the valleys whence the Rhine and the Rhone and the Reuss derive their sources, were in possession of the French; and the troops, which the latter had beaten in Italy, could no longer stand against those now before them.

This admirable expedition had brought the French eight thousand prisoners, but without altering, in any material degree, the disproportion of force between the hostile armies. The Directory was forming an army in the Alps, and another on the Rhine. The several corps which were to compose them, and the generals who were to command their columns, were both selected from among those who had fought the battles of France upon the shores of Egypt.

Ney was directed to join the second of these armies, and gave notice to Masséna of the orders he had received. But this commander was on the eve of encountering a fresh tempest. The Austrians had assembled upon his left wing, and might be expected every moment to cross the Aar, turn the lines of water which covered Masséna's forces, break the latter, cut them off, and perhaps drive them upon the Jura. These circumstances were too serious for Masséna to permit the departure of so able an officer, and he therefore begged Ney to remain until the danger was past.

> "I was aware, my dear General," he wrote to Ney, "of the order given you to join the army on the Rhine; but I must request you will defer your departure for some days. Indeed I most earnestly entreat you to do so. You are necessary, nay, indispensable to your division, and I should feel the most lively regret if you were to leave it until the arrival of the general appointed to succeed you. At all events, be assured that it is with great regret I see you taken from an army to whose success you have so powerfully contributed.
> "Head-quarters, Lentzburg, 2nd *Fructidor*, Year 7. (August 19th, 1799.)"

No request could be more flattering; but the storm burst sooner than Masséna had anticipated, for his letter had scarcely reached Ney ere the cannonading began. The archduke had taken advantage of the darkness of the night, and thrown bridges across the river at Dettingen. His columns were supported by heavy batteries. The French troops, having imprudently formed upon the bank, were immediately broken and forced to take shelter in the woods. Ney arrived in the midst of the confusion, rallied and cheered the spirits of the discouraged soldiers, but could not succeed in making them debouch.

The effect of the Austrian artillery was terrific; as soon as a file appeared it was mowed down. Fortunately Ney had discovered some Helvetian carabineers in the French army. He knew with what true aim these men used their pieces, and the immense distance at which they could hit their mark. Having placed them behind some sheds which happened to be on the ground, both French and Austrians soon perceived the superiority of a true aim over the noisy detonations of the artillery. Each ball levelled its victim with the earth—each shot reached the individual for whom it was designed. Pontonneers were soon found wanting, the time passed, the French columns came up, and the operation failed.

The Austrians being thus foiled in their undertaking, the French were about to set fire to the timbers and boats which their adversaries had collected upon the Aar. But this warm reception having cooled the courage of the imperialists, they no longer thought of crossing the river, but were content to return to their cantonments and maintain the positions they already occupied. They accordingly proposed that the French light infantry should cease firing, and they would replace everything in the same state as before the attempt which had just failed. The French commander having acceded to these terms, the boats were accordingly carried away, the rafters abandoned to the stream, and each army peaceably guarded its own side of the river. Ney then set out for Manheim.

Although he had devoted only four days to assist in maintaining these important positions, yet this short delay had well nigh led to unpleasant consequences. The organisation of the army was complete when he arrived; not a single corps nor a division was without a commander; and in addition, he found it under the command of Muller, though he had been officially informed that it was to be commanded by Moreau. General Muller was assuredly a worthy man, but he possessed neither the resolution nor the spirit of enterprise necessary in the general of an army. Having been unsuccessful in his first attempts, he was fearful of committing himself further, and aspired only to rid himself of a charge he was not qualified to bear. The distribution of the forces composing his army had already taken place, and he dared make no alteration in the columns, nor increase the number of their generals.

Ney was therefore several days without having any post assigned to him. The army consisted only of demi-brigades, formed of men from the depôts, who had neither clothes nor shoes. It therefore became necessary to make the Austrians minister to the wants of the French soldiers. Provisions must be obtained and so must money; wagons, cattle, and clothes were likewise wanted;—a spirit of enterprise must therefore be at work, parties must be sent to a distance, and the greatest dangers and difficulties encountered. As Ney had already given proofs of his ability in such matters, he was applied to, and a sort of division formed for him, by drafting a certain number of regiments, or portions of regiments, from each of the others;—thus forming a column of fourteen hundred foot and two hundred horse, the command of which was given to him, and with which, on the 27th of August, he pushed on to Heilbronn.

This was but a small force to besiege a place, almost open, it is true, but situated in the midst of a vast plain overrun on all sides by a numerous body of cavalry. Nevertheless Ney did not despair of success. The imperialists, strong in cavalry, had at their disposal only a feeble body of infantry, and not a single piece of artillery. Ney had three field-pieces, a circumstance which seemed to him to make up for his inferiority in numerical strength: he therefore marched boldly on. An action took place on the 29th. The first shock was terrific; the Austrian squadrons vied with each other in the impetuosity of their charges. But a well-supported fire was kept up; both of musketry and artillery; and the attack of the imperialists soon became less fierce, then uncertain, and soon ceased altogether.

The three guns did excellent service, and in every manoeuvre foiled the enemy, who were obliged to evacuate the field and leave Ney master of it. He defeated them solely by his superiority in artillery; and he did not despair, weak as were his forces, of striking a still more important blow by the same means. Heilbronn, by supplying provisions and paying contributions, had satisfied the most pressing wants of the French army; Ney's men were consequently in good trim, and he resolved to push on to Ulm. This expedition was perilous; but that which he had more particularly in view was the disengaging of the army of Helvetia; and nothing was so likely to produce such a result as this expedition. The Austrians had made a depôt of Ulm, where they had collected their artillery, built warehouses, and assembled all their stores. If the attempt succeeded, all these stores would fall into the hands of the French; if unsuccessful; still it would force the Austrians to advance. In every point of view it offered advantages, and Ney therefore resolved to risk it.

Unfortunately all the commanders in the French army had not his energy or his talents. The remainder of the army however followed his movement, and a column took up a position at Lauffen. The country was poor, and the troops were obliged to spread themselves through it, in order to find subsistence; but with generals as devoid of prudence as of resolution, the army lost its energy, and no sooner did the Austrian scouts come in sight than this column retrograded. This unexpected movement had well nigh led to the most fatal consequences.[1] Far from being able to push on to Ulm, Ney had great difficulty in maintaining the positions he occupied. The extent of country which the army was obliged to overrun in order to live, had rendered the French odious to the inhabitants, who acquainted the Austrians

---

1. Ney to the General-in-chief Muller.
"Steinfurt, 15th *Fructidor* (September 1st, 1799.)
"I cannot understand, my dear General, the partial retreat just effected by the ——division. It would seem as if the enemy had pushed it in close columns. The whole country is so well satisfied with this manoeuvre, that the inhabitants would soon attack and expel me with prongs, if I did not employ the means necessary to guard my forces. I should think the above-mentioned division, might easily have occupied Singen without committing itself, even had it sent only a single battalion upon this service. I might then have given a useful direction to my excursions and to my reconnoitring of the interior of the country, and I might even sometimes have passed the Necker. But if my rear is to be left open and insecure, I cannot, without being considered wanting in common prudence, so readily place my division in jeopardy. You ask me to send you the two squadrons of the third regiment of hussars, in order that they may join the cavalry reserve. "Not only, however, would they be of no use there, but you would disgust these brave men by thus sending them to the rear. Already has *Chef-d'escadron* Lenougarède, who commands them, inquired if he has lost my confidence or committed some fault, as he is to be so disgraced. I told him that the surplus of his regiment being about to join the army, the general-in-chief wished to see the regiment complete, and he would then return to me.
"Be so good, my dear General, as to leave me these men. The 20th *Chasseurs-à-Cheval* are doubtless sufficient to do the duty at Bergstadt, and I presume they would have no other to perform. "Ney."

with all the preparations and measures of their adversaries.

Sinzheim had been evacuated on the morning of the 1st of September, and scarcely had the night fallen ere the Szeckler Hussars appeared at Hilsbach. Such things were of trifling importance in themselves; but they were enterprises undertaken in consequence of information given by the peasants, and from that fact alone they derived an importance which they otherwise would not have had. They rendered the inhabitants more bold in their opposition, and less disposed to supply the provisions without which the French could not live; for in the distress which weighed upon them, the most important object was, not victory, but to prevent the men from dying of hunger, by providing against the want by which they were worn down.

Ney took immediate measures to put an end to these understandings with the Austrians, and secure his own communications. This he was not long in effecting. The enemy had been imprudent enough, on the 6th, to establish themselves at Lauffen; on the 8th he attacked, broke, and drove them upon Stuttgard. The French column which had before retreated so precipitately, now resumed its line of battle, and the original movement was followed up. But it no longer presented the same advantages: Ulm was now defended by a strong garrison, and it was as impossible to surprise as to force that place.

Still there remained another effect to be produced, and never was any operation better calculated to produce it than the movement now undertaken. The Austrian columns which had suffered defeat at Lauffen, had unsuccessfully attempted to make a stand at Wissloch and at Hoffeim. Being overthrown each time, they were unable to cover the ducal residence, and Ney, in possession at Eppingen, carried his excursions even to the walls of Louisburg. Staray was obliged in consequence to hasten up with all his forces, and thus a diversion was effected.

With so very small a force at his disposal, Ney had now before him from twenty to thirty thousand Austrian troops, and his retreat might at any time be cut off. He accordingly raised his camp, and retrograded without further delay, but without haste or precipitation. The enemy's columns attempted each day to break his lines. They were guided by the peasants, and had therefore the advantage of knowing the country, as well as an overwhelming superiority of numbers. Nevertheless, they were constantly foiled in their attempts. Ney's troops were patient and devoted; and his measures being always taken with judgement, the Austrians were beaten each time they came to action. This series of engagements somewhat damped their ardour, and they halted, became less troublesome, and the French general quietly regained the banks of the Rhine.

The army had already recrossed that river; and General Laroche alone maintained his position before Manheim. This officer belonged to a species of patriots not uncommon at that period. He was a red-hot democrat, but a cool and intrepid soldier;— he seized with rare sagacity all the advantages of a position, and skilfully counteracted its disadvantages. The position he occupied excited his apprehensions. He found it too extensive and too open, to be guarded, by his skeletons of regiments, against the dense columns which were approaching him. Ney's opinion of the position was still more unfavourable. Manheim is built upon both the Necker and the Rhine. Being situated upon the right bank of the former, it is at a little distance from the angle formed by the latter. The intermediate space, intersected with woods and canals, was capable of making a long defence.

The approaches to Manheim, on the other hand, offered no means of resistance; nevertheless it was determined to defend it; and what is inexplicable, the bridge had been thrown across the river at the precise spot where it ought not to have been placed. The Austrians had only to push a column to the conflux of the two rivers, and their success was certain; for the French generals would not venture to draw their forces from their position on the Necker. The French troops, thus deprived of the means of retreat, were uncertain and irresolute, or at best devoid of enthusiasm.

Ney therefore found the position too dangerous, and recommended its being changed. He advised that the bridge should be removed to Neckerau, and after concentrating all the disposable means within the creek, Manheim and the banks of the Necker should be guarded by posts only. Having submitted his observations to the general-in-chief, they were no better received than those of General Laroche; and nothing was now left but patient resignation. The Austrians attacked the position; their attack was resisted with spirit, but they were so numerous, and the position so bad, that the French were forced to give way, and after a complete rout, compelled to evacuate Manheim.

To complete their disaster, the Austrians attacked their communications. General Vandermassen and Adjutant-General Lefol having collected a few men, threw themselves boldly in front of the enemy; but being almost immediately surrounded, some of their soldiers were put to the sword, and the remainder called for quarter. The French were now in open flight, and the whole division would have been annihilated, had not Ney come to its assistance. He had made his men fall in and prepare to march the moment he heard the first reports of the artillery; but his cantonments were far off, and the attack had been so sudden and rapid, that he had not time to reach the spot before the rout took place.

He debouched at the head of the 16th, drove directly at the enemy, and for an instant threw their ranks into disorder. But his efforts were lost upon this immense mass of troops. All he could do was to stop and keep them in check. Part of the French prisoners rescued themselves; but the officers, and particularly Lefol, submitted to the captivity. Ney was himself twice wounded: he received a musket shot in the chest, and his thigh was dreadfully contused by a biscayan,

The French were now completely beaten. Their opponents might follow them to the left bank, in the boats which they had imprudently left, and attack them in the midst of their cantonments. Ney hastened to provide against such an occurrence. Having suffered less, he was in a condition to support General Laroche. He accordingly covered Laroche's division, and concerted with him upon future measures.

The staff officers at head-quarters, who could anticipate or decide upon nothing, were, however, very jealous of their rights. They considered that these rights had been infringed; and the cantonments, as well as the intended measures of Generals Ney and Laroche, were immediately changed. The latter was directed to guard no longer the Rhine from Spire to Neuhaufen, but to face the plain, with his right towards Spire, and his left towards Hanaufen.

Laroche was thunderstruck at receiving so singular an order. The Austrians might still come up with him, overwhelm his force, and renew the disasters, which he was then endeavouring to remedy. He immediately wrote to Ney, to acquaint him with the critical situation in which he should be placed by executing this ill-judged order; nor did he conceal from him the opinion that "it required a strong dose of patriotism not to yield to discouragement."

"I admit," was Ney's reply, "that matters are arranged in a most incomprehensible manner. It is impossible to imagine a more painful situation than yours. But we are on the eve of an invasion, and must make up our minds to endure its disgusts."

And in truth this was necessary. A considerable force was advancing upon Mayence, and another upon Offenburg. Everything clearly showed that the archduke, who had assumed the command of the Austrian army upon the Rhine, had resolved, as report already proclaimed, to act by means of his wings. One was to penetrate into Brabant for the purpose of assisting the British, and the other to make an irruption into Alsace, in order to harass and turn Masséna.

The situation of the French army was indeed critical; but it is in struggling against evil fortune that true courage shows its greatness. Ney did everything that circumstances would admit of; and fortunately for the French, the Austrians did not evince the promptitude he had anticipated. They sent, it is true, five thousand men to Manheim; but this movement, caused by the severity of the season, was unconnected with any meditated hostile attempt. But what were they doing, and what were their plans? Such inaction was not natural, and must therefore have reference to some reverses which they had encountered in Helvetia. And then again such reverses must be great and important, thus to arrest the movements of so considerable a force.

Ney was lost in conjecture; he had received no intelligence from Masséna, and could not at all account for the lengthened halt of the archduke. It might possibly conceal a snare: the prince might have conceived the project of crossing the Rhine, and extending his force along the left bank; neither was it impossible that he might descend the Necker, throw troops upon Frankenthal, and, profiting by the advantage afforded by the possession of Manheim, land at Ogersheim.

If such were his intentions, he must necessarily threaten Seltz and Brisach and attempt diversions upon numerous points. But these two places alone offered a real chance of success, and they were therefore the only points which the French general applied himself to put beyond the power of attack. This he did by inundating part of the environs of the one, and concentrating all his available force upon the other;—he then calmly awaited the issue.

CHAPTER 25

Ney Appointed to the Chief Command of the Army

The several garrisons taken from the French army having considerably reduced its strength, there remained to carry on the campaign only the skeletons of corps; and these the enemy might every moment be expected to force. Yet no orders were given, nor any thing decided upon at head-quarters. Ney, uneasy at such a state of affairs, renewed the observations which he had already submitted to the commander-in-chief. But the latter had just received his recall; and he therefore sent for Ney, to whom he delivered up the command in chief, the Directory having just appointed him to the vacant office. He at first refused to accept it.

The difficult situation in which the army was placed, and his own ill-health, his two wounds being yet unhealed, induced him to do all in his power to get rid of the perilous honour conferred upon him. But the Directory had forwarded his commission; and the generals and other officers unanimously entreated him to put himself at their head. He therefore acceded to their wishes, but rather as a self-immolated victim, than an officer whose ambition is crowned by fortune.

His first act was to claim the indulgence of his colleagues, and to invoke the aid of their talents and exertions.

"The executive Directory," said he in his circular, "has called upon me to assume the provisional command of the army, in the room of General Muller. You are aware of the inefficiency or my military talents for this important station, particularly in our present critical situation. I shall perhaps become the victim of my obedience; but under the circumstances in which we are placed, I am bound to accept the appointment. I therefore claim your kind solicitude for the safety of the troops under your command, as also your individual kindness towards myself. I must moreover inform you that I have signified to the Directory my intention of not retaining the command beyond ten days."

Nothing could be more modest than this address, nor show a stronger proof of the most devoted zeal. But every officer in the army had the strongest confidence in Ney's talents. The different commanders of corps, whose assistance he solicited, had fought with him, some in Helvetia, others in the army of Sambre-et-Meuse; all knew his ability and daring courage, and all were delighted at seeing him assume the command. General Gillot congratulated the army upon having Ney at its head;[1] and, General Legrand, though ill of fever, was impatient to receive and execute his orders.[2]

---

1. Head-quarters, Nancy, 8th Vendemiaire, Year 8 (September 29th, 1799.)
I have learnt with real pleasure your appointment to the provisional command of the army of the Rhine. The executive Directory, in conferring this office upon you, has calculated upon your talents being equal to the danger; and your modesty will give an additional value to what it expects from you.
You may depend, Citizen General, upon my vigilance for the safety of the troops under my command, and believe me when I say, that I will always exert myself to deserve your esteem and friendship
Gillot.

2. Head-quarters, Metz, 1st Vendemiaire, Year 8 (September 29th, 1799.)
The last courier, my dear General, brought me the news of General Muller's departure for Paris, and your appointment to the chief command of the army. This gives me the most lively pleasure. I must inform you that I have received from General Muller a leave of absence during two decades, to recover my health at Metz. The fever left me but a few days since, and although I am still very weak, pray let me know if you think my presence would be of service to the army before the expiration of my leave. The promptitude with which I will proceed to whatever post you may assign me, will prove to you how much pleasure I feel in serving under your orders, and the sincere attachment of your comrade and friend.
Legrand

The sincere and candid Leval, so little given to flattery, was still warmer in his congratulations. His letter, which moreover alluded to the difficulties of the situation in which the army was placed, was calculated to give Ney confidence in himself. It ran thus:—

> If in the whole course of my life, my dear comrade, I ever experienced sincere satisfaction, it was on receiving the news of your appointment to the chief command of this army. It is, of a certainty, weak, but it is composed of soldiers who greatly esteem you. You are sufficiently well acquainted with my sincerity to be assured that I do not seek to disguise my real sentiments. You are calculated to inspire confidence; and it is with redoubled zeal that I shall study to execute scrupulously the orders you may give me.
>
> I shall, in obedience to your letter of the 5th instant, immediately pursue those prompt measures which you direct concerning the storehouses in the places you mention. I thank you, General, for your approbation of the steps I took to secure two decades of pay to the men under my command, namely the 20th and 43rd Demi-Brigades, and the 17th Regiment of cavalry. I feared I had exceeded my powers: but I am sure you have admitted the purity of my intentions.
>
> To speak candidly, my dear General, I must state that if you would give orders to withdraw the letter relative to the cutting of the woods and forests belonging to the princes, you would confer the greatest service upon the unfortunate inhabitants of this country. Matters have been so managed, that the Prince of Nassau-Orange is included in the exceptions;—he who is, at this very moment, one of our most determined enemies.
>
> Believe me, General, when I say that I shall neglect nothing to prevent all kinds of oppression, and at the same time to

promote the interests of the republic. I cannot speak with the same confidence concerning the collecting of contributions, because I have not a single company to spare. Two millions of *francs* are due, and I have not the means of getting them paid into the treasury of the department. A regiment of cavalry would be of great service to me for this purpose; for we cannot conceal the fact that, in this country, force must be employed on such occasions.

I herewith enclose the last report which has just been made to me concerning the movement of the Prussians. I will take care to send you intelligence of their march, and of the motions of our enemies.

Any commander but you, my dear General, would be displeased perhaps that in this my first letter I should declare that I am entirely without funds. I think you will feel the urgent necessity of placing some at my disposal.

You may rely upon my neglecting nothing to contribute to the success of your undertakings. That is the first proof I will give you of the satisfaction I experience at being under your command.

Rely also upon my sincere devotion and friendship.

Leval.

Head-quarters, Coblentz, 7th *Vendemiaire*,
Year 8 (September 28th, 1799.)

Ney having assumed the command, it became incumbent upon him to provide for the security of the frontier, by adopting the measures which he had before recommended in vain. But nothing is more variable than the theatre upon which the interests of nations are contended for. The Austrian army, which lately threatened Holland, was now in full march towards Switzerland. Numerous bodies of troops, it is true, were collecting on the banks of the Maine and the Necker; but these corps were calculated only to cover and threaten fortresses, and not to strike any decisive blow. Every act of offensive warfare was therefore to be undertaken by the army under the command of the archduke.

The Austrian prince had accordingly assembled his bridge-equipages; and Lambesc, who had been directed to penetrate into the Low Countries, was replaced by Condé. The Imperial troops were to take no share in this latter adventurous undertaking: the French emigrants were alone to run the hazard, and brave the dangers of the attempt.

The archduke therefore concentrated his forces on the left bank for no other purpose than to make an irruption into the territory of the Upper Rhine; for with the French reserve on his right, he could not think of attempting to press upon the centre of the republican army. Mayence stopped him on one side, Landau embarrassed him on the other; and at that season of the year, he could no more blockade those places than he could take them. Seltz, at first a point of no importance, was now the only one by which he could reach his adversaries with any chance of success.

The French general, however, had no direct intelligence of the motions of the archduke's army, and in so important a matter mere conjecture was not sufficient; he therefore directed General Nansouty to observe the march and movements of the Austrians, and prevent their establishing themselves in the Hundsruck hills.

This country, the actual possession of which offered the greatest advantages, had acquired peculiar importance from the circumstances under which the French were placed. Luxemburg was almost without troops and provisions; and the archduke, if once master of these mountains, would find no further obstacle to his progress. He was trying to intercept every communication between the places which the French held on the Rhine, and was pushing on without opposition towards the Moselle. Ney endeavoured to frustrate both attempts.

Having distributed and grouped his forces, he placed himself in a situation to strike with vigour on whichever side the Austrians should appear. But his army was so weak, and the line he had to defend so extensive, that he had strong misgivings as to the course of events, which he was watching with the most intense anxiety, when he perceived the Austrian general call in his columns, and soon after ascend the Rhine. What could be the cause of so extraordinary a movement? Had there been a battle in Helvetia? Were the Austrians defeated, or was it the reverse? Was the archduke himself proceeding to consummate the overthrow of the republicans, or was he hastening to rescue the wreck of the coalition from their hands?

Ney knew not what to think. But he concluded that the march of the Austrian general could only have been undertaken with a view hostile to his own army; and he resolved, if not to make him suspend it, at least to slacken his movements. But from the point which Ney occupied, he could do nothing: Manheim was no longer in his power, and he had neither bridges nor equipages;—he had therefore no immediate means of harassing the archduke. To cross the river by main force, was totally impracticable; and he was obliged to remain inactive. But that which it was impossible to do from the position which Ney then occupied, might be effected elsewhere. The republicans were masters of Kehl, they had a strong force at Brisach, and he therefore ordered General Collaud to debouch upon these two points.

Collaud, as may be seen in a former part of these memoirs, was a cold, reserved man, without ambition or ardour. Too little enterprising perhaps, he was unable to create opportunities; but he well knew how to seize and take advantage of those which offered. This instinctive quality rarely deceived him, and his vigilance was still more rarely at fault. The movements which had aroused Ney's attention, had also excited that of Collaud. His forces were already engaged with those of the archduke, when the order reached him to harass the latter; but this attack, advantageous as it was when made, proved nevertheless inadequate to the occasion; and Ney soon became aware of this, by learning the secret of the archduke's manoeuvres.

A pitched battle had been fought under the walls of Zurich, in which the French had beaten and cut the Russians to pieces. Those among the latter who had escaped the sword, had taken refuge in the mountains. The archduke was proceeding to the assistance of the vanquished, for the purpose of assembling and saving the wreck of their once formidable army; and Ney determined to do all in his power to counteract the intention of the Austrian prince.

Success having once more returned to the French arms, each individual soldier was full of confidence and courage, and each thought that an attempt which he would not have ventured upon a few days previous, could not now be otherwise than successful. But no sooner were the Russians defeated, than a host of fresh enemies appeared. The population inhabiting the banks of the Necker had taken up arms, and the Prussians seemed disposed again to join in hostilities against the republicans.

The peasants of the Necker, seduced by the enemies of France, affected to apprehend an invasion of their country by the French armies. The Prussians, taking advantage of the aspect of affairs in Holland, pretended that it was expedient they should adopt measures of precaution against the British army, which the French did not seem strong enough to keep in check.

The forces of the former, increased by the Schwarzenbach militia, were forming in the neighbourhood of Hulsbach; those of the latter were assembling at Vesel, where five battalions of infantry and as many squadrons of horse were already collected. But these were not the only enemies against which the French army had to contend; treachery and fanaticism were at work in its very ranks.

Whenever new principles are proclaimed, men of exaggerated opinions are to be found who carry such principles to the extreme of abstract theory, as well as adroit hypocrites who affect a like exaggeration as the best means of combating them. The army of the Rhine contained many individuals of both these classes; the French troops on the left bank as well as on the right, had their fanatics, and likewise their hypocrites in patriotism. Both were equally dangerous, and both calculated to excite mutiny and dissension among the soldiers.

The army required tranquillity; it wanted a spirit of consistency and concord; and Ney determined to put down the agitation raised by these two classes of men. He refrained however from coercion; leaving it to time and victory to correct the evil. But time only increased the exaggeration of the one class and the perfidy of the other; and victory, far from keeping either in check, only hastened the explosion of their violence.

The Austrians, as usual, instead of a defeat, had announced a great triumph. This report had reached Bonn, and the people, persuaded that the archduke had crossed the Rhine at Neuwied, crowded to the banks of the river to see him arrive. Some Capuchin monks were at the head of the multitude, whom they entertained with the same fables they had employed in agitating the country-people in the departments of the Sarre and Mont-Tonnère. In vain was the untruth of their statements exposed, and facts related as they really were: these fanatics obstinately persisted, during three days, in praying for the appearance of the army which the republicans had defeated.

Matters were much worse at Coblentz, where General Leval commanded. This officer, who was somewhat of an invalid, was generous and benevolent, and he equally abhorred both turbulence and perfidy. Fond of order, and severe in matters of administration, he had managed to keep all parties under control. The pretended and the true Jacobins were obliged to contain themselves within just bounds; but both, impatient of the restraint he had imposed upon them, were only seeking an opportunity to shake it off. The news of Masséna's victory had just reached Coblentz; the city was illuminated, and the republican soldiers exulting in the event.

This seemed a favourable time for appealing to opinions which were now getting out of date. The president of the municipality had been secretary to Prince Charles. He had returned to his native country about eighteen months before; and having first glided into the municipal administration, and then subdued the other members to his will, he now reigned over it in despotic sway. His colleagues had adopted his views, were penetrated with his principles, and co-operated in all his plans. Rude towards the citizens, and brutal towards the soldiers, these men affected an exaggeration of feeling which strangely contrasted with their actions.

Though this singular patriot calculated his plans with cool deliberation, he accused those who daily exposed their lives to maintain the institutions of their country, of coldness and want of energy. His colleagues, obedient to his beck and call, like him affected exaggeration, appeared thoughtful and uneasy, put on the disguise of stern and unflinching republicans, and pretended to lament that freedom should have been placed under the protection of unworthy guardians. Popular feeling had just been excited, and they did not let this opportunity for agitation escape them. A great crowd assembled, and, headed by the municipal magistrates, proceeded through the streets crying, "Long live the Jacobins!"

They applied the most opprobrious epithets to every French soldier they met; the French officers were likewise insulted, termed aristocrats and Vendeans, and pursued with the cries of "Down with the Chouans!"

To the latter exclamation some among them replied, "And the Jacobins likewise!" This they said merely from irritation at the ill-usage they received. At this answer, which seemed very natural, the mob rushed upon them, ill-treated them, threw them on the ground, and stamped upon them. The guard, having come to their assistance, was likewise attacked, and with great difficulty succeeded in extricating itself from the riotous multitude, who, being assailed in their turn, were dispersed.

The aspect of affairs was therefore not very brilliant with the French. On the one hand the Austrians appeared with hostile demonstrations, on the other the Prussians with equivocal assurances; in front was an insurrection, and attempts at revolt in the rear. The French army was thus menaced on all sides. If it had only had to face the enemy, or guard against ambuscades, the danger would not have been greater than usual; but demagogues had suddenly sprung up among its ranks, and transforming the ardour of war into the fever of revolt, threatened to paralyse the feeble battalions which composed it. This, of all the obstacles Ney had to encounter, was the most dangerous. But he little heeded loquacity, and turbulence still less; those who gave way to them, were severely reminded of their duties.

Of two general officers who had fired the train by inflammatory speeches to the men, one was as bad a soldier as he was a furious Jacobin; and having no letters of service, was dismissed without ceremony. The other, though a bustling demagogue, was nevertheless a good and brave officer, and Ney was hesitating as to the steps he should take, when the officer himself put an end to this embarrassment. He had commanded upon the Rhine during the last war, and had a violent altercation with Moreau.

It is known that the latter general blamed the addresses of the army of Italy, and opposed such addresses in his own army. His lieutenant, the officer in question, paid no attention to Moreau's orders to this effect. The men belonging to the right wing, which was under his orders, having expressed their desire to protest against the project of Clichy, he assembled them, libelled the manifesto, and excited to a pitch of rage the hatred which they already bore to the emigrants.

Moreau, provoked at seeing his authority thus slighted, suppressed the protest. A violent quarrel ensued, and the powers of the too impetuous commander of the right wing were soon taken from him. The speedy arrival at Ney's army of the officer he accused of this disgrace, being announced, he availed himself of the repugnance he felt at being under the command of this individual, to apply for employment in a subordinate rank elsewhere. All dissensions now ceased among Ney's troops; the men resumed their warlike habits, and forgetting politics, directed their attention solely to their duties as soldiers.

The republican forces, reduced almost wholly to live upon what they could take from the enemy—being without pay, clothing, or shoes—were under that degree of irritation which leads men willingly to the field of battle. Coblentz was in a state of siege, and there were neither revolts nor insurrections to be apprehended in the rear. Ney thought he had reached the end of his difficulties, but he had only got out of one to fall into another. His forces being so feeble, he endeavoured to supply this defect by courage and promptitude. He organized his army afresh, and placed at the heads of columns young men like himself, ardent and vigorous, fearing neither fatigue nor peril. He stationed in the rear those whom age and obesity had rendered less active.

This was enough, however, to set the whole of the field-officers in a rumour. One vehemently claimed his place in action; another appealed to the tenour of his commission; a third was indignant "at being confined to one place;" a fourth could not submit "to march in the rear of the ammunition wagons." Even the members of the commissariat became angry, and invoked their rights of precedence.

In the midst of this species of mutiny, Lacombe Saint-Michael arrived from the army of the Danube, and having found Sorbier at the head of the light artillery, "fancied himself transformed into a guard-general." He would not countenance such changes, he said, and claimed his station in the line. As he had distinguished himself both in the field of battle and at the tribune, Ney considered him entitled to an explanation.

"Would you wish," said Ney, "that the muster-roll should have greater weight than the good of the service; and that for the sake of complying with vain pretensions of precedence, I should risk the success of my operations?—for, in sober earnest, are you active enough to be attached to my suite?—are you supple and strong enough to be constantly in the field? Leave then to Sorbier, the fatigues which his youth will enable him to bear; he will correspond with you, and will not cease being under your orders."

Lacombe was convinced. "It is all right, General," he cried. "I had not the honour of being known to you; and as I possessed the confidence of the whole of France, I thought it hard that you should refuse me yours. All is now explained; send me your orders, and you know how I can execute them."

CHAPTER 26

Different Engagements

The peasantry on the right bank had, as we have already stated, taken up arms, and were tumultuously assembled round Frankfort. They were already twenty thousand strong. As this movement might become serious, Ney resolved to punish these villagers for interfering in a quarrel which did not concern them, and at the same time make a useful diversion. Having settled his plans accordingly, General Leval pushed a column upon Limburg, whilst General Roussel crossed the Rhine at Seltz, and Nansouty at Frankenthal.

The Imperialists, being menaced on their wings, dared not weaken them; and General Lorcet, who led the real attack, debouched without obstacle upon the dense ranks of these unhappy peasants, whom a sort of infatuation had brought to the field of battle. They were established upon the Maine; their position was strong and well chosen; but the French troops were irritated at this rising, and rushing upon them with fury, overthrew and cut them to pieces. Those who escaped with their lives from this foolish attempt, returned peaceably to their cottages. There remained, however, about fifteen thousand in arms, whom it afterwards became necessary to punish also.

This act of energy produced a good effect. No sooner had the Austrian reserves received the news of the rout of their militia, than they ran to its assistance. Schwartzenberg, quitted Manheim with precipitation and threw himself into Frankfort with the ten thousand men he commanded.

The French thus cleared the approaches of the river; but the stores which they had hoped to seize, and the contributions they had expected to levy, escaped them with this place. Resignation was again their only remedy, and they were once more reduced to expedients to alleviate their intolerable sufferings. But this was now a more easy task. The Directory had given orders that an active and vigorous diversion should be made, and the reinforcements which it had announced for this purpose were beginning to arrive.

Ney had now from eighteen to twenty thousand men at his disposal; the field of action was consequently larger, and the operations were more extended and more certain. The enemy had established themselves upon the Necker, and Ney determined to go there and meet them. His columns were put in motion, and he was preparing to follow when news reached him that Lecourbe had been appointed to the command of the army.

He had formerly served under this general, whose sagacity, enthusiasm, and precision in conducting attacks, Ney well remembered, as he did also the praises he had received from Lecourbe. The operation which he had planned seemed sure, and he hastened to offer its direction to his new commander.

> "The Austrian troops assembled upon the Necker," he wrote to the latter, "do not amount to half the number of ours. Hasten hither, and put yourself at our head; everyone expects you, and I in particular, with the most sincere impatience. Your presence will excite fresh ardour among us. We shall, under your command, be more certain of success and proceed with greater confidence."[1]

But in warfare Lecourbe loved only the field of battle. He had just arrived at Strasburg, where he found nothing but want and misery. Having entered the town on the 10th of October, when the weather was cold and rainy, he beheld the soldiers parading about the streets in rags. Their arms were no better than their clothing: one had no musket, another no sword; all

---

1. Mayence, 19th *Vendemiaire,* Year 8. (Oct. 10th, 1799.)

bore evidence of the most cruel neglect, and all bent under the weight of distress. Nothing in this deplorable picture flattered Lecourbe's passion for military glory, and he was on the point of resigning his command. Meantime, the army was following up the advantages it had gained; it had taken Grosgerau and Treben, and was advancing upon Heidelberg. A new action was about to take place, and Ney again offered his new commander the honour of leading it. He was aware of Lecourbe's hesitation about retaining the command, and he thought he could overcome this hesitation by giving him an account of the vigour with which the troops, represented to him as so weak, had attacked the enemy.

> "Come quickly," he wrote; "do not suffer yourself to be influenced by anyone respecting the situation of the army. It is capable, whatever some may say to the contrary, of making a vigorous diversion."

It was impossible to be more pressing or more friendly; but Lecourbe having met at Strasburg all those whom Ney had sent to the rear, had listened to their statements, and replied with coldness to these kind entreaties. Ney had the Austrians in front of him, and revenged himself on them for the injustice of his commander. He attacked them on the 15th of October in front of Heidelberg, and such was the force of the shock that neither the hussars nor the hulans could withstand it. Not but that they fought with courage; indeed their resistance was heroic. Prince Lichtenstein, who commanded during the action, was overpowered, and Count Esterhazy taken prisoner, before they would give way. The different corps upon the Necker had also been defeated, and Prince Schwartzenberg, who commanded the Austrian army on the Lower Rhine, had made all possible haste to Stuttgard.

The diversion ordered by the Directory having thus been effected, Masséna, more at his ease, could now extend his operations. But these successes, far from allaying angry political feelings, tended only to inflame them the more: one did not, without rage, see his predictions fail; another was angry that the army could do without him; and wounded vanity being more powerful than a sense of duty, Ney encountered nothing but opposition and malevolence in those who ought to have given him their most strenuous support. This was lamentable; but man is so formed. Ney however was not discouraged, and only determined to push on his operations with redoubled vigour.

Philipsburg was still in the hands of the Landgrave, or, more properly speaking, in those of the Austrians; and he resolved to try whether an attempt to obtain possession of it would not be now more successful than at the beginning of the war. He accordingly marched thither, and found it as little able as formerly to offer an effective resistance. The garrison was badly provisioned, not numerous, and its ranks further thinned by desertion and sickness; so that the place could not possibly hold out six days after the trenches were opened.

Weak as Philipsburg was, it however required a certain display of force to reduce it; ammunition, artillery, and from twenty to twenty-five thousand men were requisite to cover the siege. Ney had only fourteen thousand; he therefore deemed the operation too hazardous, and contented himself with blockading the place.

His force however, though insufficient for a siege, was greater than a mere blockade required. He therefore took with him all the troops he could spare, and determined upon a fresh attempt in favour of Masséna.

Stuttgard continued the depôt of the Austrians, and he doubted not that, if he threatened that place, Prince Charles would hasten to its assistance. Having made his preparations, he sent for the commissary and the chief of his staff. The latter contented himself with eluding the order; but the former, stung to the quick at Ney's uncompromising integrity, boldly declared that all connexion between himself and this general had ceased; that both had now another commander, who retained him near his person. So long as this malevolent feeling did not lead to acts detrimental to the service, Ney took no notice of it; but as such was now its effect, he visited it with the full weight of his displeasure.

The staff officer having done duty with the army, Ney was content to treat him as a man who had forgotten himself. But the commissary, who had done nothing during the whole campaign, had provided nothing, and had left the soldiers in a state of the most dreadful destitution, he treated with greater severity, and at the same time with the most cutting contempt. He ordered him to join the army forthwith, and organize the administration attached to it; and further, to produce the order which authorised him to remain at Strasburg.

The commissary had indulged in the opposition which embarrassed Ney's operations, and given way to his malignant feelings towards this general, under the idea of receiving support from General Lecourbe, who, being dissatisfied, and naturally fond of finding fault, had left the burthen of the war to his active predecessor, and yet took a secret pleasure in the malevolent reports spread against him.

Ney could with difficulty endure that Lecourbe should encourage such opposition, and took care to let him know it. But Lecourbe was always wavering: still undecided whether or not he should accept the command, he nevertheless thwarted Ney in every possible manner. Sometimes he said that it was dangerous to cross the Rhine, at others he wanted all operations to be suspended. Thus Ney being pressed on the one hand by government, who directed that the war should be pushed to extremities, and kept back on the other by the general in-chief, who only sought to throw obstacles in his way, soon became weary of these contradictory instructions, and requested the war minister to put an end to such a state of things.

> "I beg to inform you," he wrote, "that since General Lecourbe's arrival, I experience nothing but opposition to everything I undertake. Commissary-General Lamartellière, and the General Baraguey-d'Hillers, chief of the staff, are with him at Strasburg, and are constantly throwing obstacles in my way. Have the goodness, Citizen Minister,

to force General Lecourbe immediately to exercise the honourable office with which the executive Directory has invested him, and no longer leave me exposed to the annoyances of men who would do much better in attending to the welfare of the array.

"Ney."

"Manheim, 29th *Vendemiaire*, Year 8. (October 20th, 1799.)"

Ney, having forwarded a copy of this letter to Lecourbe, set out on his expedition. His forces, though far from numerous, were composed of steady and experienced troops, each soldier being actuated by one common feeling of hatred to the Austrians and of devotion to his country. The Imperialists, with all their numerous battalions, were unable to withstand this handful of brave men, who, on the 29th of October, encountered and drove them back at Hislack. On the following day, as the French columns were advancing to Slocksberg, the *cuirassiers* of Anspach and those of Frantzmailand appeared, to give them battle.

The First Regiment of French *Chasseurs* immediately advanced, the light artillery prepared their pieces, and the action began. The attack of the French was, as usual, dreadfully impetuous; but the resistance of the Imperialists was most determined, and for a long time no advantage was obtained on either side. At length *Chef-d'Escadron* Dubois-Crancé, having at the head of his squadron charged the Austrians with extraordinary energy, succeeded in shaking them.

The Prince of Hohenlohe rode forward, rallied his men, and the action was resumed with fresh spirit, and with such determined obstinacy that neither party would give way. But the French artillery being brought to bear upon the Austrians, its fire proved so destructive that they fell back in disorder, and the prince himself made off with all haste for Louisburg, in order to effect a junction with the Duke of Wirtemberg, and rally his forces under the walls of Ulm. Ney might have pursued him, driven back the Austrian troops on his right, and seized Stuttgard; but his cavalry was too weak to venture into the vast and fertile plains through which the Necker winds its course.

Meantime Lecourbe had joined the army and assumed the command. He seemed but little disposed to second Ney's enterprises; he had not forgotten their late altercation, and it seemed his constant aim to mortify his predecessor, whom he ordered one of his *aides-de-camp* constantly to follow, under pretence of rendering his communications with head-quarters more rapid. Ney at first treated this measure with silent contempt, and feigned not to perceive the motive in which it originated; but Lorcet, who commanded one of his brigades, having complained to him of similar treatment, he determined to take the matter up. The fact is, Baraguey, the chief of the staff, pretending to entertain suspicions of Lorcet, sent an officer to observe his conduct, and more particularly to watch his proceedings in levying contributions on the villages.

So long as the insult had been confined to himself, Ney had not complained: but the moment it was directed against one of his officers he gave vent to. his anger. After expressing his feelings with regard to the chief of the staff, he arrested certain agents or spies which that officer had sent into the villages, and then addressing Lecourbe, bitterly upbraided him with these unhandsome proceedings.

> "I do not, I know, enjoy your confidence," he wrote. "Well, be it so! but then you must send me to the rear, and not subject me to the investigations of your officers; for you must know that I have the presumption to think I understand my duty and am capable of performing it. I am not, it is true, base enough to cringe to or flatter any man; but my country is the object of my sole and constant solicitude, and for it I shall find strength to make every sacrifice and support every mortification."[2]

This bold and manly expostulation produced a powerful effect: Lecourbe disavowed the acts of his staff officer, and replied to Ney's letter with kind and friendly professions. He then

---

2. Letter of the 10th *Brumaire*, Year 8. (Nov. 1st, 1799.)

seemed to restore his confidence to the brave general, and to act upon all his suggestions. Ney having several times complained of the small number of his cavalry, and of the constant delay in pursuing the enemy, Lecourbe now sent him the first regiment of cavalry, with an intimation that he was about to direct a march upon Stuttgard. As this movement required stores of provisions, and means of carriage, he directed Ney to collect all the money and horses still remaining in the villages. This was an unpleasant duty, but it was commanded by circumstances; Ney therefore directed one of his brigades upon Wimpfen, advanced upon Bruckenheim at the head of the other, and, by alternately fighting and assuming a threatening attitude, succeeded in reaching the Entz.

This bold and skilful march placed the imperial army in a very critical situation. Masséna was at Basle with a heavy column of grenadiers, and Ney had crossed the Necker; the former was about to make an irruption into Suabia, the latter to penetrate into Wirtemberg. Both the flanks and the communications of the archduke's army were thus exposed; and this prince, if he could not secure his menaced flanks from danger, was anxious at least to keep his communications open. He had marched to the assistance of Hohenlobe, and directed that Heilbronn should be occupied and maintained at any sacrifice.

Hohenlohe having pushed forward, and extended his lines from Gross-Botwar to Besigheim, Ney resolved to attempt driving them back. He accordingly threw a part of his left brigade upon Marpach, placed the remainder round Lauffen, and advanced with his right brigade upon the Austrian columns which had taken up their position at the conflux of the Entz. The weather was most unfavourable, and the inhabitants of the country, tired of the presence of the French, and otherwise discontented, were zealously devoted to the archduke; this prevented Ney from ascertaining the strength of these columns, but on the 3rd of November he formed into line in front of them, with the 1st Cavalry, the 10th Chasseurs, and two battalions of the 8th Demi-Brigade.

When the French debouched, the Imperialists were themselves about to march in pursuit of them. The Austrian force consisted of three thousand horse and four thousand foot, and they attacked the French with all the confidence inspired by a greater superiority in numbers. They rushed like an irresistible torrent upon Ney's little band; but its brave leader succeeded in checking their career. The French infantry received them with admirable coolness, and the 10th Chasseurs made some very effective charges. By degrees the action became more developed, and, notwithstanding the great disproportion of force, the French maintained the contest during six hours without any decided disadvantage.

Night was however approaching, and the strife seemed to become every instant more animated and more deadly. The French artillery fired with admirable precision; the grenadiers of the 8th Demi-Brigade evinced an extraordinary degree of courage and fortitude, and the increasing danger seemed only to stimulate them to greater daring; but a body of three thousand Wirtembergians having come up to the assistance of the Imperialists, Ney was forced to give way.

The retreat of the French was at first conducted with order and precision; and every attempt of the enemy to trouble it was frustrated. But the Austrians, vexed at seeing so small a force escape from them, made a desperate charge, and fell in overwhelming numbers upon the artillery and the infantry by which it was supported. The grape-shot of the French artillery stopped the career of the Austrian cavalry, but the republican infantry was not so fortunate. The men were exhausted by forced marches and by the fatigue of the action; they lost their steadiness at the sight of the swarms of cavalry rushing upon them, and gave way in confusion.

Ney lost six hundred men killed or made prisoners, and could no longer stem the torrent which was sweeping all before it. He therefore prolonged his movement, and took up a position with his right at Stockberg and his left at Helmstadt. Lecourbe did not think this a good position: he wished the 9th Demi-Brigade to cross the Entz and effect a junction with the right wing under the command of Legrand. But Ney having ascertained that the great mass of the Austrian forces were in front of him, and perceiving that their object was to surprise Sinzheim, represented to the commander-in-chief the importance of maintaining his position, and Lecourbe yielded to his opinion. The confidence displayed by Ney restored that of his troops; nevertheless it could not prevent the evil consequences always attendant upon defeat.

The reader may remember the attempt upon Philipsburg at the beginning of the campaign, and the causes of its failure. The Directory was now desirous of repeating this attempt, in the conviction that, with a display of force before the place, the former secret negotiations with the inhabitants, which had nearly placed the town in the hands of the French, might easily be renewed.

It was to no purpose Ney represented that the circumstances were no longer the same: that the commanding officer of engineers and the town-major had been changed. The weak and haughty Rheingrave of Salm, so fond of intriguing and plotting against the French, and so little qualified to meet them in the field, was still governor of Philipsburg; but the Austrians who, prior to the battle of Stockach, were spread through Suabia, had now a considerable force on the Rhine, and Ney feared to risk, on the opposite bank of that river, a train of artillery which he had no adequate means to protect.

Having stated the amount of his own force, and that of the Austrians, together with the number of troops which such an undertaking would require, and what was more especially necessary for the opening of the trenches, he showed the danger and probable failure of the attempt. But the Directory persisting in its orders, Ney invested Philipsburg, and defeated part of the forces employed to defend it; but this, led to no advantage. At a former period the French had been forced to retire after bombarding the place, and in the present instance a slight check forced them hastily to withdraw their artillery and convey their guns and wagons to the left bank.

Hohenlohe pursued them at the head of a numerous force, and his columns having ascended the Necker, seemed likely to reach the Elsatz. Ney therefore felt the necessity of stopping their career, and directed Montholon to assume a position in front of Waughenzel. This officer had just been appointed *chef-d'escadron*.[3] He possessed daring courage, together with a good eye; and he did his best in this emergency. But the Austrians, having debouched in great numbers, forced the position, and compelled Ney to a retrograde march.

The loss on this occasion was very trifling; nevertheless the check placed the rear of the French in jeopardy, by giving the Austrians possession of the entrance into the valley of the Necker; and this circumstance made it of some importance. Ney did not conceal from Lecourbe the consequences to which it might lead.

> "I think, my dear General," he wrote, "that you would do well to make your posts fall back from Weinheim, keep only Heidelberg, strongly barricade the bridge communicating with the right bank of the Necker, and send companies of observation to the fords at Helwesheim and Ladenberg. Your forces would be then more concentrated; Necker-Gemund might be preserved by the garrison of Heidelberg, and if the enemy were to attack me in strong force, I could easily effect my retreat upon Wislock. But is the division of General Legrand not to make a retrograde movement? Consider of it, my dear General;—the position of Obstadt, or that of Mengelsheim, keeping Bruck-

---

3. The General of Division, acting Commander-in-Chief.
Considering the advantageous reports which have reached me concerning the conduct of Citizen Montholon, captain in the 1st Regiment of *chasseurs-a-cheval;* considering, moreover, the talents and bravery which that officer displayed in the action of —— *Vendemiaire*, in which he forced and carried the bridge-head at ——, below Frankfort, defended by two thousand Austrians and peasants, I hereby, in the field of battle, appoint him *chef d'escadron* in the same regiment
.Ney
.Head-Quarters, Hoœscht, the —— *Vendemiaire*, Year 3.

sall notwithstanding, might perhaps be a suitable one for him under present circumstances!"⁴

This advice, though excellent, was but an imperfect remedy for the evil. The checks which the French troops had received had renewed with frightful energy their former destitute condition. They were in rags, without food, and constantly exposed to a beating rain, which a sharp wind rendered cruelly piercing. Discouragement and hunger now extinguished their remaining energy, and they could neither fight nor any longer struggle against their wants and privations. Masséna was however still at Basle, his preparations were nearly made, and Lecourbe felt unwilling to continue his retreat when he might every day expect succour. But the discouragement evinced by the men was by no means consistent with his firmness, and having expressed how deeply he lamented his lot, and that of his subordinate generals, in seeing the soldiers under their command fail in resolution at such a trying moment, he requested Ney to employ his influence in rekindling their courage, rousing the energy they were capable of displaying, and again exciting that confidence in themselves which had so often led them to victory.

Ney had no great difficulty in effecting this. His own men had undergone the same sufferings as the rest of the army, but had always been patient, obedient, and ready to undertake any act of daring proposed by their general. The first division had seized upon a convoy of provisions belonging to that of Ney; the men went in a body to their commander and complained of this unhandsome proceeding.

> "What would you have me do, my lads?" said Ney. "Our fellow-soldiers have certainly not treated us like friends, and it is no doubt because they know that the Austrians are followed by immense stores of provisions, and that they cannot flatter themselves to attack and capture these stores with the same courage you display."

---

4. Head-quarters, Homberg, 16th *Brumaire*, Year 8. (November 7th, 1799.)

The poor men had however been two whole days without rations, and would doubtless have preferred bread to praises; nevertheless they resigned themselves to the loss with a good grace, and determined to revenge themselves upon the Austrians for the sufferings they endured. The example of Ney's division soon restored the energies of the whole army. The Austrians had begun to form in line in front of Herberg, and Ney's forces marched up to them; but the imperial columns increased every moment in numbers, and completely turned the position, so that Ney's division was obliged to fall back, and amid the charges of the Austrian cavalry took up a position upon the skirts of the wood of Schasthausen.

Hohenlohe had been unable to prevent the retreat of Ney's division. He was defeated each time he had attacked it; but he had always returned to the charge, and from one attack to another had reached Wistock, where there was space to form his columns into line. This he did, and rushed impetuously on the position. It was defended by a very small number of men of the most determined bravery, who being aware of its importance, determined not to evacuate it till the last extremity. The first charge of the Austrians made no impression upon them; but the numbers of the foe were too unequal, and they could not long maintain the conflict.

After a most energetic resistance, they were about to give way, when Ney, appearing at the head of the remainder of his division, took the Austrians in flank and dispersed their whole force. But the reserves of the imperial army were formidable; they advanced and covered the columns which had just been routed; these rallied, came up again, and in an instant the action was resumed with tenfold energy. But the French troops, elevated by the success they had already obtained, fought with desperation: the infantry engaged part of the enemy's masses, and kept the remainder in check, whilst the 10th Chasseurs, charging the dense columns already crippled with the fire of the French musketry and artillery, overthrew them all, and even the Frantzmailland *cuirassiers*, who were proceeding in all haste to their assistance. Ney then pushed forward and re-occupied his position upon the Elsatz.

This successful action restored the confidence of the French army, and the hopes of its soldiers revived. The Austrians once more fled before them; and they again raised contributions, and enjoyed the abundance attendant upon victory. But an event of great importance now occupied their attention. Bonaparte, the conqueror of Italy, had returned from the expedition to Egypt; and his first act on landing in Europe was one of kindness and benevolence. He had sent assistance to the demi-brigades which occupied Corsica, put an end to their privations, by feeding them and covering their numerous scars with warm and comfortable clothing.

That which he had done for the troops on a distant and isolated station, he was about to do likewise for all the French forces who were fighting around the circumference of the republic. He was about to renew the wonders of Lodi and Castiglione, and also to provide for the wants of the brave men who were on the banks of the Rhine fighting the battles of the republic. Both officers and men now gave way to the most flattering anticipations.

Some of the former thought that an immediate stop would be put to the cruel agitation which pervaded the interior of the country; others expected to see the end of that series of reverses which had pursued the French arms upon the Rhine. General Boyé, who had a command in the army of the Danube, applauded the return of a man devoted to the popular cause, and enjoyed in idea the vexation which it would cause among the royalists. Baraguey, who had come from Malta to the Rhine, congratulated his brother officers and the country upon the fortunate results to which Bonaparte's arrival in France must lead.

General Championnet, who was fighting his way among the rocks of Liguria, went further than this: in his opinion Bonaparte alone could restore to the French arms, the ascendancy which their continued ill-fortune had made them lose. He hoped to see this general once more at the head of those veteran bands which he had so often led to victory, and he nobly resigned his command in Bonaparte's favour. The courage of each soldier seemed to increase in a tenfold ratio with the return of this extraordinary man: each felt that his country was on the eve of a great and favourable crisis, and that some striking event was about to take place which would restore the ancient splendour of France and attach fortune once more to her standard.

Lecourbe, eager to take advantage of this enthusiasm which was general in the ranks of his army, determined to attempt something against the enemy. Having received some reinforcements, and the weather being dry, he was able to spread his forces and keep the inhabitants of the country in check. The country itself was extremely intricate and difficult; nevertheless he resolved to make a continued series of attacks upon the Austrians.

The population evinced the most malignant feelings towards the French, who were again reduced almost to starvation, when Ney succeeded in capturing some provisions which relieved their most pressing wants, and in routing the imperial generals, who encouraged the hostility of the inhabitants and excited uneasiness and agitation among them. The republican army now prepared to push forward; for the plots of the Austrians were defeated and could injure it no longer.

The pensioned officers, post-masters, and burgomasters, who, being in constant intercourse with the French troops, had given intelligence of their movements to the Austrians, were unable to do further mischief, being all taken prisoners. The *Baily* of Hoest, more alert than his colleagues, had at first made his escape. But he was too dangerous to be left at liberty. His extreme cunning, and the influence he enjoyed in the country, rendered him a very formidable enemy, and Ney tracked, pursued, and at length succeeded in taking him. The villages, being thus deprived of men capable of exciting and leading their inhabitants, soon resumed their wonted tranquillity. The republicans had now no foe to surprise their rear, or any one to betray their plans and preparations.

They could advance in security, and they took advantage of this circumstance to march up to the Austrians. Bonnet commanded the right wing, and Rouyer the left; they came up with the imperial forces in front of Hoffheim, engaged, and drove them in disorder upon Sinzheim. The obstinacy which Ney had before displayed in defending this position, had revealed its importance to the Austrians, and they made great exertions to maintain it. He now cut off the approaches and crowned the heights, but still the defence was most determined, and the French troops were a long time in overcoming it.

At length the position was carried, and the dense bodies of Austrian cavalry which defended it, driven to Rohrbach, where, with the aid of a body of infantry already in the place, they endeavoured to make a stand. But the French grenadiers having rapidly pursued them, they were again defeated, and sought refuge at Steinfurt.

The Austrian reserve now came to their assistance, and the arrival of Prince Hohenlohe restored their confidence; but the French columns having debouched, attacked them again, and a sanguinary action was the result. For a long time the fortune of the day remained equally balanced; but Ney, at length, made an attempt to fix it to the republican standard. He manoeuvred on the left and prepared to make a tremendous charge. This the Austrians dared not withstand, but fell back and retreated towards Heilbronn. Ney was about to pursue them, when proposals for an armistice were made at head-quarters. Having in consequence received orders to stop all pursuit, he halted and took up a position.

Appendix

No. 1

Gillet, Representative Attached to the Army of Sambre-et-Meuse, to the Committee of Public Safety.

Head-quarters, Poetershem, October 1794.

My dear Colleagues,

Adjutant-General Ney does not spare the enemy's equipages. A few days since he captured all those of a foreign minister upon the Rhine. They contained a great deal of silver plate, which I have handed over to the paymaster.

Near Cleves also, he captured the courier of Holland and Vesel, who was the bearer of several letters from emigrants, and others, relating to the affairs of the day. I enclose some of them.

You will observe that several of these letters relate to La Vendée. Is it not possible to destroy this last hope of our enemies?

The traitor, D'Artois, has, it appears, just embarked for England. Is he not a manikin which the atrocious government of London intends to thrust forward for the purpose of rekindling that execrable war of La Vendée?

I am well persuaded, my dear colleagues, of your eagerness to extirpate this political cancer. But recollect that this war has become serious only from the bad choice of those selected to put an end to it. It has been perpetuated by their incapacity and corruption, and by the perfidy of some among them. Send hither well-intentioned, active, and able generals, and all will be saved. How is it that Finisterre, when revolt had burst out in so alarming a blaze, did not become a second La Vendée? Why, because Canclaux, who then commanded at Brest, put himself at the head of fifteen hundred brave soldiers, and pursued the rebels until they were dispersed and exterminated. The revolt lasted only a fortnight.

Pardon me, dear colleagues, for these observations; but the subject interests me in every way. I am indignant that a handful of rebels should dare still to lift up their heads in our country, when the whole of Europe is trembling before our victorious armies.

Health and Fraternity.

Gillet.

No. 2

The Committee of Public Safety to the Representative Gillet, Delegated to the Armies of the North and Sambre-et-Meuse.

Paris, September 21st, 1795.

Dear Colleague,

The national convention, and we ourselves, have learnt with the most lively satisfaction the constant success of the army to which your mission attaches you, since it has crossed the Rhine. We could have wished that all the brave men composing that army had witnessed the expressions of delight which burst forth at almost every sentence uttered by the reporter. But if the defenders of the republic are deprived of such enjoyment, the published report, the bulletin of the convention, and public papers, will furnish them with the proofs of esteem and gratitude which the whole nation feels towards them.

Doubtless, after such constant fatigue, the officers and men must have rest; but never let us, citizen colleague, lose sight of this fact, that nothing is yet accomplished whilst anything remains to be done. Above all, let us not forget that the blows struck up to the present day are only preparatory; for our duty is less to humble the princes of the empire, than the house of Austria, which has at all times shown itself the bitterest enemy of the French nation. And indeed, the princes of the empire must, sooner or later, throw themselves into our arms. We are necessary to their existence. With regard to the house of Austria, the more we mulct it, the farther we advance towards repose and happiness. It is therefore against the armies and dominions of that power that our efforts must be directed. We must march without delay upon Suabia, after terminating what remains to be done upon the Lower Rhine: that is to say, after having taken Ehrenbreitstein, driven the enemy beyond the Maine, and blockaded Mayence. Then, dear colleague, it will remain for the army of Rhin-et-Moselle, strengthened by its junction with that of Sambre-et-Meuse, to ascend the river in its turn and carry the war into the dominions of our real enemy.

We have learnt with much pleasure that the newly conquered territory produces more than you expected, and promises to yield still more. The time for mildness is gone by; our enemies must positively be deprived of the resources which they might one day find in these territories, and we must be provided with what we require. The English have for a time closed the sea against us; therefore the land must supply that which we cannot obtain by means of the other element.

Although we have no reason to fear being forced to recross the Rhine, still let us bring within this boundary of the republic all that is not indispensable to the daily wants of the army. Yes! citizen colleague:—to take Ehrenbreitstein, blockade Mayence, seize the states of the house of Austria situated upon the right bank, convey to France all the provisions and stores not absolutely indispensable to the wants of the inhabitants of the countries under the rule of the princes of the empire, and carry off all the produce of every kind from the hereditary provinces of the house of Austria—such is our plan, which nothing must frustrate. There lies the glory of our undertakings, and there lies the road to peace. Point out forcibly these two great objects to the generals and soldiers to whom you are delegated. Render unanimous every opinion and every will, and you will see that we shall execute with facility that which, in other times, no one would have dared to plan.

Rely upon it, citizen colleague, that the committee will neglect nothing to secure the due execution of an undertaking which alone can lead to a speedy and lasting peace.

Health and Fraternity.

Cambacérès,
Letourneur,
Merlin.

No. 3

The Committee of Public Safety to the Representatives Attached to the Army of Sambre-et-Meuse, Cologne.

September 15th, 1797.

Citizens Colleagues,

You are aware that one of the first principles of military administration is to make the war supply the wants of the war.

If ever circumstances imperiously required the strict execution of this principle, it is at the present juncture. No doubt we must spare as much as possible the countries we have conquered, and alleviate, as far as we are able, the evils which conquest always drags in her train; no doubt, we must make the inhabitants suffer the least we possibly can for the folly of their rulers; no doubt, we must make a distinction between the countries under the dominion of our most inveterate enemies, and those whose governments are ready to effect a reconciliation with us; no doubt, we must also separate from the former those which have only shown timidity or weakness: but all are not the less bound to help us with their contributions to support the burthen of a war which either their malevolence or their weakness has excited against us.

We are unable, dear colleagues, to determine either the quantity or the nature of the contribution which you are to exact from the conquered countries. Your decision on this head must depend, first, upon the political considerations above mentioned; secondly, upon the wants of your army; and, thirdly, upon the wealth of the conquered countries.

And generally let us not forget, that it is the unjust distribution of a military impost which makes its burthen more severely felt.

Let us not forget either that a dilapidation of the articles supplied by such contributions renders them of no use to those who receive them, and a grievous burthen to those by whom they are paid.

Let us always remember that the poorer classes, and those who owe their existence solely to manual labour, have the greatest claim upon republican commiseration.

Let us always have this truth present to our minds: that the greatest enemies of the French republic, throughout Europe, are the nobles and the priests.

Let us likewise never lose sight of this principle, that when a conquered country has paid the contribution imposed upon it, both the persons and property of its inhabitants ought to be held as sacred as in the centre of the republic.

Besides the contributions which you are to impose, either in produce or in money, you will doubtless take measures for securing, by right of pre-emption, all the provisions for men and horses which the conquered country can supply, without ruining its agricultural interests, and depriving its inhabitants of the articles necessary for their own consumption. By these means we can pass our assignats, and economise the produce of our own agriculture and manufactories. We want peace, and it is refused to us! Well then! let us provide for a continuance of the war by laying in great stores of provisions, and taking away the supplies of our enemies.

You will no doubt think it right, dear colleagues, after having provided, by means of storehouses built upon the right bank of the Rhine, for the momentary subsistence of the army, to send the surplus of your purchases to the left bank of that river. In so doing we shall have nothing to fear from the enemy, nor from those misfortunes to which the chances of war sometimes lead. Even were we to take up our winter quarters on the right bank, still this precaution would be advisable.

Letourneur.

No. 4

The Representative Joubert, Attached to the Army of Sambre-et-Meuse, to the Committee of Public Safety.

Hadamar, October 15th, 1795.

Dear Colleagues,

In vain did we flatter ourselves that we could maintain the position which the enemy's manoeuvres had obliged us to assume on the right bank of the Lahn, The retrograde march of the army on this occasion has convinced us of the necessity of resuming our position on the left bank of the Rhine. It is no doubt painful to be forced to give up all idea of success in so brilliant an expedition; but instead of continuing to yield to illusions, it has been the first duty of the generals, and my own, to endeavour to preserve for the republic one of its strongest and most formidable armies, which would surely have been lost, but for the steps we have taken, and upon which we have not hesitated to stake our responsibility.

The following are our reasons for doing as we have done:

In the first place, we could not but admit that the retreat upon the Lahn, regular and well combined as it was, very deeply affected the feelings of the men, who, accustomed as they were to advance, were unable to account for this retrograde movement. They could not conceive the reason for retreating without having been beaten; and it must be confessed, that there exists not among the French that blind confidence in their officers which makes soldiers look with indifference upon the various movements of an army. Exclamations were heard, taxing their commanders with treason; and, as during the first days of the war of liberty, the disorder and disorganization attendant upon defeats were greatly to be apprehended.

There has been no difficulty, it is true, in bringing the army to a proper state of feeling, by reminding it of its victories, and the fidelity and talents of its commanders; and the unfavourable impressions, arising from the natural effect of an unusual movement, were soon eradicated. But the movement itself has convinced us of the extreme weakness of our means, and the dreadful penury we are in with regard to the articles most necessary for the march of an army.

It was only with the greatest difficulty, and by the most violent means, that we were able to provide food for the troops on the banks of the Maine. The soldier's ration was reduced to a pound, three-quarters, and often half a pound of bread, and oftener still the army was three or four days without receiving any rations.

The attitude of victory, and the hope of acquiring fresh resources by enlarging the circle of our conquests, had, until the moment of our departure, kept the men within bounds, and their patience was not less admirable than their courage. On the other hand, the hope of seeing the wagons arrive which had so often been asked for, and so often promised, and the want of which alone was the cause of all our sufferings; the prospect of being seconded by a movement of the army of Rhin-et-Moselle, which would have driven the enemy from the territory of Darmstadt, and opened to us fertile countries abounding in resources of every kind; the facility which this operation would have given to the navigation both of the Rhine, and of the Maine as far as Mayence, and the communication which it would thus have been easy to open between the left bank of the Rhine and the Palatinate;—all these grounds of hope, I must confess, made us participate in the confidence of the troops, and imparted to us, under the painful circumstances in which we are placed, that patient perseverance which famine alone could overcome. My correspondence, my dear colleagues, that of the generals, and that of the chief *commissaire-ordonnateur*, must have proved to you the extent of our resolution and firmness in this respect.

But the inaction of the army of Rhin-et-Moselle has rendered our energy of no avail; and the fruit of our crossing the Rhine and of our rapid marches, has been lost.

I know not whether an absolute impossibility be the cause of the inaction of the army of Rhin-et-Moselle. I am ignorant of the resources of that army, and must not therefore hazard an opinion; but it has been clearly shown that the passage of the Rhine could not be attended with good results, and procure for the republic the advantages anticipated from it, except with the co-operation of the army of Rhin-et-Moselle. All the projects of government, and the ultimate plans of our military operations, were combined under this supposition; and it was Pichegru's place to carry the terror of the French arms into Brisgau and Suabia, cut off all communication between the armies of Wurmser and Clairfayt, force those two generals, whose troops were struck with consternation, to seek an asylum towards the Danube, yield us all the provinces bordering upon the Rhine, and give us an opportunity of surrounding Mayence by the occupation of the territory of Darmstadt. Such, it appears to me, was the duty of the army of Rhin-et-Moselle; and had this duty been performed, the enemy would have been ruined, and peace have been the fruit of this series of victories! I know not, I again repeat, whether that army was or was not in a state to pursue this plan.

Be that as it may, Clairfayt's corps was reinforced with nineteen chosen battalions of infantry, and twenty-three squadrons of cavalry, from the army of Wurmser.

Having nothing to apprehend in his rear, he bore with rapidity upon our left, crossed the Rhine at Selingenstadt, and, as I stated to you in my last, instead of risking a battle, which we impatiently expected, and in which we should have beaten him, he contented himself with a simulated attack, and with rapidly passing our left wing through the neutral territory, threatening at the same time to turn us with his numerous cavalry. We had therefore no other alternative than to retreat upon the Lahn. This measure would have produced no further consequences, had it not had the double effect of shaking, as I have before stated, the confidence of the army in its commanders, and of showing us the insufficiency of our means, particularly in provisions and wagons.

From our mode of living on the banks of the Maine, and in

the event of our being able to make further progress, no danger would have resulted from our penury; but a retrograde movement has laid open and made us sensible of all its consequences.

That which more particularly struck the troops, and has made a deep and lasting impression upon them, is, the obligation under which we found ourselves to leave behind us, for the want of the means of carriage, five hundred and fifty of our wounded, who are in the hands of the enemy,—and this after having put them to flight in their simulated attack upon us near Redda and Hochst.

The retreat was well managed, and executed with admirable precision. The firm bearing of our troops prevented the enemy from giving us much uneasiness; but some artillery wagons, four pieces of cannon and howitzers, and several tumbrels, have fallen into their hands from our want of horses, and because those which we had left, worn out with fatigue and want of forage, could not render us the service we expected, and the country could not supply our deficiency in this respect.

The troops being obliged to live by requisitions, experienced on this march the most dreadful privations. The discipline which the salutary law on the police of the army had restored, gave way to the necessity of living. The most dreadful and irremediable disorders were the consequence: many of the horses fell from fatigue, whilst many others, having lost their shoes, which there were no means of replacing, became lame and were of no further use.

Such was our situation when we reached the banks of the Lahn, and it was aggravated by the want of provisions,—an inevitable result of our being without the means of carriage.

Under these circumstances, it was found impossible to maintain this position without exposing ourselves to lose everything. The enemy are aware of our want of means, but they are also acquainted with French valour. It would have been too imprudent for them to have risked a battle, as they had with them the most certain means of completely destroying us, which means they seemed to be employing. An endeavour to turn us with a large body of light troops, and cut off our communication with the countries whence we derived our subsistence:—such would have been their tactics towards an army whose provisions are so precarious, and which has no storehouses within reach of its rear, and can get nothing for want of wagons.

These points were discussed by the generals in my presence. The chief commissaire-ordonnateur declared that he knew no means of providing for the wants of the army; the commander of the artillery repeated what he had already stated as to the utter impossibility of bringing into play the numerous artillery belonging to this great army. Every combination was discussed, in order to find one which could secure the position of the army upon the right bank; and all were unanimous in the opinion that to persevere any longer would only lead to the absolute loss of an army that had hitherto sustained no loss, and experienced no reverses, but was forced to give way before a host of untoward circumstances which no power could alter.

If the army resumes its position on the left bank of the Rhine, it may be saved for the republic, and may there await the reinforcements absolutely necessary to establish its means of carriage. Its artillery may likewise be repaired; whilst the army itself will cover the conquered territory by opposing an invincible force to every attempt the enemy may make to cross the Rhine.

However painful our situation, do not imagine, dear colleagues, that courage has deserted the soldiers of their public. They can make their colours respected; and this very evening the enemy had proof that their audacity is of no avail against our brave men.

A body of Austrian troops pressed a little too closely on the column of retreat commanded by General Lefebvre. Our troops charged it, and the enemy left upon the field of battle a somewhat considerable number of slain, and three pieces of cannon. There exists this difference between the enemy and us, that if we lose a few ammunition wagons and a few guns, the weakness of our means of carriage is the cause of it; whereas we only obtain their artillery sword in hand, and after having beaten them.

Citizen Dufalga, whose talents are known to you, is charged by the general and by me to deliver this despatch into your hands. He will give you full particulars of our situation, for in the present despatch it is impossible for me to enter into them fully.

I feel, my dear colleagues, the impression which this event must make. I feel, and the thought painfully affects me, that the enemies of the republic may derive some advantages from it; but it must be made known to Europe, that if the army of Sambre-et-Meuse has been obliged to yield to the force of circumstances, its glory has not been tarnished by a single check. It remains wholly to our country, and so soon as its means are restored to it, will become only more formidable to the enemies of France.

Health and friendship.

Joubert.

P. S. I had forgotten to say that the army will preserve the beautiful bridge-head which Dusseldorf affords it. This place, the repairs of which will be made with the greatest expedition, will be in a state to oppose a resistance of greater power, because it will be supported by the army upon the left bank. By thus preserving the two bridge-heads of Manheim and Dusseldorf, we may be able, the moment the armies are filled up, to establish ourselves without difficulty upon the right bank, or at all events keep the enemy constantly in check, and frustrate every attempt they may make to cross the Rhine.

No. 5

To the General-in-Chief of the Army of Sambre-et-Meuse.

Paris, 2nd *Messidor*, Year 4.
(June 20th, 1796.)

Citizen General,

The Directory has received your letter, dated Montabaur, the 29th of *Prairial*. The retreat which you have ordered from the Lahn to the Sieg, may not prove disadvantageous to our arms, provided it draws a portion of the enemy's forces upon you, so as thereby to disengage, for a time, the army of Rhin-et-Moselle, and enable General Moreau to cross the Rhine at Strasburg, as he purposed doing in the event of this operation, which he hoped to be able to execute on the 30th of *Prairial* (18th of June), it not having taken place at this present time when we are writing to you. But the retreat of the left wing of the army of Sambre-et-Meuse would have an injurious effect if the confidence of its soldiers were shaken, and the enemy succeeded in making us abandon the entire right bank of the Rhine.

It is a truth which it is important you should bear in mind, and which the experience of the last campaign has sufficiently proved, that you ought carefully to avoid taking up positions exactly parallel to the Sieg or the Lahn, and approaching too near the Rhine on its right bank, because by so doing you would give the enemy an extreme facility in out-flanking our left wing, and in bringing forces on that side sufficiently strong to drive us from our positions.

Another consideration deserves our most serious attention: it is that by boldness and extreme celerity alone in our military operations we can become successful in Germany. To this we owe our victories and our conquests in Italy. A single day of rest given to the enemy when defeated, often enables them to resume offensive operations, which their numerical superiority always renders them impatient to do. It is only by a succession of defeats following close upon each other that we may hope to exterminate their armies, and dictate terms of peace in the midst of astonished Germany.

The armies of Sambre-et-Meuse and Rhin-et-Moselle must likewise act together. Their combined operations must prevent the enemy from directing the whole of their force, at any time, against either, as during the last campaign.

The Directory sees all the advantages which, by forming in itself a central point of military operations, it derives in bringing about this simultaneous action of the two republican armies upon the Rhine; and it hereby instructs you as to the measures it has determined to adopt, and the execution of which it confides to you and the General-in-Chief Moreau.

The left of the army of Sambre-et-Meuse will resume the offensive on the receipt of this despatch. If the movement of the enemy should have forced it back upon the Wupper, which the Directory does not apprehend to be the case, it will immediately approach the Sieg, place its right against that river, and keep as far from the Rhine as it possibly can without danger. It will take up a position nearly parallel to the Acher, which will prevent the enemy from turning it by throwing a strong force upon its left flank.

It will remain as short a time as possible upon the Sieg, and advance with rapidity towards the Lahn, occupying positions almost parallel to that I have just mentioned. On its arrival near the latter river, it will place its right at Weilburg, or in preference at Wetzlar, and extend its left as far as Marburg, and even beyond it.

At the time of executing this movement, it will be joined by the French troops occupying the line of the Rhine, which begins opposite to the mouth of the Sieg, at its conflux, and extends as far as Coblentz, as well as by such other troops as you may think proper, Citizen General, to call to the right bank for the purpose of reinforcing this wing. A sufficient force must keep the garrison of Ehrenbreitstein in awe, and a small corps of observation be placed upon the right bank of the Lahn, from Wetzlar to its mouth, to prevent the enemy from crossing.

That part of the army of Sambre-et-Meuse now acting upon the right bank of the Rhine, will, as soon as possible, change its position from Wetzlar to Marburg, attack the enemy with impetuosity, and keep towards the Kintz, with its right upon Hanau.

The small corps of observation which it had upon the Lahn, will, after receiving reinforcement from the left bank, seize upon Frankfort and Offenbach, whilst the portion of the army of Sambre-et-Meuse remaining upon the left bank of the Rhine, shall, after having occupied Kreutnach and Bingen, march upon Seltz, in sufficient strong force to keep the garrison of Mayence in awe, and shall throw upon the heights of Hocheim a sufficient number of troops to observe this place, situated upon the right bank of the Rhine.

The army of Sambre-et-Meuse shall next enter Franconia, for which orders will, at a future period, be sent to it by the Directory.

The army of Rhin-et-Moselle will cross the Rhine at Strasburg. It will leave a corps of observation on the Pfirmm to keep the garrison of Mayence in check, and troops in front of Manheim to resist the attempts of the hostile forces which occupy that place. It will then advance with rapidity upon the Upper Necker, after having detached a sufficient force to occupy the mountain gorges of the Black Forest.

Such are the formal instructions which the Directory thinks it right to give you, and General-in-Chief Moreau; the fate of the present campaign depends upon their being implicitly followed.

It is the intention of the Directory not to suffer the French armies to undertake any siege. Its wish is that they should seek the enemy on the right bank of the Rhine, and encounter them with that boldness and impetuosity which characterize the warriors of the republic, and are sure pledges of victory.

The plan we have adopted is one of great magnitude, and requires vigour of execution. It cannot be confided to soldiers more worthy of so glorious an undertaking, or to generals who better deserve the national esteem. You have long, Citizen General, been held in the highest estimation by the Directory, and no misfortune could make you lose it.

Thus the Directory places its confidence in your probity, your patriotism, and your military talents. With a certainty of the support of the Directory, and the good wishes of all the friends of freedom, you have now only to act with boldness and rapidity, and reap those laurels which will prove harbingers of an honourable and lasting peace consequent upon our successes in Germany.

The Directory has just received intelligence that the army of

Rhin-et-Moselle obtained a marked advantage on the 26th of Prairial, before Manheim; also that the Austrians have detached twenty-five thousand men from their armies on the Rhine, to reinforce General Beaulieu in Italy.

Carnot, President.

No. 6

The Executive Directory to Adjutant-General Ney.

Paris, 5th *Messidor,* Year 4. (June 23rd, 1796.)

The passage of the Sieg, Citizen Adjutant-General, and the affair at Altenkirchen, must have raised some anticipations of your success at Montabaur. General-in-chief Jourdan has made a most satisfactory report concerning you to the executive Directory, which hastens to express its satisfaction at your conduct.

A true copy. Carnot, President.

By order of the executive Directory,

Letourneur, Secretary-General.

No. 7

Kléber, General of Division, Commanding the Left Wing of the Army of Sambre-et-Meuse, to General of Division, Collaud.

Head-quarters, Bornheim, *25th Messidor,*
Year 5. (July 13th, 1796.)

My dear General,

Your men must fall in at four o'clock this afternoon, leave their camp, advance, and at nightfall take up a position before Frankfort, so as to be perceived in their full development.

You will form the battalions in two ranks, making a wide interval between them; and if the ground should prevent any of the battalions from being seen from the city, you will place the second line at a distance of three hundred paces from the first. Let all the men stand at ease, but without stirring from their ranks.

The companies of sappers shall be immediately assembled at the toll-tower, and placed at the disposal of the artillery officers.

Kléber.

A true copy. Collaud.

From the above order, my dear Ney, you perceive that your men are to fall in at four o'clock, and that you will also have to make a demonstration. Do not, however, expose your cavalry to lose horses; but shelter it as much as you can from the enemy's artillery.

Collaud.

No. 8

Kléber, General of Division, to General Collaud.

Head-quarters, Lohrhaupton, *1st Thermido*r,
Year 4. (*July 19th*, 1796.)

My dear General,

I have just read with considerable interest the report that you have sent me from Adjutant-General Ney, who may remain at Lohr until he is relieved by the divisions of the right wing; for our plan is to file off on the left upon Schweinfurt.

I hereby authorize Ney to levy a military contribution of one hundred *louis*, on account of the sum to be hereafter exacted from that town. He will give a special receipt accordingly, which, in the event of a fresh impost, may be returned as cash. This sum shall be handed over to you for secret service money, and other extraordinary disbursements.

Direct Ney, I beg of you, to obtain the most precise information concerning Gemunden, Wurtzburg, Schweinfurt, and the nature of the roads leading to these places; and to try to discover the position, strength, and motions of the enemy.

It is stated by mistake, my dear General, that on the ground pointed out to you, your van-guard is to cover your left wing, since it is to communicate by the right with General Grenier. I am convinced that you have rectified this error, which indeed is rectified by the fact itself, since Ney is at Lohr.

Health and friendship.

Kléber.

No. 9

The Executive Directory to Brigadier-General Ney, Army of Sambre-et-Meuse.

Paris, 27th *Thermidor*, Year 4
(August 14th, 1796.)

In the battles of Zeil and Ebersbach, you have shown, Citizen General, what the impetuosity of French valour can effect. These battles do great credit to your courage and to your prudence, both of which being already well known, the executive Directory feels a lively satisfaction in assuring you of the high estimation in which it continues to hold your zeal and military talents.

A true copy.
L. M. Revellière-Lépeau, President.
By order of the Directory.
Lagarde, Secretary-General.

No. 10

General Hoche to the Directory.

Citizens Directors,

Being on the point of taking leave of you, allow me to submit to you some reflections which the good of the service has suggested to me. The state of the army which you have just placed under my command, likewise requires, that I should make you a series of requests, upon the compliance with which its interests and reputation perhaps depend.

Numerous complaints have been made and repeated to the Directory, against the French administrations established in the country occupied by the army, and which is not united to France. All the soldiers of the army loudly accuse these administrations as the cause of the famine against which it is forced to contend, if not in the seat of abundance, at least in a country not wholly unprovided with food.

Would it not be advisable to abolish these administrations, which, supposing them composed of the most honest persons in the world, are an immense expense to the country, without being in anywise useful?—for most of the commissaries who compose them are ignorant of the language of the country, and, as foreigners, have no knowledge of its productions, nor of the private fortunes of its inhabitants. Is it not, moreover, to be feared that these commissaries, whose manners, tastes, and habits cannot resemble those of the population inhabiting the banks of the Rhine, should by injudicious exaggeration, and false political or administrative principles, disgust the latter with the French revolution and the republican form of government?

Would it not be better and more useful to restore to the inhabitants of the territories occupied by the army of Sambre-et-Meuse, their natural administrators, the *bailies*?—and the ecclesiastical estates to the management of the chapters? Economy alone seems to call for this measure, which policy will not disavow. Who shall say that it will not bring back to the republic those affections which the rudeness and the errors of the French administrators have alienated?

The man who is called to the management of public affairs in his birthplace, is acquainted with the private means of each of his fellow-citizens, and he makes each share, in due and equitable proportion, the common burden imposed upon the country. Experience has proved that a chapter which, when its revenues were administered by its monks, could provide subsistence for ten thousand men, can now scarcely feed six or eight hundred. The abbey of Closterbock, near Coblentz, is an instance of this:—and let not this difference be attributed to the constant presence of armies, and to exhaustion: improper administration of the property is alone the cause of it.

Let the most enlightened men of the army be consulted on this head: Jourdan, Joubert, Kléber, Lefebvre, &c. It would therefore seem advisable to restore to these countries their administrations, their civil tribunals, their magistrates, and their own customs. Let the chief *commissaire-ordonnateur*, or his subordinates, under the inspection of the general-in-chief, make the demands of corn, cattle, horses, and generally of all things required by the defenders of the state.

But, it may be said, are you not going backward? will not public spirit be destroyed in the country? and if the territory should remain attached to France, will not hatred of the republican name remain deeply implanted there? Experience ought to have counteracted our desire to municipalize Europe. Moreover, I deny that the inhabitants can ever hate us more than they do at present; and in the supposition that a treaty of peace were to leave us strictly the left bank for our limits, I doubt the expedient of establishing the constitutional regime in the Palatinate, the Hundstruck, the Archbishopric of Treves, the Duchy of Berg, &c.

No people can become republicans in a day; and they who purchase freedom at so high a price seldom love it, after being accustomed under a monarch to pay no taxes, or at least scarcely any. Therefore, before we ascertain whether our opinions may become those of the Germans, from whom nature has formed us so different, let us wage war at their cost, since their sovereign forces us to make war. You are not going backwards. When you introduced laws into the conquered territories, which could take place only after peace, it would then be time to send commissioners thither; and as they would then have no exactions to make, they would no doubt succeed if they conducted themselves with prudence.

It is highly important that I should know what line of conduct I am to pursue towards foreign princes, whether allies, neutrals, or enemies; upon what terms I am to conclude a suspension of arms with the latter; what the intentions of the government are with regard to the opening of the campaign, and what the nature of the operations to be pursued; finally, what general officers I am to serve with, and upon what reinforcements I may depend.

Of our northern allies, the King of Prussia is certainly the principal. No doubt, his government is attentively watching events, and will take advantage of them. But whatever these events turn out to be, it appears to me presumable that, at least for some time to come, the Prussian government cannot renew its connexion with the Emperor, who has just denounced its conduct to the Germanic confederation; and it may be assumed, without fear of mistake, that the ambition of the King of Prussia, which could not be displayed more positively than during the last campaign, would lead that monarch to join us, were he assured that at the proper time we should grant him that which he is eager to obtain: namely, a province, of which Erlangen should form the centre, and which should contain Wurtzburg, Amberg, Bamberg, Nuremberg, Schweinfurt, and perhaps Frankfort. Doubtless such a conquest is worthy of defence; and he certainly intended to defend it, when, through his minister Hardenberg, he proposed to Jourdan to purchase all the artillery which the French army found in the different fortresses it had captured.

But, it may be said, you are making the King of Prussia very powerful! What matters it? Do you think that the house of Austria would ever consent to such a transaction, of which, after all, the King of Prussia must have weighed all the consequences? Your object is a continental peace, which you will obtain if your ally declares war but an instant, and you will, during a long period, get rid of the uneasiness of seeing him renew his connexion with England, whilst this power will thereby be able to economise nothing for a continuance of the war, or for the purpose of raising up new enemies against France.

I have considered it my duty to offer these reflections to the government, and to give, in some measure, the assurance that the King of Prussia is not averse to declaring war. I almost convinced myself of this, yesterday 14th, in a conversation with Sandoz, the Prussian envoy. You may suppose that I maintained the strictest reserve, so as to be able to break off when, I thought proper, a conference brought on by chance alone.

I shall not dwell upon the other points. I only beg that the Directory will be so good as to send me answers to them as soon as possible. The situation of the army, and the motions of the enemy, seem to require my immediate presence in the field.

It remains for me, Citizens Directors, to thank you for having placed the whole of Belgium under my command; I hope to derive from it the assistance of which the army is so much in want.

L. Hoche.

P.S.—It is not for me to prejudge the intentions of the government; but, if it expressed a wish to have my opinion, I would submit to its consideration some ideas which, under certain circumstances, might prove useful.

No. 11

General Laroche to General Ney.

Ogersheim, 3rd *Complementaire*, Year 7.

Doubtless I explained myself badly, my dear General, since you supposed that I guarded the Rhine from Spires to Esenhofen, whilst, on the contrary, I am to face the plain with my right at Spires and my left towards Hanofen, with a line of bridges from Otterstat as far as Schiferstat. It was this order, which must appear to you as singular as it does to me, that induced me to write to you as I did this morning.

In order that you may be convinced of its existence, which you never can be by a simple assertion, I enclose you the letter I received to this effect, and which can bear no other interpretation.

I shall establish myself tonight with my feeble division in two lines, and shall have my headquarters at Spires, in order to be able to communicate with General Collaud.

Health and friendship.

Laroche.

No. 12

General Laroche to General Ney.

Head-quarters, Ogersheim, 3rd *Complementaire*, Year 7.
My dear General,

You must have received an order which does away with the measures we determined upon. I cannot conceal from you that it requires a strong dose of patriotism and devotion to serve in this manner.

In order not to render the movement which you have begun useless, I will, if you like, commence mine, and proceed to the singular positions assigned me: my right at Spires, my left towards Hanofen, and my advanced posts at Otterstat.

I am impatient for your answer. Laroche.

P.S.—We shall no doubt receive other orders in the course of the day, which will again alter what we are going to do. Alas! alas!

No. 13

Brigadier Lery to General Ney.

Mayence, 4th *Complementaire*, Year 7.

Cassel has not been surprised, my dear General, as you were informed it had; and up to the present time no one has any knowledge of troops going that way, with the exception of a body of cavalry to take possession of Wisbaden, where there is no garrison.

We were also informed that the enemy had crossed the Rhine at Worms and at Philipsburg. All these reports had their origin in fright and malevolence.

It is certainly lamentable that in our defence of Manheim, time and circumstances have not allowed us to pursue the plans agreed upon, and that the principal defence and the retreat of the army were not concentrated in Neckerau. The most unfortunate part of this catastrophe is its moral effect upon the feelings of the men. Let us hope that more fortunate measures will soon cause a change in our situation. The news from Holland is very good: the British have been repulsed by General Brune, and it is hoped that he will force them to re-embark.

Measures are here in agitation for carrying on a siege, and I am far from thinking that these surprises can succeed.

I am delighted that the present opportunity enables me to give you the assurance of my constant and sincere friendship.

Lery.

No. 14

Lecourbe, General-in-Chief, to General Ney.

The point of Neckerels was vigorously attacked yesterday. The troops withdrew to Wissenbach and to Necker-Gemund, where they were even reinforced.

Should you take up a position farther back, that is to say upon the Elzatz, you will give notice of it to General Legrand, who ought also to fall back a little, always however occupying Gochrau and Bretten by means of advanced posts.

I am not easy with regard to the points of Dunlach and Philipsburg. The enemy will probably make attempts upon the latter; and it is expedient that you should be nearer General Legrand, in order that the latter may be able to make a movement from left to right.

I shall remain some days at Manheim; write to me often, and watch carefully the progress of the enemy upon your left, at Necker-Gemund.

We shall, in a short time, receive good accounts of Masséna. An express from him is just arrived. If a large force comes against us, so much the better; we must however maintain our positions even against wind and tide.

You know that I cannot replace the 8th for you. General Bonnet will proceed and join your division.

Health and friendship.

Lecourbe.

No. 15

Lecourbe, General-in-Chief, to General Ney.

Head-quarters, Manheim, 16th *Brumaire*,
Year 8 (Nov. 5th, 1799.)

It appears, my dear General, that the enemy are making attempts upon our left; they have even, as I am informed, forced the point of Necker-Gemund. It is important that you should co-operate in the recapture of this place, and fall upon the rear of the enemy if they are pent up in the gorge of Rorbach and

Heidelberg.

I perceive with pain that the troops are disheartened; there are many individuals in the rear of the divisions who spread alarm among them; and many others who, being gorged with booty, wish for a retreat in order to put their plunder in a place of safety.

It behoves you, my dear General, and my other assistants, to put a stop without pity to all that is immoral, and force the men to do their duty.

Should you be unsuccessful in the recapture of Necker-Gemund, send a portion of your forces down upon Heidelberg, in order to defend the Necker and succour the 4th division. The enemy cannot have collected a large force upon this point.

Fraternal salutation.

Lecourbe.

No. 16

Brigadier-General Boyé to General Ney, Commanding the Army of the Rhine.

Head-quarters, Kloten, 29th *Vendemiaire*,
Year 8. (Oct. 20th, 1799.)

I had the pleasure of writing to you, my dear General, on my arrival at the army of the Danube; and having received no answer, I presume my letter never reached you.

I congratulate you on the success obtained by the army of the Rhine whilst under your command. Bravery and able tactics are so familiar to you, that soldiers commanded by you cannot fail to conquer.

I do not mention to you our brilliant days from the 3rd to the 16th instant, as the particulars must be known to you; I shall merely state that I never beheld a more complete rout. The Russians will remember it, as will their worthy chief, Suwarrow, surnamed the Italic. The Emperor Paul was to have conferred upon him the surname of the Helvetic; and he is still mad enough to do it. Victory has at length returned to our standard, and I hope she will not again leave us. From Holland to Italy the enemy has been beaten. *Vive la Republique!*

I am very sorry Bernadotte has quitted the ministry. I know not where he is, and would thank you, my dear General, for his address, as I wish to write to him.

The return of General Bonaparte will make all good republicans rejoice, and the royalists burst with spite.

I hope to be more fortunate in this instance, and that all my letters will not be lost.

Our friend Kléber has remained in Egypt; probably General Bonaparte has left him in command of the army.

I hope that the armies of the Rhine and the Danube will soon shake hands.

Adieu, my dear General,

Believe me ever your sincere friend,

Boyé.

www.ingramcontent.com/pod-product-compliance
Lightning Source LLC
Chambersburg PA
CBHW031617160426
43196CB00006B/169